FEMINISM AND SUFFRAGE

Feminism and Suffrage

THE EMERGENCE OF
AN INDEPENDENT WOMEN'S
MOVEMENT IN AMERICA
1848–1869

Ellen Carol DuBois

CORNELL UNIVERSITY PRESS
ITHACA AND LONDON

Cornell University Press gratefully acknowledges a grant from the Andrew W. Mellon Foundation that aided in bringing this book to publication.

First published 1978 by Cornell University Press.
Second printing, 1980.

First printing, Cornell Paperbacks, 1980.
Fourth printing, 1987.

International Standard Book Number 0-8014-1043-6 (cloth)
International Standard Book Number 0-8014-9182-7 (paperback)
Library of Congress Catalog Card Number 77-90902

Printed in the United States of America

Librarians: Library of Congress cataloging information appears on the last page of the book.

The paper in this book is acid-free, and meets the guidelines for permanence and durability of the Committee on Production Guidelines for Book Longevity of the Council on Library Resources.

To my mother and father,
Mildred and Irwin,
and to my grandmother, Lilly

Contents

Acknowledgments

I worked on this book for a long time, and many people helped me. Linda Gordon, Carolyn Korsmeyer, Eric Foner, and above all Mari Jo Buhle read large sections of it and gave me the benefit of their careful and comradely criticism. I couldn't and wouldn't have finished writing it without their help. I also want to thank Nancy Cott, Ruth Myerowitz, and Judy Smith for their comments and support; I am particularly grateful for the help of Ann D. Gordon and Eli Zaretsky. Elaine Schwartz gave me valuable assistance in preparing the final manuscript. Several other people read an earlier version of this study, and I deeply appreciate their criticisms and encouragement: George Fredrickson, David Hollinger, Jesse Lemisch, Gerda Lerner, Lewis Perry, and especially Anne Firor Scott and Robert Wiebe. Many of my ideas and interpretations were developed in discussions with my students at the State University of New York at Buffalo, and I hope they recognize my debt to them.

The staff of the Arthur and Elizabeth Schlesinger Library, Radcliffe College, assisted me in my research, and just before she died, Alma Lutz opened her private library and files to me. I hope I have done honor to her concern for women's history. The Julian Park Fund of the Faculty of Arts and Letters of the State University of New York at Buffalo generously supported the preparation of the final manuscript.

John, Howard, and George Blackwell and Ethel B. J. Whidden kindly gave me permission to include quotations from unpublished writings of the Blackwell family. I am also grateful to the following for permission to quote from unpublished letters and manuscripts in their possession: the George Arents Research Library for Special Collections, Syracuse University; the Trustees of the Boston Public Library; the Buffalo and Erie County Public Library; the

Houghton Library, Harvard University; the Kansas State Historical Society, Topeka; the Massachusetts Historical Society,
Boston; the Arthur and Elizabeth Schlesinger Library on the History of Women in America, Radcliffe College; the Sophia Smith
Collection (Women's History Archive), Smith College; and the
Vassar College Library. These letters and manuscripts and their
locations are identified in the footnotes.

My final acknowledgment is to the women's liberation movement, of which I am a part and which raised the historical questions my book is intended to answer.

ELLEN CAROL DuBOIS

Buffalo, New York

Abbreviations

HWS	*History of Woman Suffrage,* ed. Elizabeth Cady Stanton, Susan B. Anthony, Matilda Joslyn Gage, et al. (Rochester: Susan B. Anthony; New York: National American Woman Suffrage Association, 1881–1922), 6 vols.
LC	Library of Congress, Manuscript Division, Washington, D.C.
NAW	*Notable American Women,* ed. Edward T. James, Janet Wilson James, and Paul S. Boyer (Cambridge, Mass.: Harvard University Press, 1971), 3 vols.
NAWSA	National American Woman Suffrage Association.
SL	The Arthur and Elizabeth Schlesinger Library on the History of Women in America, Radcliffe College, Cambridge, Massachusetts.
Stanton Letters	*Elizabeth Cady Stanton as Revealed in Her Letters and Reminiscences,* ed. Theodore Stanton and Harriot Stanton Blatch (New York: Harper, 1922).

FEMINISM AND SUFFRAGE

We thoroughly comprehended for the first time and saw as never before, that only from woman's standpoint could the battle be successfully fought, and victory secured. . . . Our liberal men counseled us to silence during the war, and we were silent on our own wrongs; they counseled us again to silence in Kansas and New York, lest we should defeat "negro suffrage" and threatened if we were not, we might fight the battle alone. We chose the latter, and were defeated. But standing alone we learned our power; we repudiated man's counsels forevermore; and solemnly vowed that there should never be another season of silence until woman had the same rights everywhere on this green earth, as man.

We would point for [the young women of the coming generation] the moral of our experiences: that woman must lead the way to her own enfranchisement, and work out her own salvation with a hopeful courage and determination that knows no fear nor trembling. She must not put her trust in man in this transition period, since, while regarded as his subject, his inferior, his slave, their interests must be antagonistic.

—*History of Woman Suffrage,* 1881

Introduction

This book is a study of the origins of the first feminist movement in the United States, the nineteenth-century woman suffrage movement. For three-quarters of a century, beginning in 1848, American women centered their aspirations for freedom and power on the demand for the vote. At its height, the movement involved hundreds of thousands of women. Along with the black liberation and labor movements, woman suffrage is one of the three great reform efforts in American history.[1]

To appreciate the historic significance of the woman suffrage movement, it is necessary to understand the degree to which women expected the vote to lead to a total transformation of their lives. This expectation had to do with changes taking place in the family, its relation to society, and women's role within it. Historically, woman's role has been shaped by her position in the family. Because the traditional family was the site of production and closely integrated with all forms of community life, women

1. The major histories of the movement are: Eleanor Flexner, *A Century of Struggle: The Women's Rights Movement in the United States* (New York, 1968); Alan Grimes, *The Puritan Ethic and Woman Suffrage* (New York, 1967); Aileen S. Kraditor, *Ideas of the Woman Suffrage Movement, 1890–1920* (New York, 1965); William O'Neill, *Everyone Was Brave: The Rise and Fall of Feminism in America* (New York, 1969); Ross Evans Paulson, *Women's Suffrage and Prohibition: A Comparative Study of Equality and Social Control* (Glenview, Ill., 1973); and Anne F. Scott and Andrew M. Scott, *One Half the People: The Fight for Woman Suffrage* (Philadelphia, 1975). Also of great importance are two histories generated within the movement itself: Carrie Chapman Catt and Nettie Rogers Shuler, *Woman Suffrage and Politics* (New York, 1923); and the monumental, six-volume *History of Woman Suffrage,* ed. Elizabeth Cady Stanton, Susan B. Anthony, Matilda Joslyn Gage, et al.; the first three volumes were published and distributed by Anthony herself (Rochester, 1881–1886). The *History of Woman Suffrage* is evidence of the extraordinary commitment of these feminists to documenting and preserving the records of their political efforts and passing them on to future generations of women. It embodies their unusually acute sense of their place in and responsibility to history.

were recognized as participants in the larger world of the society. However, the family's central importance in social organization meant that the patriarchal relations between men and women which characterized family life were carried into all other aspects of society as well.

With the growth of industrial capitalism, production began to move outside the home. Yet woman's place, her "sphere," remained within the family. Outside it there arose a public life that was considered man's sphere. Although public life was based on the growing organization of production outside the home, its essence was understood not as economic experience, but as political activity. Beginning in the 1820's and 1830's, an enormous upsurge of popular political energies took place—among working men, in the antislavery societies, and in almost every other aspect of antebellum life. The woman suffrage movement was women's response to these developments. Driven by their relegation to a separate, domestic sphere, which had always been marked by inequality, especially their own, women were also drawn, like the men of their time, by the promise that political activity held for the creation of a truly democratic society.

Until the development of women's rights and woman suffrage politics, the major approach to improving women's status came from domestic reformers, such as Catharine Beecher. To retrieve some of the social recognition that women were losing as production and other aspects of social life moved away from the home, domestic reformers called for an elevation of women's status in the family, and for increased recognition of the contribution that domestic relations made to community life in general. They did not challenge the relegation of women to the domestic sphere, but only the relationship between that sphere and the rest of society. The demand for suffrage represented a much more advanced program for improving women's position. Suffragists recognized that the locus of community life had shifted away from the family and that women's aspirations for a greater voice in the conduct of community affairs could be satisfied only by their moving into the public realm. Moreover, the demand for woman suffrage raised the prospect of sex equality in a way that proposals for domestic reform never could. Notwithstanding domestic reformers' assertions that the influence women wielded as wives and mothers was great, the fact remained that women in the family were dependent on men. Domestic reformers could aspire merely to modify women's subordinate status, never to eliminate it. Women hoped, however, that in the public realm men would be forced to face them as equals. In the mid-nineteenth century, enfranchisement offered women a route to social power, as well as the clearest possible vision of equality with men.

Suffragism has not been accorded the historic recognition it deserves, largely because woman suffrage has too frequently been regarded as an isolated institutional reform. Its character as a social movement, reflecting women's aspirations for and progress toward radical change in their lives, has been overlooked. Abstracting the demand for the vote from its social context, feminists and historians alike have seriously underestimated its relevance for contemporary women. It is certainly true that the Nineteenth Amendment did not emancipate women, and that rediscovering the revolutionary hopes that feminists had for the ballot has a bitter edge for us today. However, it is a mistake to conclude that the woman suffrage movement was a useless detour in women's struggle for liberation because the vote did not solve the problem of women's oppression.[2] The vote did not have the inherent capacity to emancipate women as individuals, isolated from the collective struggles of their sex. Like all institutional reforms, it required an active social movement to give it meaning and make it real. Approached as a social movement, rather than as a particular reform, suffragism has enormous contemporary

2. O'Neill, for instance (pp. 55–64), occasionally slips into an appreciation of the political foresight of antisuffragists for anticipating his own analysis that the vote accomplished very little. The most recent example of this tendency to dismiss suffragism is Carroll Smith Rosenberg's comment that "women's suffrage has proved of little importance either to American politics or American women" ("The New Woman and the New History," *Feminist Studies* 3 (1975), 186).

relevance. It was the first independent movement of women for their own liberation. Its growth—the mobilization of women around the demand for the vote, their collective activity, their commitment to gaining increased power over their own lives— was itself a major change in the condition of those lives. My concern is less with how women won the vote than with how the vote generated a movement of increasing strength and vitality. In other words, this book is intended as a contribution, not to the history of woman suffrage, but to the history of the feminist movement.[3]

The word "movement" should, I think, be taken seriously as a description of the emergence of suffragism and similar historical processes. It suggests an accelerating transformation of consciousness among a group of oppressed people and a growing sense of collective power. The overwhelming majority of challenges to established power are stillborn, but a few generate movements. Prior to a movement's emergence its coming into being is difficult to imagine, but once it begins the initial problem of radical social change is solved and how people could have ever accepted their own powerlessness becomes increasingly difficult to imagine. The early history of woman suffrage vividly demonstrates this phenomenon. The movement started with a handful of mid-nineteenth-century women—scattered, isolated, and handicapped by the limited sphere of their sex—who began to demand political parity with men. Within a generation, they had organized their demand for enfranchisement into a powerful political force that was able not only to sustain itself over a half-century, but to challenge the structures of American political and social life until its goals were met. "We solemnly vowed," Elizabeth Cady Stanton declared on behalf of the first generation of suffragists, "that there should never be another season of silence until woman had the same rights everywhere on this green earth, as man."

3. Linda Gordon makes the same distinction about birth control in her brilliant study, *Woman's Body, Woman's Right: A Social History of Birth Control in America* (New York, 1976).

Because my concern is to trace the development of the suffrage movement, I have chosen to focus on its earliest period, and to uncover the process by which women's discontent crystallized into the political demand for women's emancipation. The beginnings of this process lie in the dozen years before the Civil War, primarily among women associated with the antislavery movement. They laid the groundwork for a feminist movement by articulating a set of demands for women's rights and by acquiring the skills and self-confidence necessary to offer political leadership to other women. However, the development of feminism before the war was restrained by the organizational connection of its leaders with the antislavery movement, which kept them from concentrating on the mobilization of women around a primary commitment to their own rights.

Postwar politics provided the setting within which feminists came to recognize that the only force capable of bringing about radical change in the condition of women's lives was the organized power of women themselves. From the perspective of feminists, postwar politics had two important aspects. One was the general flowering of radical ambitions for social change that accompanied the defeat of slavery and encompassed demands for racial equality, sexual equality, and labor reform. The other was the process by which the power of the Republican party was marshaled in behalf of only one of these reforms, the demand for black suffrage.[4] Stimulated by the former and thwarted by the latter, feminists came to realize that they needed an independent political base if they were to demand women's enfranchisement with any real force. The particular historical conditions under which they came to this realization shaped the nature of the movement they began to build in response to it.

At the center of the postwar development of the woman suffrage movement—and therefore the central characters in this

4. In developing this analytical framework, I learned a great deal from David Montgomery's history of Reconstruction politics from the perspective of the labor reform movement, *Beyond Equality: Labor and the Radical Republicans, 1862–1872* (New York, 1967).

book—were Elizabeth Cady Stanton and Susan B. Anthony. It was they who realized most clearly the limitations that political dependence on abolitionism imposed on feminism, and who took the lead in finding a new political context for woman suffrage. Their decision to end their twenty-year alliance with abolitionism led to a break with many other leading advocates of woman suffrage, prominent among them Lucy Stone. After the failure of efforts to convince abolitionists to support a Reconstruction program that included woman suffrage as well as black suffrage, Stanton and Anthony attempted to forge an alliance with labor reformers and to build a new reform coalition on that basis. From political cooperation with labor reformers they moved quite naturally into efforts to organize a feminist movement among working women. The failure of these efforts set the stage for their decision to form an organization of women dedicated first and foremost to securing political equality with men. That decision marks the emergence of woman suffrage as an independent feminist movement, and it is with the events surrounding it that the book concludes. While suffragism went through many changes over the next fifty years, reflecting the variety of its political contexts, its basic characteristics were set in the Reconstruction period: it was an independent reform movement, composed primarily of white, middle-class women, which defined women's emancipation and equality largely, although not exclusively, in terms of the franchise.

I hope that this book leads to other histories of the woman suffrage movement, especially at the local level, where its growth can be observed in its most human dimensions. Beyond that, I have written this study because I am a feminist and a radical, and present it as a contribution to our understanding of the ways in which politics emerges out of and transforms common social life and consciousness.

Chapter One

Women's Rights before the Civil War

For many years before 1848, American women had manifested considerable discontent with their lot. They wrote and read domestic novels in which a thin veneer of sentiment overlaid a great deal of anger about women's dependence on undependable men. They attended female academies and formed ladies' benevolent societies, in which they pursued the widest range of interests and activities they could imagine without calling into question the whole notion of "woman's sphere." In such settings, they probed the experiences that united and restrained them—what one historian has called "the bonds of womanhood."[1] Yet women's discontent remained unexamined, implicit, and above all, disorganized. Although increasing numbers of women were questioning what it meant to be a woman and were ready to challenge their traditional position, they did not yet know each other.

The women's rights movement crystallized these sentiments into a feminist politics. Although preceded by individual theorists like Margaret Fuller, and by particular demands on behalf of women for property rights, education, and admission to the professions, the women's rights movement began a new phase in the history of feminism. It introduced the possibility of social change into a situation in which many women had already become dissatisfied. It posed women, not merely as beneficiaries of change

1. Nancy F. Cott, *The Bonds of Womanhood: "Woman's Sphere" in New England, 1780–1835* (New Haven, 1977). On the early nineteenth century, see also Kathryn Kish Sklar, *Catharine Beecher: A Study in American Domesticity* (New Haven, 1973); Carroll Smith Rosenberg, "Beauty, the Beast and the Militant Woman: A Case Study in Sex Roles and Social Stress in Jacksonian America," *American Quarterly*, 23 (1971), 562–584; and Keith Melder, "The Beginnings of the Woman's Rights Movement in the United States, 1800–1840" (doctoral diss., Yale University, 1964).

in the relation of the sexes, but as agents of change as well. As Elizabeth Cady Stanton said at the meeting that inaugurated the movement, "Woman herself must do the work."[2] The pioneers of women's rights pointed the way toward women's discontent organized to have an impact on women's history.

The women's rights movement developed in the dozen years before the Civil War. It had two sources. On the one hand, it emerged from women's growing awareness of their common conditions and grievances. Simultaneously, it was an aspect of antebellum reform politics, particularly of the antislavery movement. The women who built and led the women's rights movement combined these two historical experiences. They shared in and understood the lives of white, native-born American women of the working and middle classes: the limited domestic sphere prescribed for them, their increasing isolation from the major economic and political developments of their society, and above all their mounting discontent with their situation. Women's rights leaders raised this discontent to a self-conscious level and channeled it into activities intended to transform women's position. They were able to do this because of their experience in the antislavery movement, to which they were led, in part, by that very dissatisfaction with exclusively domestic life. Female abolitionists followed the course of the antislavery movement from evangelicism to politics, moving from a framework of individual sin and conversion to an understanding of institutionalized oppression and social reform. This development is what enabled them and other women's rights pioneers to imagine changing the traditional subservient status of women. Borrowing from antislavery ideology, they articulated a vision of equality and independence for women, and borrowing from antislavery method, they spread their radical ideas widely to challenge other people to imagine a new set of sexual relations. Their most radical demand was enfranchisement. More than any other element in the women's rights program of legal reform, woman suffrage em-

2. As quoted in Flexner, *Century of Struggle,* p. 77.

bodied the movement's feminism, the challenge it posed to women's dependence upon and subservience to men.

The first episode of the women's rights movement was the 1848 Seneca Falls Convention, organized by Elizabeth Cady Stanton, Lucretia Mott, and several other women. As befitted an enterprise handicapped by the very injustices it was designed to protest, the proceedings were a mixture of womanly modesty and feminist militancy. When faced with the task of composing a manifesto for the convention, the organizers, in Stanton's words, felt "as helpless and hopeless as if they had been suddenly asked to construct a steam engine." Nor was any woman willing to chair the meeting, and the office fell to Lucretia Mott's husband. Yet the list of grievances which the organizers presented was comprehensive. In retrospect, we can see that their Declaration of Sentiments and Resolutions anticipated every demand of nineteenth-century feminism. To express their ideas about women's rights and wrongs, they chose to rewrite the Preamble of the Declaration of Independence around "the repeated injuries and usurpations on the part of man towards woman." On the one hand, this decision reflected their need to borrow political legitimacy from the American Revolution. On the other, it permitted them to state in the clearest possible fashion that they identified the tyranny of men as the cause of women's grievances.[3]

The Seneca Falls Convention was consciously intended to initiate a broader movement for the emancipation of women. For the women who organized the convention, and others like them, the first and greatest task was acquiring the skills and knowledge necessary to lead such an enterprise. In Elizabeth Cady Stanton's words, they had to transform themselves into a "race of women worthy to assert the humanity of women."[4] Their development as feminists, as women able to bring politics to bear on the condition of their sex, had as its starting point the experience they shared with other women. While many accounts of this first

3. On the Seneca Falls convention, see *HWS,* I, 68–73.
4. Stanton to Gerrit Smith, January 3, 1856, *Stanton Letters,* p. 64.

generation of feminist activists stress what distinguished them from other women—their bravery and open rebellion—it is equally important to recognize what they had in common with nonfeminists: lack of public skills; lives marked by excessive domesticity; husbands and fathers hostile to their efforts; the material pressures of housekeeping and child-rearing; and the deep psychological insecurity bred by all these factors. A movement is a process by which rebellion generates more rebellion. The women's rights pioneers did not begin their political activities already "emancipated," freed from the limitations that other women suffered. Many of the personal and political resources they drew on to challenge the oppression of women were developed in the course of mounting the challenge itself.

"The Infancy of our Movement"

Even the most committed and militant of the first-generation women's rights activists hesitated on the brink of the public activity necessary to build a feminist movement. Although a successful writer, Frances Dana Gage was as homebound as other women, when she was asked to preside over a women's rights convention in Akron in 1851. She was reluctant, but accepted the responsibility. "I have never in my life attended a regular business meeting," she told her audience, whose vistas were even more circumscribed than hers.[5] When Clarina Nichols delivered the first women's rights address before the Vermont legislature in 1850, her voice broke and her supporters feared that she would fail. Spurred on by "the conviction that only an eminently successful presentation of her subject could spike the enemy's batteries," she finished her speech, "though her voice was tremulous."[6] Daring to speak out at the first women's rights convention she had ever attended, in 1852, Matilda Joslyn Gage was inaudible to her audience and "trembling in every limb." The

5. *HWS*, I, 111.
6. *HWS*, I, 174.

mother of four young children at the time, Gage did not plunge seriously into political work until after the war, when her children had grown and domestic responsibilities were less insistent.[7] Abigail Bush spoke for an entire generation of feminists committed to acquiring political skills in service to their sex. When the audience at a convention in Rochester in 1848 called down the women speakers with cries of "louder, louder!" Bush responded: "Friends, we present ourselves here before you, as an oppressed class, with trembling frames and faltering tongues, and we do not expect to be able to speak as to be heard by all at first, but we trust we shall have the sympathy of the audience, and that you will bear with our weakness now in the infancy of our movement. Our trust in the omnipotency of right is our only faith that we shall succeed."[8]

Compared to many other women, Antoinette Brown was relatively self-confident as she prepared herself for public life and women's rights leadership. For three years, she resisted Oberlin College's attempts to drive her from its theological course. Nonetheless, the objection of a respected mentor to her women's rights ideas "put me into such an agony . . . I did wish God had not made me a woman."[9] The opposition of men, particularly the fathers and husbands on whom they were dependent, reinforced women's lack of public experience to restrain their feminist activism. Excluded from the World's Anti-Slavery Convention in London in 1840, Mary Grew returned to Pennsylvania to circulate petitions for a married women's property act. Her abolitionist father, who had encouraged her to do similar work in behalf of the slave, vigorously opposed her.[10] Elizabeth Cady Stanton, who was singularly unafflicted with psychological insecurity, faced her greatest obstacles in her husband and her father. Henry

7. Elizabeth B. Warbasse, "Matilda Joslyn Gage," *NAW*, II, 4.
8. *HWS*, I, 76.
9. Antoinette Brown Blackwell, "Autobiography," unpublished manuscript, 1909, SL, p. 117.
10. Ira V. Brown, "Mary Grew," *NAW*, II, 91.

Stanton stubbornly opposed his wife's desire to join in the 1855–1856 canvass of New York, and her father, whom she adored, temporarily disinherited her when she began public lecturing. Her convictions only deepened. "To think," she wrote, "that all in me of which my father would have felt a proper pride had I been a man, is deeply mortifying to him because I am a woman . . . has stung me to a fierce decision—to speak as soon as I can do myself credit. But the pressure on me just now is too great. Henry sides with my friends, who oppose me in all that is dearest to my heart. They are not willing that I should write even on the woman question. But I will both write and speak."[11]

During the late 1850's the focus of Stanton's "domestic bondage" shifted from the opposition of husband and father to the demands of her seven children. "I seldom have one hour undisturbed in which to sit down and write," she complained, while nursing her daughter. "Men who can, when they wish to write a document, shut themselves up for days with their thoughts and their books, know little of what difficulties a woman must surmount to get off a tolerable production."[12] By sharing both political and domestic work with Anthony, she was able to continue leading the women's rights movement for most of this period. But Stanton's last pregnancy was enough to undermine even her exceptional self-confidence and physical strength. "You need expect nothing from me for some time," she wrote to Anthony after the birth of 12½-pound Robert. "I can scarcely walk across the room . . . and have to keep my mind in the most quiet state in order to sleep. . . . He seems to take up every particle of my vitality, soul and body."[13] Four months later, she was still "in no situation to think or write," but succumbed to Anthony's blandishments to prepare a memorial for the New York State

11. Stanton to Anthony, September 10, 1855, *Stanton Letters*, pp. 59–60. Also see Stanton to Elizabeth Smith Miller, September 20, 1855, *ibid.*, pp. 60–62.
12. Stanton to Anthony, December 1, 1853, *ibid.*, p. 55.
13. Stanton to Anthony, April 2, 1859, Autograph Collection, Vassar College Library.

legislature. "We have issued bulls under all circumstances," she conceded. "I think you and I can do more even if you must make the pudding and carry the baby."[14]

Unlike Stanton, Lucy Stone and Antoinette Brown assumed domestic responsibilities after they had become prominent women's rights advocates. Stone married Henry Blackwell in 1855, and Brown married his brother Samuel a year later. Brown had seven children; Stone had one, which kept her out of political work for over a decade. "I wish I felt the old impulse and power to lecture . . . , but I am afraid and dare not trust Lucy Stone," Stone wrote to Brown, when her daughter was a year and a half old. "I went to hear E. P. Whipple lecture on Joan d'Arc. It was very inspiring and for the hour I felt as though all things were possible to me. But when I came home and looked in Alice's sleeping face and thought of the possible evil that might befall her if my guardian eye was turned away, I shrank like a snail into its shell and saw that for these years I can be only a mother."[15] Brown experienced this same dilemma. Unable even to keep up a political correspondence because of the press of household obligations, she wrote to Anthony, "This, Susan, is 'woman's sphere.' "[16] Anthony was unsympathetic to her comrade's preference for what she called "the ineffable joys of Maternity," and resentful of the political responsibilities that devolved on her. She wrote to Brown in frustration over Stone's preparations for an important debate: "A woman who *is* and *must* of necessity continue for the present at least the representative woman has no right to *disqualify* herself for such a *representative occasion*. I do feel that it is so foolish for her to put herself in the position of *maid of all work* and *baby tender*. What man would dream of going before the public on such an occasion as this one night-tired and worn from such a multitude of en-

14. Stanton to Anthony, July 15, 1859, *ibid*.

15. Stone to Antoinette Brown Blackwell, February 20, 1859, Blackwell Family Papers, SL.

16. Antoinette Brown Blackwell to Anthony, October 25, 1859, as quoted in Blackwell, "Autobiography," p. 228.

grossing cares."[17] Indeed, even though Brown and Stone had
foresworn marriage while young girls, Anthony was the only first-
generation national women's rights leader who remained single.
"Where are you Susan and what are you doing?" Stanton wrote
when she hadn't heard from Anthony for some time. "Are you
dead or married?"[18]

In the face of such obstacles, the major resource on which
women's rights activists drew to support themselves and advance
their cause was one another. Like many nineteenth-century
women, they formed intense and lasting friendships with other
women. Frequently these were the most passionate and emotion-
ally supportive relationships that they had. While feminists'
mutual relationships were similar to other female friendships in
emotional texture, they were different in their focus on the public
and political concerns that made their lives as women unique.
The most enduring and productive of these friendships was undoubtedly that of Elizabeth Cady Stanton and Susan B. Anthony,
which began in 1851. The initial basis of their interdependency
was that Anthony gave Stanton psychological and material support in domestic matters, while Stanton provided Anthony with a
political education. In an episode repeated often in their first
decade together, Anthony called on Stanton when she found herself unable to write a speech for a New York teachers' convention: "For the love of me and for the saving of the reputation of
womanhood, I beg you, with one baby on your knee, . . . and
four boys whistling, buzzing, hallooing 'Ma, Ma,' set yourself
about the work. . . . I must not and will not allow these school-
masters to say, 'See, these women can't or won't do anything
when we do give them a chance.'"[19]

17. Anthony to Martha Coffin Wright, June 6, 1856, Garrison Family
Papers, Sophia Smith Collection (Women's History Archive), Smith College
Library; Anthony to Antoinette Brown Blackwell, April 22, 1858, as quoted
in Blackwell, "Autobiography," p. 223.
18. Stanton to Anthony, January, 1856, Autograph Collection, Vassar College Library.
19. Anthony to Stanton, June 5, 1856, *Stanton Letters,* pp. 64–65. See
Carroll Smith Rosenberg, "The Female World of Love and Ritual: Relations

Antoinette Brown and Lucy Stone were also bound by an intense friendship, formed when they were both students at Oberlin. They turned to each other to fortify their common feminism against the assaults of friends and teachers, and, as Brown remembered it, "used to sit with our arms around each other . . . and talk of our friends and our homes and of ten thousand subjects of mutual interest until both our hearts felt warmer and lighter."[20] Their relationship continued to sustain them after they left Oberlin and became abolitionists and women's rights agitators. When Stone was subject to particularly intense harassment for wearing bloomers, Brown offered her support. "Tonight I could nestle closer to your heart than on the night when I went through the dark and the rain and Tappan Hall and school rules—all to feel your arm around me," she wrote, "and to know that in all this wide world I was not alone."[21]

An important aspect of these relationships was overtly political. Given the strength of men's commitment to maintaining their political monopoly, the few women who were fortunate enough to have acquired a political education had to share their skills and knowledge with others. Stanton's contribution to Anthony's political development has already been noted. When Brown and Stone first met, they organized six other women students into "an informal debating and speaking society" to provide the oratorical experience they were denied in Oberlin's "ladies" course. They were so afraid of official intervention that they met in a black woman's home "on the outskirts of town," and occasionally in the woods, with a guard posted "against possible intruders." When Brown returned home to Michigan for a year, she organized another group to discuss women's sphere and women's rights. "We are exceedingly careful in this matter and all move on together step by step," she wrote to Stone. "Some will un-

between Women in Nineteenth-Century America," *Signs: Journal of Women in Culture and Society,* 1 (1975), 1–29.

20. Brown to Stone, sometime in 1848, as quoted in A. B. Blackwell, "Autobiography," p. 128.

21. Brown to Stone, February 18, 1854, as quoted in *ibid.,* p. 172.

doubtedly shrink back when they come to find where they stand
and believe they must have been mistaken . . . and a few I hope
and believe will go out into the world pioneers in the great reform which is about to revolutionize society."[22]

There were limits, however, to the support women's rights
pioneers could offer one another. One such constraint was physical distance. As reformers they traveled to a degree unheard of
among pre–Civil War women and, when unmarried, could
scarcely be said to have a home. They were usually alone. In
addition, the attacks on them for stepping outside women's sphere
were constant, severe, and beyond the power of friends to halt
or counteract. Brown described for Stone the response she elicited
from the townspeople of Oberlin: "Sometimes they warn me not
to be a Fanny Wright man, sometimes believe I am joking, sometimes stare at me with amazement and sometimes seem to start
back with a kind of horror. Men and women are about equal and
seem to have their mouths opened and their tongues loosed to
about the same extent." Surrounded on all sides by hostility,
women's rights agitators had to work most of the time without
the companionship and sisterhood they so prized. "You know we
used to wish sometimes that we could live on and have no need
of the sympathy of anyone," Brown reminded Stone, after she
had left Oberlin, "I have learned to feel so." "What hard work it
is to stand alone!" she wrote a few years later. "I am forever
wanting to lean over onto somebody but nobody will support
me."[23]

In the face of such pressures, some women could not maintain
their resolve to challenge women's sphere. One such woman was
Letitia Holmes, who was Antoinette Brown's classmate at Oberlin and, like her, committed to becoming a religious teacher.
Holmes married a minister, moved with him to Portsmouth, New
Hampshire, and found herself in a role she had not anticipated,
isolated from any source of support. "You know I have been

22. *Ibid.*, pp. 54 and 119.
23. *Ibid.*, pp. 127 (1848), 129 (1848), and 137 (August 4, 1852).

looked upon as a pastor's wife with the incumbent duties to perform . . . ," she wrote to Brown. "I have been (I was going to say tired to death) receiving calls." An educated woman, she had ambitions beyond her sphere, which were not well received in Portsmouth. "There are but few here who think of women as anything more than slave or a plaything, and they think I am different from most women," she wrote. "I tell them I think not." Despite a sympathetic husband, she could not find an outlet for her talents or knowledge. Her long letter describing her situation to Brown, who was already achieving some prominence as a public lecturer, was a mixture of jealousy and a plea for help. Holmes regretted that she did not have another woman "who seems to be one of us you might say . . . another self of my own sex." She asked Brown for "a list of what books would be advantageous for me to read and study with a view to assist me in preparing for public duties." She also asked for Brown's lectures on women's rights, and offered a glimpse into the pressures operating against her Oberlin education and her strong-minded aspirations: "The thing is just this. I do not see it all as clearly as I should to explain to others and when they bring forward the scriptures I fear for myself." In the end, Holmes continued to believe that she would "go forth," which she never did, and could not understand why she was so "long in beginning."[24]

Abolitionist Politics

The abolitionist movement provided the particular framework within which the politics of women's rights developed. From the 1837 clerical attack on the Grimké sisters, through the 1840 meeting of Lucretia Mott and Elizabeth Cady Stanton at the World's Anti-Slavery Convention, to the Civil War and Reconstruction, the development of American feminism was inseparable from the unfolding of the antislavery drama. In tracing the sources of the women's rights movement, Stanton and Anthony cited abolitionism "above all other causes." Mistaking political

24. Holmes to Brown, March 9, 1851, SL.

rhetoric for historical process, historians commonly identify the connection between the two movements as women's discovery of their own oppression through its analogy with slavery.[25] Certainly women's rights leaders made liberal use of the slave metaphor to describe women's oppression. Yet women's discontent with their position was as much cause as effect of their involvement with the antislavery movement. What American women learned from abolitionism was less that they were oppressed than what to do with that perception, how to turn it into a political movement. Abolitionism provided them with a way to escape clerical authority, an egalitarian ideology, and a theory of social change, all of which permitted the leaders to transform the insights into the oppression of women which they shared with many of their contemporaries into the beginnings of the women's rights movement.

Women's involvement in abolitionism developed out of traditions of pietistic female benevolence that were an accepted aspect of women's sphere in the early nineteenth century. The feminist militance of Sarah and Angelina Grimké and the women who succeeded them was rooted in this common soil. The abolitionist movement was one of the many religious reforms that grew out of evangelical Protestantism. For the movement's first half-decade, the role women had in it was consistent with that in other benevolent religious efforts such as urban missionary activities and moral reform. Women organized separate antislavery auxiliaries, in which they worked to support men's organizations and gave particular attention to the female victims and domestic casualties of slavery. The Grimkés entered abolitionism on these terms.[26] Unlike other pious activisms, however, abolition had an unavoidably political thrust and a tendency to outgrow its evan-

25. *HWS*, I, 52. Women's antislavery activities are surveyed in Alma Lutz, *Crusade for Freedom: Women of the Antislavery Movement* (Boston, 1968). Andrew Sinclair locates the origins of women's discontent in the abolitionist movement in *The Emancipation of the American Woman* (New York, 1966), p. 37. Also see Flexner, *Century of Struggle*, p. 40. The most notable exception to this approach is Melder, "Beginnings of the Woman's Rights Movement."

26. On the evangelical origins of abolitionism, see Bertram Wyatt-Brown, *Lewis Tappan and the Evangelical War against Slavery* (Cleveland, 1969), and Ronald G. Walters, *The Antislavery Appeal: American Abolitionism*

gelical origins. As the movement became secularized, so did the activities of benevolent women in it. "Those who urged women to become missionaries and form tract societies . . . have changed the household utensil to a living, energetic being," wrote domestic author and abolitionist Lydia Maria Child, "and they have no spell to turn it into a broom again."[27]

The emergence of the Garrisonian wing of the abolitionist movement embodied and accelerated these secularizing processes. In 1837 William Lloyd Garrison was converted by utopian John Humphrey Noyes to the doctrine of perfectionism, which identified the sanctified individual conscience as the supreme moral standard, and corrupt institutions, not people, as the source of sin. In particular, Garrisonians turned on their churchly origins and attacked the Protestant clergy for its perversion of true Christianity and its support of slavery.[28] Garrisonians' ability to distinguish religious institutions from their own deeply-felt religious impulses was an impressive achievement for evangelicals in an evangelical age. The reformulation of antislavery strategy around these beliefs drew Hicksite Quakers, liberal Unitarians, ultraist come-outers, and a disproportionate number of women activists.

The clergy was the major force that controlled women's moral energies and kept pietistic activism from becoming political activism. Garrisonian anticlericalism was therefore critical to the emergence of abolitionist feminism and its subsequent development into the women's rights movement. This was clear in the

---

after 1830 (Baltimore, 1976). On women's early antislavery benevolence, see Keith Melder, "Ladies Bountiful: Organized Women's Benevolence in Early Nineteenth Century America," *New York History,* 48 (1967), 231–254. On the Grimké sisters, see Gerda Lerner, *The Grimké Sisters from South Carolina: Rebels against Slavery* (Boston, 1967).

27. Child, July 23, 1841, *The Liberator,* as reprinted in Aileen S. Kraditor, *Means and Ends in American Abolitionism: Garrison and His Critics on Strategy and Tactics, 1834–1850* (New York, 1967), p. 47. Kraditor is excellent on the emergence of the women's rights issue within abolitionist circles in the late 1830's.

28. Wyatt-Brown, *Lewis Tappan,* and Lewis Perry, *Radical Abolitionism: Anarchy and the Government of God in Antislavery Thought* (Ithaca: Cornell University Press, 1973).

1837 confrontation between the Grimké sisters and the Congregational clergy of Massachusetts. In this episode, Garrisonian perfectionism and the limits of women's sphere were inseparable matters. Like women in moral reform and other pious activisms, the Grimkés had been led by their religious vocation to step outside their traditional role. At that point, like other benevolent women, they were confronted by clerical authority and ordered to return to more womanly pursuits. Yet the fact that they were Garrisonians enabled them to hold fast to their religious convictions, reject clerical criticism, and instead indict the churches for being institutional bulwarks of slavery and women's oppression.[29]

Against the power of clerical authority, which had long restrained women's impulses for a larger life, Garrisonian abolition armed women with faith in their own convictions. Although restrained by the fact that her husband was a political abolitionist, Elizabeth Cady Stanton's allegiances were with the Garrisonians. Throughout her young adulthood, she had wrestled unsuccessfully with religious orthodoxy from which Garrisonian anticlericalism liberated her.

In the darkness and gloom of a false theology, I was slowly sawing off the chains of my spiritual bondage, when, for the first time, I met Garrison in London. A few bold strokes from the hammer of his truth, I was free! Only those who have lived all their lives under the dark clouds of vague, undefined fears can appreciate the joy of a doubting soul suddenly born into the kingdom of reason and free thought. Is the bondage of the priest-ridden less galling than that of the slave, because we do not see the chains, the indelible scars, the festering wounds, the deep degradation of all the powers of the God-like mind?[30]

29. Lerner, *Grimké Sisters*, chap. 12. The 1837 Pastoral Letter of the Massachusetts Congregational clergy and the Grimkés' responses are excerpted in *Up from the Pedestal: Selected Writings in the History of American Feminism*, ed. Aileen S. Kraditor (Chicago, 1968), pp. 50–66. For the restraining influence that clerical authority had on women's protofeminism, see Sklar, *Catharine Beecher*, chap. 3.

30. Stanton, "Speech to the 1860 Anniversary of the American Anti-Slavery Society," Elizabeth Cady Stanton Papers, LC.

Almost until the Civil War, conflict with clerical authority remained a central issue for the women's rights movement. The 1854 national convention resolved: "We feel it a duty to declare in regard to the sacred cause which has brought us together, that the most determined opposition it encounters is from the clergy generally, whose teachings of the Bible are intensely inimical to the equality of women with man." Representatives of the clergy pursued their fleeting authority onto the women's rights platform. However, Garrisonian women had learned the techniques of Biblical exegesis in numerous debates over the scriptural basis of slavery. They met clergymen on their own ground, skillfully refuting them quote for quote. "The pulpit has been prostituted, the Bible has been ill-used . . . ," Lucretia Mott contended at the 1854 convention. "The temperance people have had to feel its supposed denunciations. Then the anti-slavery, and now this reform has met, and still continues to meet, passage after passage of the Bible, never intended to be so used."[31] When ministers with national reputations started to offer their support to the women's rights movement in the 1850's, the issue of clerical authority began to recede in importance. It was not a major aspect of postwar feminism, because of changes in both the movement and the clergy.

Women in the Garrisonian abolitionist movement not only absorbed its anticlericalism, but also drew on its principle of the absolute moral equality of all human beings. Because the Garrisonian abolitionists' target was Northern racial prejudice and their goal the development of white empathy for the suffering slave, they focused their arguments on convincing white people of their basic identity with black people. The weakness of this emphasis on the ultimate moral identity of the races was its inability to account for their historical differences. Garrisonians did not develop an explanation for the origins and persistence of racism, and as a result many abolitionists continued to believe that there were biological causes for the inferior position of black

31. *HWS*, I, 383 and 380.

people. Instead, Garrisonian abolitionism stressed the common humanity of blacks and whites. Garrisonians formulated this approach as a moral abstraction, but its basis was the concrete demands of the agitational task they faced as abolitionists.[32]

Abolitionist feminists appropriated this belief and applied it to women. The philosophical tenet that women were essentially human and only incidentally female liberated them from the necessity of justifying their own actions in terms of what was appropriate to women's sphere. In other words, Garrisonianism provided an ideology of equality for women to use in fighting their way out of a society built around sexual difference and inequality. The degree to which abolitionist feminists ignored the demands of women's sphere is particularly remarkable because they did so at the same time that the ideology of sexual spheres was being elaborated by benevolent women, in other ways very much like them. To the Congregational clergy's demand that she return "to the appropriate duties and influence of women," Sarah Grimké responded: "The Lord Jesus defines the duties of his followers in his Sermon on the Mount . . . without any reference to sex or condition . . . never even referring to the distinction now so strenuously insisted upon between masculine and feminine virtues. . . . Men and women are CREATED EQUAL! They are both moral and accountable beings and whatever is right for man to do is right for woman."[33] Her belief in sex equality took added strength from Hicksite Quaker doctrine and practices. The Grimkés were followed by other Garrisonian feminists who also refused to justify their efforts in terms of women's sphere. "Too much has already been said and written about woman's sphere," Lucy Stone said in 1854. "Leave women, then, to find their sphere." The 1851 women's rights convention resolved that: "We deny the right of any portion of the species to decide for another portion . . . what is and what

32. Kraditor, *Means and Ends, passim,* esp. p. 59.
33. Sarah Grimké, *Letters on the Equality of the Sexes and the Condition of Woman: Addressed to Mary S. Parker* (Boston, 1837), p. 16.

is not their 'proper sphere'; that the proper sphere for all human beings is the largest and highest to which they are able to attain."[34]

Just as the Garrisonian emphasis on the moral equality of the races could not account for their historical inequality, the conviction that men and women were morally identical had serious analytical limitations. The women's rights belief in the moral irrelevance of sexual spheres ignored the reality of women's domestic confinement, which made them different from and dependent on men, and gave credence to the doctrine of spheres. Indeed, Garrisonian feminists ignored the question of women's sphere while simultaneously believing in its existence. A women's rights convention in Ohio in 1852 simultaneously resolved: "Since every human being has an individual sphere, and that is the largest he or she can fill, no one has the right to determine the proper sphere of another," and "In demanding for women equality of rights with their fathers, husbands, brothers, and sons, we neither deny that distinctive character, nor wish them to avoid any duty, or to lay aside that feminine delicacy which legitimately belongs to them as mothers, wives, sisters, and daughters."[35] Like other women, women's rights activists believed in the particular suitability of their sex for domestic activities and did not project a reorganization of the division of labor within the home. They believed that domestic activities were as "naturally" female as childbearing, and as little subject to deliberate social manipulation.[36] The abstract quality of their belief in the moral identity of the sexes did not help them to confront this contradiction in their feminism. Indeed, while permitting the prewar women's rights movement to establish sexual equality as its goal, Garrisonian premises simultaneously held it

34. *HWS,* I, 165 and 826.
35. *HWS,* I, 817.
36. For an account of how these domestic beliefs affected the life of one abolitionist-feminist, see Ellen DuBois, "Struggling into Existence: The Feminism of Sarah and Angelina Grimké," *Women: A Journal of Liberation,* 1 (1970), 4–11.

back from the critical task of examining the sources of sexual inequality.

Along with a philosophical basis, Garrisonian abolitionism provided the women's rights movement with a theory and practice of social change, a strategy that gave direction to its efforts for female emancipation. The core of Garrisonian strategy was the belief that a revolution in people's ideas must precede and underlie institutional and legal reform, in order to effect true social change. "Great political changes may be forced by the pressure of external circumstances, without a corresponding change in the moral sentiment of a nation," Lydia Maria Child wrote in 1842, "but in all such cases, the change is worse than useless; the evil reappears, and usually in a more exaggerated form."[37] Some historians, notably Stanley Elkins and Gilbert Barnes, have mistaken this radical and democratic approach to reform as an anarchistic disregard for the institutional structures of social reality.[38] Garrisonians were not indifferent to institutions, but it is true that they did not specify how changes in popular ideology could be translated into institutional reform. They left this up to the politicians. Instead, they saw themselves as agitators concentrating their energies on provoking public sentiment. While Garrisonian agitation did not develop political mechanisms for ending slavery, it was well suited to the early years of the antislavery movement when the primary problem was overcoming public apathy.

Faced with an equally stubborn and widespread indifference to the oppression of women, women's rights leaders drew on this abolitionist precedent and formulated their task as the agitation of public sentiment. "Disappointment is the lot of woman," Lucy Stone wrote in 1855. "It shall be the business of my life to deepen this disappointment in every woman's heart until she bows down to it no longer."[39] Ernestine Rose described the work as "breaking

37. Child, "Dissolution of the Union," *Liberator,* May 20, 1842, as quoted in Kraditor, *Means and Ends,* p. 23. Kraditor provides an excellent analysis of the Garrisonians' agitational approach to social change.
38. Elkins, *Slavery* (Chicago, 1959), and Barnes, *The Antislavery Impulse, 1830–1844* (New York, 1964).
39. *HWS,* I, 165.

up the ground and sowing the seed."[40] To Lucy Stone and Susan
B. Anthony, both of whom were paid agents of the American
Anti-Slavery Society, the role of itinerant feminist agitator came
quite naturally. However, it was Elizabeth Cady Stanton who
developed the strategy of women's rights agitation most fully, and
this was one of the bases of her leadership. Throughout her long
political career, she consistently believed that anything that
focused public attention on women's oppression was desirable.
She wrote in her diary in 1888, "If I were to draw up a set of
rules for the guidance of reformers . . . I should put at the head
of the list: 'Do all you can, *no matter what,* to get people to think
on your reform, and then, if the reform is good, it will come
about in due season.' "[41] She did not care whether her efforts
generated sympathy or antipathy, as long as they undermined
public apathy. Nor did she believe that translating agitation into
reform was her function. "I am a leader in thought, rather than
numbers," she wrote late in her life, when her methods had become alien to young feminists.[42]

Garrisonian agitation was built around the demand for unconditional, immediate abolition. The intention was both to achieve
a concrete reform and to launch an ideological attack on the
slaveholding mentality. With this program Garrisonians were
able to work simultaneously for the legal abolition of slavery and
a revolution in the racial consciousness of whites to give abolition
meaning. As Aileen Kraditor has interpreted it, immediate abolition was both the means and the end for Garrisonian anti-
slavery.[43] The demand for woman suffrage functioned in a similar fashion in the women's rights movement. It aimed at both a
concrete reform in women's legal status and the education of
public opinion to the principle of the equal humanity of the sexes.
The goal was necessarily twofold because, like unconditional
abolition, woman suffrage was a radical idea, acknowledged

40. *HWS,* I, 693.
41. Diary entry, August 20, 1888, *Stanton Letters,* p. 252.
42. Stanton to Olympia Brown, May 8, 1888, Olympia Brown Willis
Papers, SL.
43. Kraditor, *Means and Ends, passim.*

inside and outside the movement as the capstone of women's emancipation.

The Demand for Woman Suffrage

From the beginning, gaining the franchise was part of the program of the women's rights movement. It was one of a series of reforms that looked toward the elimination of women's dependent and inferior position before the law. The women's rights movement demanded for married women control over their own wages, the right to contract for their own property, joint guardianship over their children, and improved inheritance rights when widowed. For all women, the movement demanded the elective franchise and the rights of citizenship. Compared to legal reforms in women's status articulated before 1848, for instance equal right to inherit real property, the women's rights program was very broadly based, and intentionally so.[44] In particular, the right to control one's earnings and the right to vote were demands that affected large numbers of women—farm women, wives of urban artisans and laborers, millgirls and needlewomen.

While part of this general reform in women's legal status, the demand for woman suffrage was always treated differently from other women's rights. In the first place, it initially met with greater opposition within the movement than other demands did. At the Seneca Falls Convention, Elizabeth Cady Stanton submitted a resolution on "the duty of the women of this country to secure to themselves the sacred right to the elective franchise." Lucretia Mott thought the resolution a mistake, and tried to dissuade her from presenting it. Mott's position may have been based on her Garrisonian objections to involvement in the world of electoral politics, but surely others recoiled from the woman suffrage demand because it seemed too radical. Although the

44. For an excellent account of the pre–Seneca Falls efforts to improve women's legal position see Margaret M. Rabkin, "The Silent Feminist Revolution: Women and the Law in New York State from Blackstone to the Beginnings of American Women's Rights Movement" (doctoral diss., State University of New York at Buffalo, 1975).

convention passed all other motions unanimously, it was seriously divided over the suffrage. Frederick Douglass, who, himself disfranchised, appreciated the importance of membership in the political community, was Stanton's staunchest supporter at Seneca Falls. The woman suffrage resolution barely passed.[45]

Soon, however, woman suffrage was distinguished from other reforms by being elevated to a preeminent position in the women's rights movement. After the Seneca Falls Convention, there is no further evidence of reluctance within the movement to demand the vote. On the contrary, it quickly became the cornerstone of the women's rights program. A resolution passed at the 1856 national convention may be taken as representative: "Resolved, that the main power of the woman's rights movement lies in this: that while always demanding for woman better education, better employment, and better laws, it has kept steadily in view the one cardinal demand for the right of suffrage: in a democracy, the symbol and guarantee of all other rights."[46]

In keeping with the truth of this resolution, the demand for woman suffrage also generated much more opposition outside the movement. Public opinion and politicians were more sympathetic to feminists' economic demands than to their political ones. In the mid-1850's, state legislatures began to respond favorably to women's lobbying and petition efforts for reforms in property law. By 1860, fourteen states had passed some form of women's property rights legislation. Encouraged by these victories, the movement escalated its demands and shifted its emphasis from property rights to the suffrage. This was clearest in the case of New York. Initially, to gain maximum support for the less con-

---

45. On the Seneca Falls Convention see *HWS*, I, 63–75, and Elizabeth Cady Stanton, *Eighty Years and More: Reminiscences, 1815–1897* (New York, 1899), pp. 143–154. In 1849, Lucretia Mott publicly supported woman suffrage, while very clearly maintaining her distance from electoral politics: "Far be it from me to encourage women to vote or take an active part in politics in the present state of our government. Her right to the elective franchise, however, is the same, and should be yielded to her, whether she exercise that right or not" (*HWS*, I, p. 372).

46. *HWS*, I, 634.

troversial demand, activists there circulated separate petitions for property rights and for the vote. As the movement gained strength, however, they included both economic and political demands on a single petition, and, in 1857, presented a unified program to the legislature.[47] Three years later, the New York legislature passed the most comprehensive piece of women's rights legislation in the United States, the Married Women's Property Act. This law granted New York women all the economic rights they demanded, but still refused women the right to vote.[48]

To both opponents and advocates of women's rights, therefore, the demand for woman suffrage was significantly more controversial than other demands for equality with men. Why was this the case? Like the overwhelming majority of their contemporaries, nineteenth-century feminists believed that the vote was the ultimate repository of social and economic power in a democratic society. They wanted that power for women and relied on well-developed natural rights arguments and the rhetorical traditions of the American Revolution and the Declaration of Independence to make their demand. "In demanding the political rights of woman," the 1853 national convention resolved, "we simply assert the fundamental principle of democracy—that taxation and representation should go together, and that, if the principle is denied, all our institutions must fall with it."[49]

The widespread belief in the importance of the ballot which feminists drew on to make their case for woman suffrage is a somewhat elusive aspect of the American political tradition because the extension of the franchise to the masses of white men

47. *HWS,* I, 588–589 and 676–677. The fourteen states were: Massachusetts, Vermont, New Hampshire, Rhode Island, Ohio, Illinois, Indiana, Wisconsin, Connecticut, Texas, Maine, Iowa, Kansas, and Alabama.

48. *HWS,* I, 686–687.

49. *HWS,* I, 834. As one kind of evidence that woman suffrage was considered more radical than other women's rights demands, note that, in Ohio in 1850, a petition for "equal rights" for women received four times as many signatures as a petition for equal suffrage (*HWS,* I, 122). Similarly, at the 1853 National Women's Rights Convention, Clarina I. H. Nichols explained that "the propriety of woman voting" had been the last obstacle to her conversion to women's rights (*ibid.,* p. 355).

had been such a gradual process. No organized political movement was required as Chartism had been in Britain. As a result, what the vote meant and promised to antebellum American men was not formalized into an explicit ideological statement, and is that much harder for us to assess in retrospect. However, American white working men seem to have attached considerable importance to their franchise. Even though they did not have to organize to win the vote, they did form working men's parties in every northern state to protect it and give it power. Believing that the vote "put into our hands the power of perfecting our government and securing our happiness," they organized against obstacles to its use, such as indirect elections and caucus nominations.[50] In addition, working men saw the democratic franchise, divested of property qualifications, as a victory against privilege. As a British Chartist put it in 1834, "With us Universal suffrage will begin in our lodges, extend to the general union, embrace the management of trade, and finally swallow up political power."[51] To the degree that organized working men believed that universal white manhood suffrage established the necessary preconditions for social democracy, they looked to their own shortcomings for their failure to achieve such a society. "Our fathers have purchased for us political rights and an equality of privileges," a July Fourth orator chastised the trade unions of Boston in 1834, "which we have not yet had the intelligence to appreciate, nor the courage to protect, nor the wisdom to employ."[52]

Yet these general ideas about the power and importance of the

50. Frederick Robinson, "An Oration Delivered before the Trade Unions of Boston," (1834) in *Labor Politics: Collected Pamphlets*, ed. Leon Stein and Philip Taft, (New York, 1971), I, 28–29. Also see Walter Hugins, *Jacksonian Democracy and the Working Class: A Study of the New York Workingmen's Movement, 1829–1837* (Palo Alto, Calif., 1960). The one instance during the nineteenth century in which white men had to organize politically to get the vote was in Rhode Island. See Marvin Gettleman, *The Dorr Rebellion* (New York, 1973).

51. Ray Boston, *British Chartists in America, 1838–1900* (Manchester, 1971), p. 2.

52. Robinson, "Oration," p. 6.

ballot are not sufficient to explain the special significance of the suffrage issue for women. The ideas of democratic political theory were not systematically applied to women until feminist leaders, anxious to challenge the subservient position of women, appropriated those ideas and demanded the vote. Like black men, women were excluded from the actual expansion of the suffrage in the late eighteenth and early nineteenth centuries, but the exclusion of women from political life went even further. Women were so far outside the boundaries of the antebellum political community that the fact of their disfranchisement, unlike that of black men, was barely noticed. The French and American Revolutions greatly intensified awareness of the educational, economic, and social inequality of the sexes, but few Revolutionary leaders considered the inclusion of women in the franchise, and even fewer—perhaps only Condorcet—called for it.[53] Further back in the democratic political tradition, the radical Levellers of seventeenth-century England made the same distinction between women's civil and moral rights, which they advocated, and women's political rights, which they never considered.[54] In large part, the awareness that women were being excluded from the political community and the need to justify this disfranchisement came after women began to demand political equality. Prior to the women's rights movement, those who noticed and commented on the disfranchisement of women were not advocates of woman suffrage, but antidemocrats, who used this exception to disprove the natural right of people to self-government.[55]

On what basis were women excluded from any consideration in the distribution of political power, even when that power was organized on democratic principles? At least part of the answer seems to lie in the concept of "independence," which was the

53. Marguerite Fisher, "Eighteenth Century Theorists of Women's Liberation," in *"Remember the Ladies": New Perspectives on Women in American History,* ed. Carol V. R. George (Syracuse, N.Y., 1975), pp. 39–47.

54. C. B. Macpherson, *The Political Theory of Possessive Individualism: Hobbes to Locke* (London, 1962), p. 296.

55. See, for instance, Francis Bowman, "Recent Contest in Rhode Island (1834)," in Stein and Taft, *Labor Politics,* I, 421.

major criterion for enfranchisement in classical democratic political theory, and which acted to exclude women from the political community. Even the radical Tom Paine thought that servants should not have the vote because they were economically and socially dependent on their masters, and "freedom is destroyed by dependence."[56] A contemporary political theorist, C. B. Macpherson, has defined the core of this concept of "independence" as self-ownership, the individual's right to possess his own person: "The essential humanity of the individual consisted in his freedom from the will of other persons, freedom to enjoy his own person and to develop his own capacities. One's person was property not metaphorically, but essentially; the property one had in it was the right to exclude others from its use and enjoyment."[57] Women's traditional relationships to men within their families constituted the essence of dependence. When John Adams considered the question, "Whence arises the right of men to govern the women without their consent?" he found the answer in men's power to feed, clothe, and employ women and therefore to make political decisions on their behalf.[58] Not only were eighteenth- and early nineteenth-century women prohibited from owning real property or controlling wealth; they could not be said even to hold property in themselves. Law and custom granted the husband ownership, not only of his wife's labor power and the wages she earned by it, but of her physical person as well, in the sexual rights of the marriage relation. No people, with the exception of chattel slaves, had less proprietary rights over themselves in eighteenth- and early nineteenth-century America than married women.[59] Until the emergence of feminism, the dependent status that women held was considered natural, and if not right, then inescapable.

Thus, the demand that women be included in the electorate

56. Eric Foner. *Tom Paine and Revolutionary America* (New York, 1976), pp. 142–144.
57. Macpherson, *Political Theory*, p. 153.
58. Cited in Scott and Scott, *One Half the People*, p. 4.
59. Rabkin, "The Silent Feminist Revolution," *passim*.

was not simply a stage in the expansion and democratization of the franchise. It was a particularly feminist demand, because it exposed and challenged the assumption of male authority over women. To women fighting to extend their sphere beyond its traditional domestic limitations, political rights involved a radical change in women's status, their emergence into public life. The right to vote raised the prospect of female autonomy in a way that other claims to equal rights could not. Petitions to state legislatures for equal rights to property and children were memorials for the redress of grievances, which could be tolerated within the traditional chivalrous framework that accorded women the "right" to protection. In 1859 the *New York Times* supported the passage of the New York Married Women's Property Act by distinguishing the "legal protection and fair play to which women are justly entitled" from "the claims to a share of political power which the extreme advocates of Women's Rights are fond of advancing."[60] By contrast, the suffrage demand challenged the idea that women's interests were identical or even compatible with men's. As such, it embodied a vision of female self-determination that placed it at the center of the feminist movement. "While we would not undervalue other methods," the 1851 national women's rights convention resolved, "the Right of Suffrage for Women is, in our opinion, the corner-stone of this enterprise, since we do not seek to protect woman, but rather to place her in a position to protect herself."[61]

The feminist implications of the suffrage demand are further evident in the reverberations it sent through the ideology of sexual spheres, the nineteenth-century formulation of the sexual division of labor. Most obviously, woman suffrage constituted a serious challenge to the masculine monopoly of the public sphere. Although the growing numbers of women in schools, trades, professions, and wage-labor were weakening the sexual barriers around life outside the family, most adult women remained at

60. "Property of Married Women," *New York Times*, April 8, 1859, p. 4.
61. *HWS*, I, p. 825.

home, defined politically, economically, and socially by their family position. In this context, the prospect of enfranchisement was uniquely able to touch all women, offering them a public role and a relation to the community unmediated by husband or children. While the suffrage demand did not address the domestic side of the nineteenth-century sexual order directly, the connections between public and private spheres carried its implications into the family as well. In particular, the public honor of citizenship promised to elevate women's status in the home and raised the specter of sexual equality there. Women's rights leaders were relatively modest about the implications of the franchise for women's position in the family, anticipating reform of family law and improvement in the quality of domestic relations. Their opponents, however, predicted that woman suffrage would have a revolutionary impact on the family. "It is well known that the object of these unsexed women is to overthrow the most sacred of our institutions . . . ," a New York legislator responded to women's rights petitions. "Are we to put the stamp of truth upon the libel here set forth, that men and women, in the matrimonial relation, are to be equal?"[62] In the introduction to the *History of Woman Suffrage*, Elizabeth Cady Stanton penetrated to the core of this antisuffrage response. "Political rights, involving in their last results equality everywhere," she wrote, "roused all the antagonism of a dominant power, against the self-assertion of a class hitherto subservient."[63]

Obstacles to Growth

The process by which women's rights ideas were spread was a highly informal one. As the first activists reached the small towns of New York, Massachusetts, Ohio, and Indiana, their example drew local women out of their isolation. A speech by Lucy Stone impelled two Rockland, Maine, women to become printers.[64]

62. *HWS*, I, 613.
63. *HWS*, I, 16.
64. Alice Stone Blackwell, *Lucy Stone: Pioneer of Women's Rights* (Boston, 1930), pp. 101–102.

Olympia Brown was brought into the movement when, still a student at Antioch College, she heard author and abolitionist Frances Gage. "It was the first time I had heard a woman preach," she recalled, "and the sense of victory lifted me up."[65] Frances Ellen Burr, who went on to lead suffrage forces in Connecticut, attended a women's rights convention in Cleveland when she was twenty-two. She was surprised at how attracted she was to the militance of the speakers and noted in her diary, "Never saw anything of the kind before." "Lucy Stone . . . is independent in manner and advocates woman's rights in the strongest terms," she wrote; "scorns the idea of *asking* rights of man, but says she must boldly assert her own rights, and *take* them in her own strength."[66] Reports of the Seneca Falls Convention stirred Emily Collins to gather fifteen neighbors into an equal rights society, and draw up a petition to the legislature. "I was born and lived almost forty years in South Bristol, Ontario County—one of the most secluded spots in Western New York," she explained,

but from the earliest dawn of reason I pined for that freedom of thought and action that was then denied to all womankind. I revolted in spirit against the customs of society and the laws of the State that crushed my aspirations and debarred me from the pursuit of almost every object worthy of an intelligent, rational mind. But not until that meeting at Seneca Falls in 1848, of the pioneers in the cause, gave this feeling of unrest form and voice, did I take action.[67]

Of all the pre–Civil War activists, Susan B. Anthony was the most deliberate about introducing new women to women's rights. Between 1854 and 1860 she made several canvasses of New York. In the innumerable small towns she visited, she tried to locate the people most sympathetic to women's rights. She particularly cul-

65. Lawrence L. Graves, "Olympia Brown," *NAW*, I, 257, and Olympia Brown Willis, *Acquaintances Old and New among Reformers* (Milwaukee, 1911), p. 10.
66. *HWS*, III, 335.
67. Collins, "Reminiscences," *HWS*, I, 88.

tivated the women, encouraging the boldest of them by asking them to preside over the meetings she organized or by staying in their homes overnight. Occasionally, she discovered a genuinely strong-minded woman, waiting for the women's rights movement to take her up. In Aurora, she found three women wearing bloomers, one of whom she asked to conduct the meeting. "It does my heart good to see them," she wrote in her diary.[68]

Nonetheless, the movement grew slowly. As Stone rationalized after a particularly disappointing lecture tour, "I sell a great many of the tracts, so seed is being scattered that will grow *sometime*."[69] In the wake of their lectures and conventions, Stone, Anthony, and others left a trail of strong-minded women behind them. Sarah Burger attended a women's rights convention in 1853, when she was sixteen. What she heard there convinced her that the University of Michigan should be opened to women and "that women themselves should move in the matter." She located twelve other girls to join with her and in 1858 petitioned the university for admission. She continued her campaign for several years, and, although she had to attend a normal school, the University of Michigan finally admitted women in 1869.[70] Two Ellsworth, Maine, women organized a lecture series on women's rights. Despite threats to the livelihood of one of them, they persisted and the lectures were held.[71] Other local activists, more than we may ever know, launched their own protests, but often the women's rights movement was too small and weak to sustain them. In 1859, Mary Harrington of Claremont, New Hampshire, refused to pay her taxes because she was disfranchised. The tax collector seized her furniture and the local newspaper editor attacked her in print. She was too isolated to do anything more, and her rebellion went underground for the time being. "Such unjust treatment seemed so cruel that I sometimes felt I could

68. Diary entry, January, 1855. Susan B. Anthony Papers, SL.
69. Stone to Susan B. Anthony, November 8, 1855, Blackwell Family Collection, LC.
70. *HWS*, III, 527.
71. *HWS*, III, 365.

willingly lay down my life," she wrote later, "if it would deliver my sex from such degrading oppression. I have, every year since, submissively paid my taxes, humbly hoping and praying that I may live to see the day that women will not be compelled to pay taxes without representation."[72]

Prewar women's rights agitation had an impact on a large number of women who were not ready to speak or act publicly but were convinced that the position of their sex demanded reform. A friend of her sister's invited Antoinette Brown to visit her "to introduce you to my friends here and let them see that you have not got horns. . . . I think I see more and more clearly that the Lord has a work for females to do that they have not understood," she continued, "and I am glad that there are some that are willing to learn and to do what He requires of them."[73] Anthony reported to Stanton that she had been to dinner with Mrs. Finney, the wife of the president of Oberlin. After her husband denounced women's rights, "Mrs. Finney took me to another seat and with much earnestness inquired all about what we were doing and the growth of our movement. . . . Said she you have the sympathy of a large proportion of the educated women with you. In my circle I hear the movement much talked of and earnest hopes for its spread expressed—but these women dare not speak out their sympathy."[74] Women's rights agitators barely knew how many women they were affecting, much less how to encourage their halting sympathies.

Ironically, the Garrisonian politics and abolitionist alliance that had enabled the women's rights movement to develop in the first place were beginning to restrain its continued growth. Like the abolitionists before them, women's rights activists saw themselves as agitators, stirring up discontent. However, they had no way to consolidate the feminist sentiment that their agitation was beginning to create. Once the level of their discontent was raised,

72. *HWS,* III, 373–374.
73. Unknown correspondent to Antoinette Brown, November 5, 1852, SL.
74. Anthony to Stanton, May 26, 1856, Elizabeth Cady Stanton Papers, Vassar College Library.

there was nothing for most women to do with it. Women's rights activities were organized around a small group who were politically skilled, willing to shoulder the opprobrium of "strongmindedness," and able to commit a great deal of their energies to the movement. Women who were just beginning to develop political skills and sensibilities could not normally find an active role to play. The limitations to growth inherent in the agitational focus of prewar women's rights were embodied in the movement's organizational underdevelopment. There were no national or state organizations. Annual conventions were planned by an informal and constantly changing coordinating committee. Speaking tours and legislative campaigns were highly individualistic matters, which put a premium on personal initiative and bravery. The movement's close political relationship with abolitionism further restrained its organizational growth, in that its ability to rely on the organizational resources of the American Anti-Slavery Society meant that it did not develop its own. Women's rights articles were published in antislavery newspapers, and its tracts were printed with antislavery funds. The surrogate political coherence that abolitionism provided women's rights permitted the movement's leaders to indulge their propensities for individualism without risking the entire women's rights enterprise. The 1852 national convention rejected a proposal for a national women's rights society on the grounds that formal organizations "fetter and distort the expanding mind."[75]

Above all, the prewar women's rights movement depended on abolitionism for its constituency. It is impossible to estimate how many women were touched by women's rights, and how many of these were abolitionists. Still, the movement's strongest, most reliable, and most visible support came from abolitionist ranks, particularly from the women. This dependence on an organized constituency borrowed from abolitionism was particularly marked on the national level. The call for the first national women's rights convention was timed to coincide with the annual meeting

75. *HWS,* I, 540–542. The speaker was Angelina Grimké Weld.

of the American Anti-Slavery Society.[76] Abolitionist women provided women's rights with an audience well suited to its first, highly controversial years. Their antislavery activity had already put them outside the pale of respectable womanhood, where they were less likely to be frightened by public hostility. However, the availability of an audience among antislavery women kept feminist leaders from a systematic effort to reach the many women who were not reformers. At the worst, it gave them a kind of disdain for the nonpolitical preoccupations of most women. The fearlessness of female abolitionists sheltered the women's rights movement from a confrontation with the very real fears of male opposition and public disapproval that lay between it and the mobilization of large numbers of women.

Although primarily a source of strength, the relation of women's rights to abolitionism was thus a potential liability as well. The partnership was unequal, with women's rights dependent on abolitionism for essential resources and support. The basic precepts, strategic methods, and organizational forms of Garrisonian abolitionism had sustained the women's rights movement through its first dozen years. On this basis, feminist leaders were able to transform insights into the oppression of women that they shared with many other women into a social movement strong enough to have a future. This achievement raised other political problems—the extent of the movement's reforming ambitions, the nature of its constituency, the organizational form it would take, and above all, its relation to abolitionism. The resolution of these matters was interrupted by the outbreak of the Civil War. Women's rights activists subordinated all other interests to the fate of slavery, and suspended feminist activity for the length of the war. When they returned, four years later, to consider the future of women's rights, the political context within which they did so had been completely altered.

76. *HWS*, I, 216.

Chapter Two

The Fourteenth Amendment
and the
American Equal Rights
Association

The liberation of four million black people from slavery revolutionized the postwar political world. For the reformers who had worked thirty years toward that end and knew the depths of American racism, the abolition of slavery seemed a miracle. Those who did not trust in miracles, among them many women's rights leaders, did what they could to ensure total and permanent emancipation. Immediately after Lincoln issued the Emancipation Proclamation, Stanton and Anthony organized the National Loyal Women's League to push for a constitutional amendment abolishing slavery. Senator Charles Sumner credited their work in collecting four hundred thousand signatures on petitions with much of the impetus behind the Thirteenth Amendment.[1] The brilliant reality of slavery's final defeat encouraged reformers' hopes of even greater changes in the future. "The millennium is on the way," Theodore Tilton, editor of the *New York Independent,* wrote to Anthony. "Three cheers for God!"[2] Elizabeth Stanton's millennial vision was more exact. "Out of this struggle we must come with higher ideas of liberty, the masses quickened with thought, and a rotten aristocracy crushed forever," she wrote. "I have no misgivings as to the result."[3]

1. *HWS,* II, 50–89.
2. Theodore Tilton to Anthony, January 11, 1863, as quoted in Ida H. Harper, *The Life and Work of Susan B. Anthony* (Indianapolis, 1899), I, 225.
3. Stanton to Elizabeth Smith Miller, no date, as cited in Alma Lutz, *Created Equal: A Biography of Elizabeth Cady Stanton, 1815–1902* (New York, 1940), p. 123.

Above and beyond the general encouragement it provided to reformers, the abolition of slavery reshaped the postwar feminist movement in several critical ways. To begin with, it reinforced the movement's tendency to focus on woman suffrage by making the issue of political rights a question of national political significance. Emancipation immediately raised the issue of the political status of black people, who were no longer slaves but not yet citizens. Along with the readmission of southern states, with which it was closely connected, black suffrage became the pivotal issue of postwar Reconstruction politics. This in turn encouraged a shift in emphasis among women's rights advocates toward the suffrage demand. After the war feminist activists began to refer to themselves as "the woman suffrage movement," rather than the "women's rights movement."[4] Moreover, the fact that abolitionists played a major role in the drive to enfranchise the freedmen greatly intensified the impact that the new level of national attention to black suffrage had on woman suffrage. In 1865 the American Anti-Slavery Society reorganized around the demand for black suffrage, bringing the goals of the two movements much closer together. Perhaps most important to the future of woman suffrage, the defeat of slavery not only altered abolitionists' goals; it also significantly enhanced their political influence. The defeat of slavery was like an earthquake in American political life, and moved abolitionists much closer to the center of national political power. Certainly, other factors such as southern intransigence, the freedmen's own actions, and partisan realignments pushed the issue of black suffrage forward in the years after the Civil War. However, the deliberate political leadership provided by abolitionists and their allies in Congress was central to the drive for racial equality in Reconstruction. To feminists, all these changes, but especially the emergence of their long-time allies as

4. Paulina Wright Davis commented on this change in her speech on the history of the women's rights reform, delivered in 1870. See Davis, *A History of the National Women's Rights Movement for Twenty Years, from 1850 to 1870* (New York, 1871), p. 10. Martha Coffin Wright wished the movement had retained "the good, old name of Woman's Rights" (Wright to Stanton, December 14, 1870, Garrison Family Papers, Sophia Smith Collection [Women's History Archive], Smith College Library).

influential actors on the national political scene, made the achievement of woman suffrage seem no longer a visionary demand, but a real possibility.

Contrary to feminist leaders' expectations, however, the national attention focused on black suffrage and the new political prominence of abolitionists did not automatically benefit woman suffrage. Abolitionists' increased political power made them more reluctant to support feminist demands than they had been before the war. They were no longer agitators on the periphery of American society, whose primary goal was to raise popular consciousness. Instead, they were in a real position to affect the shape of congressional Reconstruction. The political requirements of their new position drove a wedge between their primary objective, which had always been the liberation of black people, and their more general reform goals, which included the emancipation of women. This development in turn led feminists to question the junior status and dependent position they held in the Garrisonian reform coalition, and to challenge abolitionsts for the right to formulate their common goals. The initial political strategy that feminists developed for Reconstruction attempted to make black suffrage and woman suffrage equal and inseparable demands. This strategy, rather than leading abolitionists back to support woman suffrage, drove them further away. However, feminists' efforts to fulfill the promise of their abolitionist alliance had an important impact on their own development and moved them much further along the path of political autonomy.

The demand that black men be enfranchised had been a minor but insistent theme of antebellum black protest. Northern free blacks protested their disfranchisement as early as the National Negro Conventions of the 1830's, but their primary goal remained the abolition of slavery.[5] After Lincoln issued the Emancipation Proclamation, the demand for black suffrage intensified, especially among abolitionists. Frederick Douglass and Wendell

5. Leon Litwack, *North of Slavery: The Negro in the Free States, 1790–1860* (Chicago, 1961), and Sterling Stuckey, *The Ideological Origins of Black Nationalism* (Boston, 1972).

Phillips were particularly active in pointing out that the question of the black man's political status followed directly from the fact of his emancipation. Phillips argued that if the ex-slaves did not have the political weapons to protect themselves against their former owners, the abolition of slavery would prove a worthless victory. He expected the American Anti-Slavery Society to lead the drive for political equality as it had the efforts against slavery. Garrison disagreed, insisting that the society's historical mission ended with abolition. At the May 1865 American Anti-Slavery Society annual meetings, abolitionists considered the matter and voted in favor of Phillips's position. Garrison resigned the presidency, Phillips assumed the society's leadership, and all its resources were redirected toward enfranchising the freedmen.[6] As Parker Pillsbury, editor of the *National Anti-Slavery Standard,* observed, "suffrage for the negro is now what immediate emancipation was thirty years ago," the cutting edge of radical racial change.[7]

The abolitionist advocates of black suffrage made their case in a variety of ways, some of which coincided with arguments for woman suffrage, others of which emphasized the difference between the two demands. On the one hand, they argued that black men should be enfranchised because the suffrage was a right of all citizens and a source of self-respect and social power. Douglass described the psychological impact of disfranchisement on black men with great eloquence and in terms that could have been taken to apply equally to women. By disfranchising black people, he explained, "you declare before the world that we are unfit to exercise the elective franchise, and by this means lead us to undervalue ourselves, and to feel that we have no possibilities like other men."[8] More frequently, however, supporters of black

6. "American Anti-Slavery Society Anniversary," *National Anti-Slavery Standard,* May 13, 1865, p. 2.

7. As quoted in James M. McPherson, *The Struggle for Equality: Abolitionists and the Negro in the Civil War and Reconstruction* (Princeton, 1964), p. 306.

8. Douglass, "What the Black Man Wants," in *Negro Social and Political Thought, 1850–1920,* ed. Howard Brotz (New York, 1966), pp. 277–284.

suffrage insisted on the special historical significance and unique strategic position of the ex-slaves. Southern blacks were a pro-northern force in the heart of the Confederacy and this linked their enfranchisement to the preservation of the Union's victory and the protection of the Republican party's power. Black suffrage, its supporters argued, was the only secure basis for Reconstruction.[9] Feminists could make no such claims of partisan benefit or political expediency for woman suffrage.

Abolitionists worked for the enfranchisement of the freedmen primarily within the framework of the Republican party. This represented a major shift in their strategy for social change and their approach to partisan politics. Before 1860 the American Anti-Slavery Society and the antislavery forces within the major parties had kept a deliberate distance from each other. Once the war began, however, the black man's fate was bound up with that of the Republican party, and abolitionists' practice of remaining outside partisan politics became unfeasible. Instead, abolitionists and their counterparts in the Republican party, the Radicals, began to collaborate closely and openly. In many ways, the position of abolitionists outside Congress and Radicals inside converged on each other. From one side, Radical Republicans brought the principles of Garrisonian agitation onto the floor of Congress. In particular, Charles Sumner linked the passage of strong Reconstruction legislation to growth in popular antiracist sentiment. From the other side, abolitionists increasingly functioned as the Republican party's left wing, pushing it to adopt a more and more extensive program of racial equality. Together, abolitionists and Radicals struggled to dictate the Republican party's postwar program and fulfill the promise of Reconstruction. "These are no times for ordinary politics; these are formative hours," Phillips advised Sumner. "The national purpose and thought grows and ripens in thirty days as much as ordinary

9. See, for instance, the comments of Charles Sumner and Thaddeus Stevens as quoted in W. E. B. DuBois, *Black Reconstruction in America, 1860–1880* (New York, 1969), pp. 192–199.

years bring it forward. We *radicals* have all the elements of national education in our hands."[10]

The Fourteenth Amendment, first introduced into Congress in December 1865, and finally passed on to the states for ratification in June 1866, represented the midpoint in the drive to make black suffrage the program of the Republican party. The amendment introduced the issue of the political rights of the freedmen into the Constitution, but it did so indirectly and did not commit the federal government to protect them. Instead, as a condition for readmission, it required the former Confederate states either to enfranchise their ex-slaves or to have their Congressional delegations cut proportionately. The major thrust of the amendment was for civil, not political, rights. It concentrated on defining national citizenship and establishing its supremacy over state provisions.[11] Abolitionists were deeply dissatisfied with the Fourteenth Amendment but ultimately could not oppose it. Their response to it indicates that while the Republican party provided them with a framework for influencing the shape of Reconstruction policy, it also imposed limitations on how their influence could be exercised. Most abolitionists considered the Fourteenth Amendment an inadequate response to their demands for political power for the freedmen and an unacceptable basis on which to readmit the former Confederate states. Phillips publicly criticized its provisions, and expressed the hope that state legislatures would not ratify it.[12] Nonetheless, abolitionists' commitment to the Republican party as the ultimate framework for the freedmen's enfranchisement made it difficult for most of them actually to oppose the amendment. The Republican party formally adopted the Fourteenth Amendment as its platform for the 1866 congressional elections. Despite misgivings, the American Anti-

10. As quoted in Michael Les Benedict, *A Compromise of Principle: Congressional Republicans and Reconstruction, 1863–1869* (New York, 1974), p. 106.

11. The authoritative history of the amendment is Joseph B. James, *The Framing of the Fourteenth Amendment* (Urbana, Ill., 1965).

12. Phillips, "The Nation's Disappointment," *Standard,* June 16, 1866, p. 1; Phillips, "Precautions," *Standard,* September 29, 1866, p. 2.

Slavery Society conceded the supreme importance of keeping Republicans in power. Accordingly, rather than advance a more forthright position on black suffrage, they accepted the party's campaign strategy and with it the Fourteenth Amendment. The *Standard* called for the election of Republicans, gambling that a Republican victory at the polls would permit the party to support black suffrage in the future. "I hope the Republican party will succeed. I know no other channel . . . in which to work," Phillips reluctantly explained to other abolitionists in July 1866. "I cannot tell you to desert the Republican party; I know nowhere else for you to go."[13]

Abolitionists' commitment to women's rights was a casualty of their new political strategy and relationship to the Republican party. From the very beginning of Reconstruction, abolitionist leaders indicated that woman suffrage would not be part of their efforts. They believed that the demand for women's enfranchisement was a burden they could not carry if they were going to overcome the enormous opposition to black suffrage. Because the women's rights movement had accepted the political leadership of the American Anti-Slavery Society in the past, abolitionists expected it to continue to do so during Reconstruction and to defer its demands until the freedmen's were achieved. As early as the 1865 antislavery meetings when he assumed leadership, Phillips informed women's rights activists that he thought it best to set aside woman suffrage for the time being and work only for an amendment that would prohibit disfranchisement on the grounds of race, color, and previous condition: "I hope in time to be as bold as Stuart Mill and add to that last clause 'sex'!! But this hour belongs to the negro. As Abraham Lincoln said, 'One War at a time'; so I say, One question at a time. This hour belongs to the negro."[14] Phillips's declaration of strategic intentions was made months before feminists began to press their claims for suffrage, either among abolitionists or before Congress.

13. "Anti-Slavery Celebration in Framingham, July 4, 1866," *Standard*, July 14, 1866, p. 1.
14. "American Anti-Slavery Anniversary," *Standard*, May 13, 1865, p. 2.

It seems to have been unprovoked, and suggests how obvious and compelling the connection between woman suffrage and black suffrage was in the first years of Reconstruction. "May I ask just one question based on the apparent opposition in which you place the negro and the woman?" Stanton wrote angrily to Phillips a few days later. "My question is this: Do you believe the African race is composed entirely of males?"[15] Privately she expressed her deepest fears to Anthony. "I have argued constantly with Phillips and the whole [antislavery] fraternity, but I fear one and all will favor enfranchising the negro without us. Woman's cause is in deep water."[16]

When first reports about the Fourteenth Amendment reached her in late summer, 1865, Stanton's worst fears were confirmed. Not only was the proposed amendment concerned with the political rights of the freedmen to the exclusion of the demands for woman suffrage. It strengthened the disfranchisement of women by making explicit their exclusion from its provisions. Two decades of women's rights agitation had destroyed the centuries-old assumption that political rights applied only to men. Accordingly, the Republican authors of the Fourteenth Amendment, including Sumner, had to decide between enfranchising women or specifying male citizens as the basis of representation.[17] They chose the latter, writing the word "male" into the amendment and introducing an explicit sexual distinction into the Constitution for the first time. Woman suffrage advocates protested vigorously, but they could not get their abolitionist comrades to join them. Frances Gage wrote a scathing attack against abolitionists for their sudden change of heart toward women's rights: "Can any one tell us why the great advocates of Human Equality . . . forget that when they were a weak party and needed all the womanly strength of the nation to help them on, they always

15. Stanton to Phillips, May 25, 1865, *Stanton Letters*, p. 105.
16. Stanton to Anthony, August 1, 1865, *ibid.*
17. "Charles Sumner said, years afterward, that he wrote over nineteen pages of foolscap to get rid of the word 'male' and yet keep 'negro suffrage' as a party measure intact; but it could not be done" (*HWS*, II, 97).

united the words 'without regard to sex, race, or color?' Who ever hears of sex now from any of these champions of freedom?"[18] Feminists claimed that the amendment insulted and degraded women, that it gave constitutional authority to their disfranchisement, and that its ratification would significantly increase the obstacles to political equality for women. "If that word 'male' be inserted," Stanton predicted ominously, "it will take us a century at least to get it out."[19]

During the early months of Congressional debate, while the amendment was still in its formative stages, Stanton and Anthony tried to avert this impending catastrophe. They drew up a petition for woman suffrage, the first ever directed to Congress rather than the state legislatures. It read in part: "As you are now amending the Constitution, and, in harmony with advancing civilization, placing new safeguards round the individual rights of four million of emancipated ex-slaves, we ask that you extend the right of Suffrage to Woman . . . and thus fulfill your constitutional obligation 'to guarantee to every State in the Union a Republican form of Government.' "[20] Initially, they found that other supporters of woman suffrage were reluctant to intrude on "the negro's hour" by circulating this petition, but by January 1866 they had collected ten thousand signatures to submit to Congress.[21] The opposition of Radicals was an insurmountable barrier, however. Although the woman suffragists tried to direct their petitions to friendly Democrats to spare Republicans the burden, a few petitions made their way to Radical Republicans, who withheld them. "There are petitions in the hands of several republican members of the House from which the public hears

---

18. "Letter from Frances Gage," *Standard,* November 25, 1865, p. 3.
19. Stanton to Gerrit Smith, January 1, 1866, Gerrit Smith Collection, George Arents Research Library for Special Collections, Syracuse University.
20. *HWS,* II, p. 91.
21. Alma Lutz, *Susan B. Anthony: Rebel, Crusader, Humanitarian* (Boston, 1959), p. 118. For early opposition to the woman suffrage petition, see Lucretia Mott to Martha Coffin Wright, November 2, 1865, Garrison Family Papers, Sophia Smith Collection (Women's History Archive), Smith College Library, and Stanton to Wright, January 6, 1866, *Stanton Letters,* p. 111.

not a word . . . ," Anthony charged. "The Republicans are cowardly."[22] The most serious incident involved Sumner, dean of antislavery radicals in Congress, who received a petition for woman suffrage from the venerable abolitionist, Lydia Maria Child. Sumner presented Child's petition to the Senate under protest, commenting that it was "most importune."[23] Without any help from Radicals or abolitionists, woman suffrage advocates were powerless to affect the formulation of the Fourteenth Amendment. By early spring, it was clear that the amendment had reached its final stages, and that it would exclude woman suffrage and include the adjective "male."

Faced with the evidence of the Fourteenth Amendment that their influential allies intended to leave them out of Reconstruction, feminists decided to take the lead in articulating a more ambitious postwar program that included women's emancipation along with the freedmen's. They called for the unification of the black suffrage and woman suffrage movements in a single campaign for Reconstruction on the basis of universal adulthood suffrage. "When the war came to an end . . . and those who had been our most professed friends forgot us," Lucy Stone explained, "then we resolved to make common cause with the colored class—the only other disfranchised class—and strike for equal rights for all."[24]

Feminists were determined to challenge the secondary status to which abolitionists and Radicals had relegated them in Reconstruction. The ratification of the Thirteenth Amendment, in December, 1865, left blacks and women in the same anomalous position, citizens without political rights. A universal suffrage campaign recognized their common demand for enfranchisement. Strategically, feminists disagreed with abolitionists' argument that now was "the negro's hour." "The whole question of 'time' is so clear to me . . . ," Stanton wrote privately. "As it is now in the

22. Anthony to Caroline Dall, January 30, 1866, Caroline Healey Dall Papers, Massachusetts Historical Society.
23. HWS, II, 97.
24. "Equal Rights," New York World, November 21, 1866, p. 2.

interest of the Republican party to give the black man the suffrage, reformers may as well pass on to some other position a
round higher." "Would it not be wiser," she urged other women,
". . . when the constitutional door is open, [to] avail ourselves of
the strong arm and blue uniform of the black soldier to walk in
by his side?"[25] Most significant, feminists' universal suffrage
strategy reflected their history within the abolitionist movement.
It embodied the Garrisonian conviction that because all radical
social change was of one piece, there need be no antagonism
between the demands of women and blacks. However, before the
war, abolitionist leaders had determined the particular conditions
within which this reform unity was forged. The universal suffrage proposal represented feminists' first serious attempt to take
the lead in directing the abolitionist/women's rights coalition. As
they pursued their campaign for universal suffrage, they learned
the limits of that alliance, and were eventually forced to abandon it.

The feminists' first step was to invite the American Anti-
Slavery Society to merge with the women's rights movement into
a single national organization for equal rights and universal suffrage. Lucy Stone and Susan B. Anthony brought this proposal
to a January 1866 antislavery meeting in Boston. Although some
abolitionists were willing to entertain the idea, Phillips continued
to believe that "success was best obtained by doing one thing
at a time." As presiding officer, he was able to prevent a vote on
the issue.[26] When Phillips's actions made a merger impossible,
feminists responded by mounting a joint campaign for black and
woman suffrage on their own.

Their campaign was inaugurated at the first women's rights
convention since the Civil War, which was held in New York

25. Stanton to Martha Coffin Wright, January 20, 1866, *Stanton Letters,*
p. 113; Stanton, "This is the Negro's Hour," *Standard,* November 26, 1865,
as reprinted in *HWS,* II, 94.

26. Harper, *Life and Work of Susan B. Anthony,* I, 256; "Special Meeting of the American Anti-Slavery Society in Boston, January 24, 1866,"
Standard, February 3, 1866, p. 1.

City in May 1866. The postwar revival of women's rights and its transformation into what Anthony called a movement for human rights was an event of great significance, and every effort was extended to ensure that the proceedings reflected this. Invitations went out to the great lights of the prewar movement as well as to personalities that had emerged since 1860. Antoinette Brown Blackwell assured Stanton that she would come although she was occupied with domestic and child-rearing duties. Anna Dickinson, the young woman whose spectacular oratory on behalf of the Republican party was the pride of feminists, promised she would attend. Henry Ward Beecher, one of the most powerful clergymen in the United States, agreed to make his first appearance on a women's rights platform.[27] At the end of the convention's second day, Martha Coffin Wright moved that "the time has come for an organization that shall demand UNIVERSAL SUFFRAGE, and that hereafter we shall be known as the 'AMERICAN EQUAL RIGHTS ASSOCIATION!' " Her resolution was adopted unanimously, and the new organization proceeded with the work of "burying the black man and the woman in the citizen."[28]

Feminists were optimistic about the new American Equal Rights Association. The formation of their own organization constituted a significant political advance. It increased their ability to agitate, lobby, and speak in their own voices. The local equal rights groups that eventually formed in Kansas, Pennsylvania, Missouri, Ohio, New Jersey, Iowa, and the District of Columbia gave the organization depth.[29] Equal rights leaders were confi-

27. Antoinette Brown Blackwell to Stanton, Elizabeth Cady Stanton Papers, Vassar College Library; Dickinson to Anthony, no date, as reprinted in Harper, *Life and Work of Susan B. Anthony,* I, 258; *HWS,* II, 156.

28. For the proceedings of the convention, see *HWS,* II, 153–177. The quote is from Stanton, *ibid.,* p. 174.

29. For equal rights activity in Iowa, see Louise Noun, *Strong-Minded Women: The Emergence of the Woman Suffrage Movement in Iowa* (Ames, 1970). The District of Columbia equal rights society was called the Universal Franchise Association and is mentioned in *HWS,* III, 809. For Missouri, see *HWS,* III, 599; for Pennsylvania, *HWS,* II, 184; for Ohio, *HWS,* III, 491. New York and Kansas equal rights activities are discussed in Chap. 3 below.

dent that a strong drive for universal suffrage would force abolitionists to abandon their parochial campaign for black suffrage and join in a united effort. Elizabeth Cady Stanton hoped that "the desire of [my] heart to see the Anti-Slavery and Woman's Rights organizations merged into an Equal Rights Association" might still be achieved. "What is so plain to me, may, I trust, be so to all before the lapse of many months," she said at the founding convention, "that all who have worked together thus far, may still stand side by side in this crisis in our nation's history."[30]

A month after the Equal Rights Association was founded, the Fourteenth Amendment was passed by Congress. With the exception of one brief attempt before the New York legislature,[31] the association chose not to work actively against its ratification. The amendment was so unsatisfactory from the perspective of black suffrage that the Equal Rights Association found it difficult to make its feminist criticisms heard above those of abolitionists and Radicals. The lone equal rights memorial against the amendment, submitted to the New York legislature, insisted that "the introduction of the word 'male' three times repeated in the constitutional amendment . . . is a gross outrage . . . and *on that ground alone were there no other reason* we earnestly hope it will be repudiated."[32] Moreover, the association needed to take more positive steps to demonstrate that woman suffrage was indeed compatible with black suffrage as a radical program for Reconstruction. Therefore, leaders concentrated their efforts on creating a universal suffrage campaign on the state level, leaving the federal arena, for the time being, to the supporters of black suffrage.

Under the banner of the Equal Rights Association, a whole series of lobbying and petition campaigns was launched in 1866 and 1867 to remove racial and sexual restrictions from state constitutions. Most of these efforts demanded both woman suffrage

30. *HWS,* II, 174.
31. "Petition to the New York Legislature," *Standard,* January 26, 1867, p. 3.
32. "Equal Rights," *New York World,* November 22, 1866, p. 2 (emphasis mine).

and black suffrage. Lucy Stone appeared before a committee of
the New Jersey legislature to call for the removal of the phrase
"white male" from the state constitution. Elizabeth Cady Stanton did the same in New York. Similar proposals were submitted
to the legislatures of Kansas, Maine, Massachusetts, and Ohio.[33]
In a few exceptional cases, equal rights activities were limited to
woman suffrage: in the former slave state of Missouri, and in the
District of Columbia, where black men were enfranchised in
January 1867, before the equal rights campaign there began.[34]

The two major campaigns took place in Kansas and New
York. In Kansas, the electorate was scheduled to vote in November 1867 on two separate referenda, one removing the word
"male" and the other the word "white" from the state's constitution. The New York constitutional convention was scheduled for
June 1867. Equal rights leaders were determined to get the word
"male" removed from the state constitution and to abolish the
discriminatory property qualification on black male voters. Drawing on her experience in the 1850's when she canvassed the state
for the Married Women's Property Act, Anthony made plans to
cover New York comprehensively. "We mean to hold a County
Convention at the County Seat of each of the 60 Counties of the
State," she wrote to Anna Dickinson, ". . . and make sure that
our petition to [the] Constitutional Convention will be thoroughly
circulated in every School District."[35] A grand two-day meeting
in Albany opened the New York canvass, and the rhetoric there
revealed the hopes for success: "The spirit of the age impels an
onward step. The people, everywhere . . . roused from the lethargy of the ages, are demanding an extension of rights. The
reconstruction of this Union is a broader, deeper work than the
restoration of the rebel states. It is the lifting of the entire nation
into the practical realization of our Republican Idea."[36]

33. *Standard,* May 16, 1867, p. 3; *HWS,* II, 184.
34. *HWS,* III, 599 and 809.
35. Anthony to Dickinson, December 2, 1866, Anna Dickinson Papers, LC.
36. "Equal Rights Convention in New York State," leaflet in Gerrit
Smith Collection, George Arents Research Library for Special Collections,
Syracuse University.

From Syracuse the equal rights team went to New York City and then to Utica. They continued their tour until April, concluding with a rally in Buffalo and 28,000 signatures on their petitions.[37]

Despite vigorous efforts and great enthusiasm, however, the Equal Rights Association could not escape the political dilemma that had forced feminists to organize it. The progress of Reconstruction politics continued to work against the introduction of woman suffrage into the debate on political rights, and to drive apart the association's twin goals of black and female enfranchisement. The passage of the Fourteenth Amendment accelerated the drive for black suffrage. In the summer and fall of 1866, violent anti-black riots in New Orleans and Memphis and southern hostility to the Fourteenth Amendment strengthened the position of those who insisted that the freedmen must be enfranchised to preserve the Union's victory. After the strong Republican showing in the November 1866 elections, supporters of black suffrage resumed their drive with new vigor. In January Congress voted to enfranchise black men in the District of Columbia and the territories, and the 1867 Reconstruction Act, which required rebel states to include black suffrage in their new constitutions, was passed over the president's veto.[38] These developments increasingly drew the black man alone to the center of the national political stage. Republicans and Democrats, abolitionists and racists agreed—the major issue of Reconstruction was the freedmen's political status. In the face of this consensus, the universal suffrage vision of the Equal Rights Association became more and more problematic.

This tension between black suffrage and woman suffrage was structured into the Equal Rights Association through its membership. Most of the officers, activists, and spokespeople, of whom

37. Willis, *Acquaintances Old and New* pp. 39–41; Catt and Shuler, *Woman Suffrage and Politics,* p. 53.
38. Kenneth M. Stampp, *The Era of Reconstruction, 1865–1877* (New York, 1967), chap. 5. My account of early Reconstruction is also drawn from Montgomery, *Beyond Equality,* and McPherson, *The Struggle for Equality.*

the majority were women, were also abolitionists.[39] The largest
group were the women who had worked for two decades along-
side and within the Anti-Slavery Society to build women's rights:
Martha Coffin Wright, Lydia and Lucretia Mott, Ernestine Rose,
Frances Gage, Antoinette Brown Blackwell, Amelia Bloomer,
Josephine S. Griffing, Caroline Severance, and, of course, Stone,
Anthony, and Stanton. There were antislavery men, who had
supported women's rights for many years: Stephen Foster, Frederick Douglass, Samuel J. May, Parker Pillsbury, and Theodore
Tilton. Another category was that of women abolitionists who
had not been very active in prewar feminism, including Elizabeth
Neall Gay, Elizabeth Buffum Chace, Abbie Hutchinson Patten,
and Sarah Hallock. Finally, there were a few women in the association who were not reformers on their own, but married to
prominent male abolitionists: Anna Rice Powell, Mrs. Isaac
Sturgeon, Mary F. Gilbert, and Elizabeth Tilton. Some of these
women and men had a primary commitment to black suffrage.
Others suffered divided loyalties between women and the
freedmen.

The most creative response of equal rights leaders to this contradiction in their midst was to turn their attention to black
women. The black woman's double disfranchisement transcended
the hostility that Reconstruction politics were generating between
the black and woman suffrage movements. The special advocacy
of black women's political rights was led by Frances Gage. In a
letter to the *Standard*, she declared herself committed to the
"cause of woman, without regard to color."[40] Gage had worked
in the Port Royal experiment in 1862 and after the war became
chief agent of the Washington, D.C., Freedmen's Bureau. More
than any other white leader of the Equal Rights Association, she
was immersed in the life of the black community. Given her
feminism, she was particularly interested in the postwar prospects

39. The names of equal rights activists were determined from lists of
officers and convention speakers, *HWS*, II, *passim*.
40. "Letter from Mrs. Gage," *Standard*, July 21, 1866, p. 2; Eugene
H. Rosenboom, "Frances Gage," *NAW*, II, 2–4.

of the freedwoman, and introduced this concern into the Equal Rights Association.

Other equal rights spokespeople followed her lead. At a meeting of Pennsylvania abolitionists, Anthony pleaded the cause of the black woman. "Mr. Phillips said to us yesterday afternoon that the result we should demand as the price of this war was the equality of the races," she challenged. "What to the slave woman is the equality of the races?" Using information gathered by Gage in her Freedmen's Bureau work, she claimed that freedwomen, who had shared equally in the obligations and suffering of slavery, were refusing legal marriage and the submission to men that emancipation seemed to require. Anthony added that the black man, trained in the ways "of tyranny and despotism," might be expected to take exceptionally well to the privileges of being a husband.[41] Similarly, Stanton argued that, without the ballot, the black woman was doomed "to triple bondage that man never knows." Olympia Brown also championed the black woman, who "needed the ballot more than anyone in the world."[42]

The attention paid to black women was more rhetorical than real, however. Black women actually took part in the Equal Rights Association only to the same small degree that black men had in the prewar Anti-Slavery Society. Among the more than fifty national officers and speakers at equal rights conventions during the association's three-year history there were only five black women and an equal number of black men. Two of the women, Hattie Purvis and Sarah Remond, were daughter and sister respectively of Robert Purvis and Charles Lenox Remond, two of the half-dozen black men prominent in white abolitionist circles. In addition, Frances Watkins Harper, Sojourner Truth, and Mattie Griffith, all ex-slaves and nationally known orators,

41. "Twenty-ninth Annual Meeting of the Pennsylvania Anti-Slavery Society," *Standard,* December 1, 1866, p. 2.
42. Stanton, "Reconstruction," unpublished manuscript speech, Elizabeth Cady Stanton Papers, LC; "Shall Women Vote?" *New York World,* December 9, 1866, p. 8.

were active in the association. The positions these women held
were not particularly powerful. Purvis and Harper served on the
finance committee, the primary task of which was to solicit do-
nations to cover the organization's expenses. Griffith was appointed one of three corresponding secretaries, an important
position and one always retained by whites in the Anti-Slavery
Society. Her appointment, however, seems to have been largely
symbolic; Anthony, who shared the post with her, performed
most of its functions. Three blacks, all men, were among the
many vice-presidents, but these too were primarily symbolic positions. No blacks served on the important business committee,
which drew up the resolutions, and only one, George Downing,
was a member of the policy-making executive committee.[43]

This sparse record is not surprising. Before the war the slave
woman had been a central symbol in antislavery propaganda,
but blacks of both sexes had been relegated to a peripheral role
in the management of the national antislavery movement.[44]
Moreover, blacks themselves were divided over this new attempt
to join the woman question with their struggle. While Robert
Purvis and Sojourner Truth warmly supported the Equal Rights
Association's universal suffrage strategy, other black abolitionists
did not.[45] Olympia Brown reported tension with Charles Remond,
one of three blacks in the equal rights team that canvassed New
York in the winter of 1866–1867. She claimed that he frequently
portrayed "the injustice done to the negro as so much greater
than the wrongs of women," and "seemed to have no patience
with the presentation of our claims."[46] Lucy Stone reported a
similar conflict in Philadelphia. There, male abolitionists, among

43. See Clifton J. Phillips, "Frances Harper," *NAW*, II, 137–138;
Dorothy B. Porter, "Sarah Remond," *NAW*, III, 136–137; Saunders
Redding, "Sojourner Truth," *NAW*, III, 479–481.
44. For the role of black men and women in the American Anti-Slavery
Society, see August Meier and Elliott Rudwick, "The Role of Blacks in the
Abolitionist Movement," in *Blacks in the Abolitionist Movement*, ed. John
Bracey, Meier, and Rudwick (Belmont, Calif., 1971), pp. 108–122.
45. For Sojourner Truth's position, see *HWS*, II, 193; on Robert Purvis'
attitude to the Equal Rights Association, see Lucy Stone's letter to Abby
Kelley Foster, January 24, 1867, Blackwell Family Collection, LC.
46. Willis, *Acquaintances Old and New*, p. 41.

them eight blacks, prevented the introduction of the woman suffrage issue onto the floor of the local Anti-Slavery Society.[47] The suspicion between black male and white female reformers was mutual, and black women, caught in the middle, had no control over the outcome. These first years of the Equal Rights Association were the one period in which woman suffragists gave consistent attention to black women. As the possibilities for a joint struggle for black and woman suffrage evaporated, and as the woman suffrage forces became increasingly independent of abolitionism, the image of the black woman—for she had never been much more than an image—receded into the background.

Despite abolitionist leaders' early rebuffs to the demand for woman suffrage and the American Anti-Slavery Society's initial refusal to join in the formation of the Equal Rights Association, feminists continued to work hard to win abolitionists to their expansive vision of Reconstruction. They were still dependent on the world that abolitionists had made, the people, organizations, principles, and political language that the two reforms shared. However, organized abolitionism yielded no ground to equal rights appeals. Its leaders evaded the claims of feminists, even while they tried to maintain a neutral stance and avoid any appearance of antifeminism.

Advocates of equal rights tried to awaken individual abolitionists to the contradictions inherent in their parochial drive for black suffrage, but they met with little success. "I sit down to write you with a feeling of despair which never came to me before where a principle is involved," Lucy Stone wrote passionately to Abby Kelley Foster on behalf of universal suffrage. Stone and Foster had shared the first struggles for women's rights within the American Anti-Slavery Society, but Foster now opposed the introduction of woman suffrage into Reconstruction. "Oh Abby, it is a terrible mistake you are making!" Stone criticized Foster for the "strange blindness" of preferring "the poor half loaf of justice for the Negro" to the grand principles of equal

47. Stone to Abby Kelley Foster, January 24, 1867, Blackwell Family Collection, LC.

rights and universal suffrage. "I really believe this is 'the negro's hour,' " Foster answered, unconvinced. "I should look on myself as a monster of selfishness if, while I see my neighbor's daughter held and treated like a beast—as thousands still are all over the rural districts of the south . . . —I would turn from helping them to secure to my daughter political equality."[48]

An equally emotional confrontation between the abolitionist and equal rights positions took place at the 1867 annual meeting of the New England affiliate of the American Anti-Slavery Society. In this episode, Abby Foster's husband, Stephen, joined with the leading male feminist, Parker Pillsbury, to bring the equal rights question before abolitionists once and for all. The debate was heated and featured the Fosters on opposing sides, Abby denying married freedwomen the same right to political independence from their husbands that she was exercising from hers. If the case for black men's suffrage was to protect them from reenslavement, Stephen Foster wanted to know, "Who is going to save the black woman from slavery?" The answer, from the floor, "Her husband." "Her husband!" Pillsbury exclaimed in frustration, "I say, God pity her then! It is time we had done with this trifling. The right of suffrage, if it came from God, came for woman as well as man."[49]

Wendell Phillips's position, here and elsewhere, was to avoid any open discussion of woman suffrage on an abolitionist platform. The 1867 meeting of the New England Anti-Slavery Society agreed, voted against Pillsbury and Stephen Foster, and rejected their bid to consider universal suffrage.[50] Most leading abolitionists responded to the appeals of the Equal Rights Association in an equally evasive way. They tried to avoid outright opposition to universal suffrage, while at the same time not endorsing it. The long history of cooperation between antislavery and women's rights worked against an open confrontation be-

48. *Ibid.;* Foster to Stone, February 10, 1867, NAWSA Collection, LC.
49. "Proceedings of the New England Anti-Slavery Convention," *Standard,* June 15, 1867, pp. 1–3.
50. *Ibid.*

tween them now. So too did the subordination of feminism to abolitionism that had characterized their alliance. Antislavery leaders may well have expected the Equal Rights Association eventually to accept black suffrage as its priority.[51] Certainly, the National Loyal Women's League, which Stanton and Anthony had formed during the war, provided a precedent for the organization of women primarily around the black man's emancipation and only secondarily around their own. Martha Coffin Wright had to remind the equal rights founding convention that the new association was being formed to expand feminists' work, not "to get rid of the odious name of Woman's Rights."[52] "We have so long held Woman's claims in abeyance," Anthony believed, "that the mere naming them now is reckoned an impertinence."[53]

The leaders of the Anti-Slavery Society worked to avoid an open debate between their strategy for Reconstruction and that of the Equal Rights Association. In particular, they blocked access to the political resources which they controlled and on which feminists had depended for many years. Equal rights spokespeople claimed that the pages of the abolitionist journal, the *Standard*, were being closed to them. When universal suffrage was debated at antislavery and other reform conventions, the *Standard* often published an edited version of the proceedings, omitting all mention of the Equal Rights Association. Following this editorial policy, the *Standard*'s stenographic account of the 1867 Equal Rights meeting, at which abolitionists and feminists fought openly, omitted all references to the conflict.[54] The *Standard* ceased reporting on equal rights activities alto-

---

51. See, for instance, *Standard*, June 9, 1866, pp. 2–3.
52. *HWS*, II, 175.
53. Anthony to Caroline Dall, January 30, 1866, Caroline Healey Dall Papers, Massachusetts Historical Society.
54. This can be seen by comparing the report of the convention in the *Standard*, June 1, 1867, pp. 1–3, with the report published in *HWS*, II, 182–224. Also see "Letter from Mrs. Gage," *Standard*, July 21, 1866, p. 2, in which she accuses the *Standard* of editing out the debate on woman suffrage from its account of a reform meeting.

gether in the months before the crucial elections of 1866, in line with Republicans' conservative campaign strategy. Parker Pillsbury, at the time editor of the *Standard* and one of the few men to stand with the women through the entire equal rights ordeal, resigned his position in protest.[55] Whether the *Standard*'s policy was intended to weaken the equal rights position by denying it public exposure, or only to repress evidence of a major political conflict among reformers, it indicated abolitionists' reluctance to confront the demand for universal suffrage.

Abolitionists who opposed the Equal Rights Association's efforts judged the strategic prospects of black suffrage and woman suffrage according to different models of social change. They argued that the major obstacle to woman suffrage was public apathy, particularly among women themselves. The *Standard* claimed that if the majority of women "were sufficiently alive" to the significance of the vote, "it is morally certain" that they would be enfranchised promptly.[56] Such an argument blamed women for their own disfranchisement, and represented a much more naive analysis of the sources of tyrannical power than abolitionists applied to the situation of the freedmen. Abolitionists understood that the major threat to the black man came not from his own ignorance and apathy, or even from the hostility of northern whites to his welfare, but from the power of the southern ruling class. They were committed to dismantling that power through Congressional action. They were not deterred by the fact that black suffrage had been rejected in every popular referendum in which it had been submitted. Nor did they see themselves following public opinion, but forming and creating it. Yet they did not approach woman suffrage in the same fashion. In response, Stanton protested that it was not "public sentiment," but abolitionists and Radicals, who were responsible for keeping

55. Louis Filler, "Parker Pillsbury: An Antislavery Apostle," *New England Quarterly,* 19 (1946), 333.

56. "The State Convention," *Standard,* March 23, 1867, p. 2.

woman suffrage out of Reconstruction: "If it be true that public sentiment is not prepared for this just and beneficent measure, then it is the duty of our leaders, instead of stereotyping the ignorant prejudices of the people into statutes and constitutions, to educate this public sentiment, . . . by the example of honest actions. When God gives new truths to the few, it is that they may win the response of the many."[57]

The continued resistance of abolitionists to the entreaties of equal rights leaders reflected the different relationships that the two groups were evolving to the Republican party and its program for Reconstruction. After the elections of 1866, the Republican party moved toward an endorsement of black suffrage, and this drew abolitionists even closer to it. Increasingly, abolitionists functioned as the Republican party's left wing, and were bound to it as a kind of loyal opposition. However, the Republicans' refusal to embrace woman suffrage remained firm. While the supporters of black suffrage were winning their struggle to shape the Republican party to their demands, feminists grew increasingly critical of Republicans and looked elsewhere for support.

As early as the founding convention of the Equal Rights Association, Connecticut feminist Frances Burr urged women to reassess the faith in Republicans that they shared with other Garrisonians. Referring to the impending Fourteenth Amendment, she charged the "chief ones of that party—now that there is any chance of attaining [woman suffrage]—utterly refuse all efforts in that direction, and, worse than that, give indications of taking positive measures in the opposite direction."[58] The passage of the amendment one month later accelerated the pace of the Equal Rights Association's alienation from the Republican party. Stanton ran as an independent candidate for the Senate in the November elections, to "rebuke . . . the dominant party for its

57. *HWS,* II, 305–307.
58. *HWS,* II, 913.

retrogressive legislation in so amending the National Constitution as to make invidious distinctions on the ground of sex."[59] Olympia Brown recalled feminists' bitter perspective on the liberal pretensions of Republicans: "One would have expected that the 'Liberal' and 'Progressive' party would be most favorable to the advancements of women, but such was not the case. Young men who could scarcely find words sufficiently strong to express their feelings on the subject of liberty for all were the ones who led the way in the effort to drive out the first woman who dared to invade the sacred precincts of the [Harvard] Divinity School."[60]

Frustrated by Republicans, equal rights leaders found Congressional Democrats willing to support their petitions and bills. Because Radicals refused to endorse woman suffrage, Democrats saw it as a way to embarrass advocates of black suffrage.[61] Similarly, while the Republican press ridiculed the Equal Rights Association and the *Standard* refused to report its activities, Democratic papers, happy to publicize any split in the abolitionist ranks, gave the association generous coverage and helped to spread its message.[62] The Equal Rights Association had little to lose by accepting the aid of Democrats since, as Olympia Brown reported, its refusal to acknowledge the leadership of the Republican party was already earning it the reputation of Copperheadism.[63] Its leaders were under no illusions as to Democrats' motives. "If the Democrats advocate a grand measure of public policy which they do not believe, they occupy much higher ground than Republicans who refuse to press the same measure which they claim to believe," they argued. "At all events, the

59. *HWS*, II, 181.
60. Willis, *Acquaintances Old and New*, pp. 29–31.
61. See the comments of Democrats, especially Senator Edgar Cowan of Pennsylvania, during the December 1866–January 1867 congressional debates on suffrage, (*HWS*, II, 103–151).
62. See, for example, the different attitudes expressed in the *New York Tribune*, a Republican paper, and the Democratic *New York World*.
63. Willis, *Acquaintances Old and New*, pp. 29–31.

hypocrisy of Democrats serves us a better purpose in the present emergency than does the treachery of Republicans."[64]

The problem of Reconstruction for feminists was how to make progress for women suffrage in the face of abolitionists' reluctance to support them. The American Equal Rights Association was their first solution. It was never a very stable organization or a viable political strategy. It represented feminists' efforts to alter their position in the Garrisonian reform coalition at a time when Reconstruction politics were destroying the conditions on which that unity was premised. The Equal Rights Association period was nonetheless a significant one in the development of the woman suffrage movement. It was the culmination of the abolitionist phase of American feminism, in which women's ambitions for liberation developed in conjunction with the movement for black emancipation. It was both the fullest and finest expression of the politics that feminists had developed through their alliance with abolitionists, and a revelation of the limitations that being dependent on other reformers' political initiatives placed on them. In the process of trying to strengthen their connections with abolitionists, feminists began to move beyond them. They began to make their own strategic assessments and lay their own political plans, which was the only way the woman suffrage movement could grow. The American Equal Rights Association was intended to have an impact on the advocates of black suffrage; instead, it was the advocates of woman suffrage who were the most affected by it.

The tension between abolitionism and feminism, which was embedded in the American Equal Rights Association, deepened until it destroyed the organization. Ultimately, it forced feminists to abandon their efforts to anchor woman suffrage to black suffrage and led them to make an open break with abolitionists. The immediate background for this change of course was the Kansas campaign of 1867, where the Equal Rights Association

64. *HWS,* II, 322.

brought all its resources to bear in a final major effort for universal suffrage. In Kansas, Republicans' refusal to advocate woman suffrage became an overt attack on feminists for doing so, and still the abolitionist supporters of black suffrage remained bound to the party. The Kansas campaign of 1867 both exemplified the process that was splitting the Equal Rights Association, and led feminists to abandon the organization in favor of building an independent woman suffrage movement.

Chapter Three

The Kansas Campaign
of 1867

In March 1867, the Kansas legislature authorized two popular referenda for the November election. The issues to be presented to the people of the state were black suffrage and woman suffrage. The Equal Rights Association committed all its limited resources to the Kansas campaign. For nine months, equal rights workers stumped the scattered settlements of Kansas on behalf of these referenda. The work was begun by Lucy Stone and her husband, Henry Blackwell. After three months of exhausting speaking, during which time Stone's voice was ruined, they returned east and were replaced by Olympia Brown and Bessie Brisbee, two less experienced agitators. Stanton and Anthony covered the state for the last two and a half months of the campaign. The eastern workers were aided by well-organized local activists and by enormous amounts of written propaganda. All these efforts were conducted with the most meager financial resources. Speakers from out of state paid their own expenses, and some made additional contributions as well.[1]

The effort extended by the Equal Rights Association in Kansas reflected the significance it attached to winning both referenda. Kansas was the first popular test ever made of woman suffrage, and victory there would counter the charge that public opinion did not support the enfranchisement of women. Moreover, it would provide the Equal Rights Association with the evidence it needed to convince Republicans that woman suffrage could be safely linked to black suffrage. Furthermore, Kansas seemed a

---

1. The general sources on the Kansas equal rights campaign are: *HWS*, II, chap. XIX; Harper, *Life and Work of Susan B. Anthony*, I, chap. XVII; Stanton, *Eighty Years and More*, chap. XVI; and Sister Jeanne McKenna, "With the Help of God and Lucy Stone," *Kansas Historical Quarterly* 36 (1970), 13–26.

particularly promising field for testing universal suffrage. Its
people were veterans of the battles of the 1850's, many of them
committed abolitionists. The antislavery heritage and principles
on which the Equal Rights Association rested were common currency in Kansas. Kansas had an especially strong record on
women's rights; only in New York was the legal position of
women more advanced. "Success in Kansas means success everywhere," Henry Blackwell wrote early in the campaign. "For the
first time, we have got the word 'male' submitted to the people.
. . . In my judgment, if we fail to get the people's vote, we shall
none of us live ever to see the word submitted to the people
anywhere again."[2]

The Kansas campaign did not strengthen the Equal Rights
Association, however, but shattered it and the abolitionist feminism that it embodied. The organization's reward for bringing its
universal suffrage philosophy before the voters of Kansas was an
overtly antifeminist countercampaign waged by the state Republican party. While Republicans attacked, prominent national abolitionists remained inactive, caught between their past affiliation
with women's rights and their present connection with the Republican party. The equal rights campaign that had begun with
such promise ended nine months later in chaos. Attacked by
Republicans, feminists turned for help to Democrats and the
racist weapons they offered. Both black and woman suffrage,
now set in opposition to each other, were defeated.

The most permanent effect of the Kansas debacle was that it
completed the split between abolitionists and feminists and
brought the conflict into the ranks of feminists themselves. Kansas
marked a major turning point in the development of an independent feminist movement. Faced with the utter collapse of
hopes for linking woman suffrage to the forces working in behalf
of black suffrage, one group of suffragists conceded to the Republican party's political dictatorship over Reconstruction. This

2. Blackwell to Olympia Brown, May 30, 1867, Olympia Brown Willis
Papers, SL.

of course meant accepting the postponement of woman suffrage until some indeterminate time in the future. Another group, led by Anthony and Stanton, came to the opposite conclusion. They held firm to their desire for an immediate victory, and therefore for finding a route other than Republican party power and protection for winning woman suffrage. This position meant an open break with organized abolitionism, the end of thirty years of close cooperation. After Kansas, Stanton and Anthony began to establish woman suffrage as an independent political movement and to search for an alternate strategic context for its victory. Ultimately, the development of a politically autonomous woman suffrage movement was feminism's greatest achievement in the postwar period.

The Equal Rights Association was invited into Kansas in 1867 by Sam Wood, leader of a rebel faction of the state Republican party. Wood was the man responsible for the woman suffrage referendum. When a bill authorizing a popular vote on black enfranchisement was presented to the Republican-dominated legislature, Wood moved to amend it to include the question of votes for women as well. Party leaders refused to permit woman suffrage to be linked so closely to black suffrage, and insisted that the two questions be submitted separately to the people. Otherwise, they yielded to Wood's initiative, and his bill authorizing a popular referendum on woman suffrage passed the legislature, along with the bill for a black suffrage referendum.[3]

Other than allowing a popular referendum, Kansas Republicans did nothing to advance the cause of woman suffrage. Despite lobbying by Stone and Blackwell, the state Republican committee endorsed only the black suffrage referendum. In a state as heavily Republican as Kansas, the absence of an official party endorsement was a serious handicap. Furthermore, early in the campaign, a group of Republicans tried to redirect the

3. Letter from Susan B. Anthony, March 12, 1867, *Standard*, March 16, 1867, p. 2; Helen Ekin Starrett, "Reminiscences," *HWS*, II, 250–251.

State Impartial Suffrage Association, the local equal rights affiliate organized by Wood, to drop woman suffrage and campaign for black enfranchisement alone. However, Wood's faction was able to secure its control. Stone and Blackwell, who arrived in Kansas in February 1867, were influential in this struggle.[4] As representatives of a national organization that was both committed to the unity of black and woman suffrage and historically affiliated with abolitionism, they strengthened Wood's hand by their presence. Although the equal rights forces won this early skirmish, it revealed that many Kansas Republicans were hostile to woman suffrage. "There are a great many silent enemies among the Republicans who are *paralyzed* by our bold strokes and waiting for a lull in our breeze to raise a *reaction*," Blackwell warned. "This must not be permitted."[5]

To head off their "silent enemies" and to augment their limited resources, the Equal Rights Association looked to the abolitionist community outside the state. But they were as disappointed in their expectations of aid in Kansas as they had been the year before with respect to the Fourteenth Amendment. Thomas Wentworth Higginson, Douglass, Tilton, and Phillips all refused their invitations to come to Kansas and join the campaign.[6] The equal rights teams in Kansas were most frustrated by the refusal of the abolitionist and Radical press to assist or even recognize their efforts. The *Independent,* edited by Theodore Tilton, was widely read in Kansas, and Stone believed it could move public opinion there. "If the *Independent* would take up this question, and every week write for it, as it does for the negro," she wrote to Stanton, "that paper alone could save this State."[7] The *National Antislavery Standard,* then edited by Phillips, had a much smaller readership, but as the official journal

4. Blackwell to Stanton, April 5, 1867, *HWS,* II, pp. 232–233; Blackwell to Olympia Brown, June 18, 1867, Olympia Brown Willis Papers, SL.

5. Blackwell to Olympia Brown, June 8, 1867, Olympia Brown Willis Papers, SL.

6. Letter from Higginson, *Standard,* June 5, 1867, p. 1; Henry Blackwell to Stanton, as quoted in Lutz, *Created Equal,* p. 145.

7. Stone to Stanton, April 20, 1867, *HWS,* II, 235.

of the American Anti-Slavery Society, it had considerable influence, especially with the Republican press. Although the newspapers urged Kansas voters to approve black suffrage, neither the *Independent,* nor the *Standard,* nor the most important Republican paper in the country, Horace Greeley's *New York Tribune,* endorsed woman suffrage or even reported on the equal rights campaign there. "What a power to hold and not use!" Stone wrote in frustration from a town on the Missouri-Kansas border. "I shall see them the very first thing when I go home."[8] As soon as she left Kansas, she went to New York to urge Tilton and Greeley to endorse woman suffrage, but she failed.[9] Anthony unsuccessfully appealed to Phillips at the *Standard.*[10] "The editors of the *New York Tribune* and the *Independent* can never know how wistfully, from day to day, their papers were searched for some inspiring editorials on the woman's amendment," Stanton and Anthony recalled "but naught was there; there were no . . . eloquent letters from an Eastern man that could be read to the people; all were silent."[11]

Despite these serious disappointments, the reception the equal rights teams received from the people of Kansas encouraged them. Their audiences were large, attentive, and terribly eager for political literature. The canvassers were particularly impressed with the women of Kansas. Elizabeth Cady Stanton admitted that she went west filled with illusions about the pioneer experience.

Heretofore my idea had been that pioneer life was a period of romantic freedom. When the long, white-covered wagons, bound for the far West, passed by, I thought of the novelty of a six-months' journey through the bright spring and summer days in a house on wheels, meals under shady trees and beside babbling brooks, sleep-

---

8. Stone to Anthony, May 1, 1867, *ibid.,* p. 237.
9. Alice Stone Blackwell, unpublished manuscript reminiscences of Lucy Stone, undated, Blackwell Family Collection, LC. Also see Elinor R. Hays, *Morning Star: A Biography of Lucy Stone* (New York, 1961), p. 207.
10. Stone to Anthony, May 1, 1867, as reprinted in *HWS,* II, 237.
11. *HWS,* II, 264–265.

ing in the open air, and finding a home, at last, where land was cheap, the soil rich and deep, and where the grains, vegetables, fruit, and flowers grew bountifully with but little toil. But a few months of pioneer life permanently darkened my rosy ideal.

Instead, she met women who left settled farms to come west, with "no reason for going except that the husband had the Western fever." Some had lost children on the way. Others arrived, only to be "disappointed in not finding the much talked of bonanzas," tied by housework and children to hardscrabble farms "in solitary places, miles from any neighbors." Many women were destroyed in mind and body by the deprivation, but others survived with a sense of personal strength and independence. Stanton wrote that "the courage and endurance of the women, surrounded by dangers and discomforts, surpassed all description."[12]

Kansas also offered an unusually experienced group of local feminists to support the equal rights work. Women such as Helen Ekin Starrett, Susan Wattles, and Clarina I. H. Nichols, had come to the territory in the abolitionist migration of the 1850's. Active in the struggle to keep Kansas free soil, they were exceptionally politicized and intensely Republican. "These Kansas women are ready for the new doctrine of woman suffrage," Stanton wrote in 1867. "You need not wonder said one of them to me the other day if after all the difficulties and dangers we have encountered, standing sentinels alone at our doors many nights for the last twelve years, that we should come to think that 'our divinely constituted heads' are on our shoulders. We should have been in a poor fix if they had not been."[13] Such women had formed the Moneka Woman's Rights Association in 1858. The organization's goal was to ensure that women had their rights when Kansas applied for statehood. The association commissioned Clarina Nichols, a veteran agitator, to lobby for women's rights at the 1859 Wyandotte constitutional convention. Nichols

12. Stanton, *Eighty Years and More,* pp. 250–253.
13. Stanton to Theodore Tilton, September 15, 1867, Gluck Collection, Buffalo and Erie County Public Library.

secured women equal rights to property and guardianship of children, but was unable to win woman suffrage. She claimed that a majority of Republicans in the convention supported women's enfranchisement, but did not want to include it for fear that Democrats would use it to defeat the entire constitution. In exchange for withholding their demand for full political equality, the women of Kansas were offered a constitutional provision granting them the right to vote in school elections, and the firm promise of future support.[14]

After the war, Kansas feminists expected the promises made at Wyandotte to be redeemed. Their situation was like that of other Union women intensified. They believed that a triumphant and principled Republican party would reward them for their ideological constancy and wartime sacrifice. When the state legislature began to consider a woman suffrage referendum in 1867, Nichols wrote with the utmost confidence: "The hour of universal freedom is coming for us without violence. Those who have fought the oppressor, and freed the slave and demand suffrage for him, will not forget the women who prayed and wept and wrought for them. . . . We have been on a political equality with the negro too long not to be lifted with him now."[15] Local women worked hard for the 1867 canvass. Nichols gave four weeks to the campaign although she was farming at the time and there was no money to pay her.[16] Martha Brinkerhoff, not previously active but later a suffragist leader in the midwest, organized her own tour of Kansas.[17] Other feminists, whose domestic duties prevented them from traveling, contributed what they could. "Old Mrs. Dr. Updegraff," wife of the first speaker of the Kansas legislature, lectured, lobbied, and organized in her home district

14. Susan Wattles to Anthony, December 30, 1881, *HWS,* II, 255; Nichols to Anthony, April 14, 1868, in "The Papers of Clarina I. H. Nichols, 1854–1884," Part IV, ed. Joseph G. Gambone, *Kansas Historical Quarterly,* 39 (1973), 547–548.

15. Nichols to the editor of the *Vermont Phoenix,* February 24, 1867, "Papers of Clarina Nichols," pp. 515–516.

16. *HWS,* I, 200; "Papers of Clarina Nichols," p. 529.

17. Noun, *Strong-Minded Women,* pp. 97–99.

of Osawatomie County. She wrote to Sam Wood that she looked forward to debate that would be *"hot, personal* and *bitter.*"[18] In the summer, local activists called on the masses of Kansas women to reject artificial femininity and demand political equality instead: "Whatever, then, may be the opinion of fair ladies who dwell in ceiled houses in our older Eastern States and cities, who like lilies, neither toil nor spin, whose fair hands would gather close their silken apparel at the thought of touching the homelier garments of many a heroine of Kansas—whatever they may say in reference to this question, we, the women of the Spartan State, declare, we want the vote."[19]

The situation in Kansas was decisively altered when, three months into the equal rights campaign, the Republican party moved to attack woman suffrage efforts there and elsewhere. The black suffrage referendum in Kansas was a Republican party measure and represented the success Radicals were having by 1867 in making the freedmen's enfranchisement part of the Republican program. At the same time that the party was moving to a firmer commitment to black suffrage, however, the Equal Rights Association's efforts in Kansas and elsewhere were beginning to gain a hearing for the universal suffrage approach to political rights. The more visible the Equal Rights Association could make its demand for woman suffrage, the more pressure it put on the Republican party to take a stand on the issue. Although a few Republicans suggested that the party take up woman suffrage, antifeminist counsel prevailed and the party moved from implicit opposition to explicit attack.[20] Republicans'

18. Mrs. Dr. Updegraff to Wood, May 27, 1867, Woman Suffrage Collection, Kansas Historical Society. I wish to thank Joseph Gambone, archivist of the Kansas Historical Society, for calling this letter to my attention.

19. Address by the Women's Impartial Suffrage Association of Lawrence, Kansas, to the women of Kansas, September 24, 1867, *HWS,* II, 932–933.

20. For efforts to halt the antifeminist tendencies in the state Republican party, see the comments of R. B. Taylor, editor of the *Wyandotte Commercial Gazette,* March 16, 1867, as reprinted in "Papers of Clarina Nichols," p. 520.

justification for their outright antifeminism was that it was part of their efforts to ensure the enfranchisement of the freedmen; once again they charged that Democrats were supporting women's demands in order to weaken black suffrage.[21] In the 1820's and 1830's the enfranchisement of nonpropertied white men had frequently been accompanied by an attack on the black man's political rights.[22] In a similar way, the Republican party's campaign against woman suffrage in 1867 developed in conjunction with its assumption of responsibility for black suffrage.

The signal for this shift in Republican policy was given in New York. There, a constitutional convention was considering the enfranchisement of women and the removal of the discriminatory $250 property qualification on black men. The Equal Rights Association worked hard for both propositions, lobbying within the convention and organizing support outside it. Black and white speakers canvassed the state from January to April 1867 and collected over 20,000 signed petitions.[23] These were presented to the committee charged with reporting to the convention on revisions of the suffrage provisions. The suffrage committee was chaired by Horace Greeley, who was considered a friend of women's rights. On June 25, 1867, Greeley's committee made its report. It recommended the removal of the $250 property qualification on black men, and it recommended against women suffrage.

Your committee does not recommend an extension of the elective franchise to women. However defensible in theory, we are satisfied that public sentiment does not demand and would not sustain an innovation so revolutionary and sweeping, so openly at war with a

21. The charge that Democrats were using woman suffrage to attack black suffrage was reported by Olympia Brown in her manuscript account of the Kansas campaign, written c. 1868 (Olympia Brown Willis Papers, SL).

22. This was the case in Rhode Island; see Gettleman, *The Dorr Rebellion,* pp. 46–47.

23. See Chap. 2. Elizabeth Cady Stanton wrote to her daughter, Margaret, "Kind regards to the 'white males' of the household & ask your Father to lobby a little for us if he knows any of the [New York] suffrage committee" (June 24, 1867, Autograph Collection, Vassar College Library).

distribution of duties and functions between the sexes as venerable and pervading as government itself, and involving transformations so radical in social and domestic life.[24]

When presented to the convention a month later, Greeley's report against woman suffrage was supported by a vote of 125 to 19.[25]

Equal rights leaders were enraged, particularly at Greeley. Stanton, pursuing a very personal kind of revenge, arranged for his report to the convention to be followed by an equal rights petition headed with the name of Mrs. Horace Greeley.[26] The *Standard,* which was inclined to take an exceptionally long view of the struggle for women's enfranchisement, did not share this outrage. While regretting the convention's decision to reject woman suffrage, it considered the equal rights campaign "a good beginning," that would "bring forth in due season an abundant harvest of success." By contrast, it protested in the strongest terms possible the convention's decision to submit black suffrage separately from the rest of the new constitution to New York voters.[27] When Stanton was asked much later why Greeley had used his power in the convention against woman suffrage, "when he had always before been in favor of that reform," her answer was that "he feared it might embarrass his party in their efforts to carry 'negro suffrage,' the great republican measure of that time."[28]

The rejection in New York strengthened the position of those Kansas Republicans who opposed woman suffrage. Henry Blackwell reported that as a result of Greeley's report, the women's "enterprise was crushed. Even the Republicans in Kansas, after witnessing this example, set their faces against the extension of suffrage to women."[29] In August, for instance, a Republican

24. Report of the Committee on Suffrage, June 28, 1867, *HWS,* II, 285.
25. *Standard,* August 3, 1867, p. 2.
26. Harper, *Life and Work of Susan B. Anthony,* I, 280.
27. *Standard,* July 20, 1867, p. 3.
28. Typescript of newspaper article written by Stanton in 1895, Elizabeth Cady Stanton Papers, Vassar College Library.
29. *HWS,* II, 309.

meeting in Emporia passed a resolution that condemned the woman suffrage referendum in language quoted directly from Greeley's New York report.[30] The roster of official Republican canvassers in Kansas was loaded with men notorious since the 1850's for their opposition to woman suffrage. One Republican speaker claimed that Lucy Stone "and that seed-wart she carries around with her—called Blackwell" were practicing free-lovers. Another, a black man named Charles Langston, claimed to represent the freedmen in his opposition to woman suffrage. Olympia Brown described a third man, who asked his audiences if "they wanted every old maid to vote" and rebuked the audiences with " 'preferring every old thing that had a white face' to the negro."[31] Encouraged to see antifeminism as a strategy for ensuring the victory of black suffrage, these local Republicans launched a formal campaign to defeat the woman suffrage referendum. On September 5 they called a meeting in Lawrence to formulate "the best method to defeat the proposition to strike the word 'male' from the Constitution of the State of Kansas." They resolved "that we are unqualifiedly opposed to the dogma of 'Female Suffrage,' and while we do not recognize it as a party question, the attempt of certain persons within the State, and from without it, to enforce it upon the people of the State, demands the unqualified opposition of every citizen who respects the laws of society, and the well being and good name of our young Commonwealth." An "Anti Female Suffrage Committee" was formed

30. Undated clipping from *Atchison Daily Champion,* Olympia Brown Willis Papers, SL.

31. Charles Eskridge, article in the *Emporia News,* June 7, 1867, as reprinted in "Papers of Clarina Nichols," p. 522; unknown correspondent to Olympia Brown, September 24, 1867, Olympia Brown Willis Papers, SL; Willis, *Acquaintances Old and New,* p. 242. For more information on the Republican antifeminist campaign, see Starrett, "Reminiscences," *HWS,* II, 255. In October, the Republican State Committee issued a statement instructing its antifeminist representatives to work for "the great question of manhood suffrage" and "to express their own sentiments on other questions" ("Address of Republican State Committee," *Standard,* October 5, 1867, p. 1).

and instructed to coordinate its plans with those of the Republican State Committee.[32] "This at once antagonized the two questions," Kansas worker Helen Starrett recalled, "and we all felt that the death blow had been struck at both."[33]

The actions of the Kansas Republicans finally woke abolitionist leaders from what Olympia Brown called their "lethargy."[34] They had tried to put off woman suffrage, ignored the Equal Rights Association's arguments for universal suffrage, and permitted Greeley's repudiation of the franchise for women to pass by with little criticism. Their inaction had undoubtedly contributed to Republicans' open hostility. The tightrope of neutrality abolitionists had been walking in regard to the question of woman suffrage had broken. Now they found themselves confronted with a viciously antifeminist campaign being conducted by Kansas Republicans. In the face of accelerating antagonisms between supporters of black and woman suffrage, abolitionists acknowledged the woman suffrage referendum in Kansas, but their support was too late and nearly useless.

Months after the Equal Rights Association had first solicited their aid, the *Standard,* the *Independent,* and even the *Tribune* finally endorsed the woman suffrage referendum in Kansas. The *Standard* was the first of the three, publishing its endorsement on September 14, after Kansas Republicans had launched their antifeminist campaign. Phillips, who wrote the editorial, supported woman suffrage by way of the temperance issue, which he argued would be less disruptive to the Republican party if women were among the voters.[35] Three weeks later, the *Independent* endorsed the referendum, and predicted its victory, a forecast that no one close to the situation was making.[36] Neither editorial indicated

32. The resolution from the Lawrence meeting is quoted in McKenna, "With the Help of God and Lucy Stone," p. 23; "Manhood Suffrage," *Atchison Daily Champion,* August 8, 1867, clipping in Olympia Brown Willis Papers, SL.
33. Starrett, "Reminiscences," *HWS,* II, 253.
34. Brown, unpublished manuscript account of the Kansas campaign, 1868, Olympia Brown Willis Papers, SL.
35. *Standard,* September 14, 1867, p. 2.
36. "Right and Wrong in Kansas," *Independent,* October 3, 1867, p. 4.

much familiarity with the actual situation in Kansas, and this
gave their endorsements an abstract and unreal character. The
Tribune's editorial was the most grudging and least useful of the
three. Published on October 1, it seemed more an argument
against the referendum than for it: "We decidedly object to
having ten women in every hundred compel the other ninety to
vote, or allow the ten to carry elections against the judgement of
the ninety; but, if the great body of the women of Kansas wish
to vote, we counsel the men to accord them the opportunity.
Should the experiment work as we apprehend, they will soon be
glad to give it up. . . . It is plain that the experiment of Female
Suffrage is to be tried," Greeley conceded, "and, while we regard
it with distrust, we are quite willing to see it pioneered by
Kansas."[37]

Similarly, an "Appeal to the Voters of Kansas" on behalf of
the referendum appeared late in the Kansas campaign. It urged
"good men of all parties . . . to apply the principles of the
Declaration of Independence to women," and was signed by
nationally prominent Radicals and abolitionists such as George
W. Julian, Benjamin F. Wade, Samuel C. Pomeroy, Phillips,
Tilton, Gerrit Smith, and Henry Ward Beecher.[38] It would have
been a great help to the Equal Rights Association if it had appeared in the summer. The Equal Rights Association had started
soliciting the appeal, as it had the editorial endorsements, many
months earlier. In June Henry Blackwell drafted the document,
and circulated it "to get [it] signed *only* by men of National
eminence."[39] However, he was unable to secure enough signatures, and the appeal was not issued for three months. When it
finally appeared in October, it was in response to the deteriorat-
ing situation in Kansas and was too late to have any impact on
Kansas Republicans, who had already launched their antifeminist

37. *New York Tribune*, October 1, 1867, reprinted in *HWS*, II, 248–249.
38. "Appeal to the Voters of Kansas," *New York Tribune*, October 1,
1867, p. 5.
39. Blackwell to Henry Wadsworth Longfellow, June 28, 1867, Houghton
Library, Harvard University.

campaign. By that time, in Anthony's words, "the mischief done was irreparable."[40]

By late summer the equal rights campaign in Kansas had almost disintegrated. In addition to its attacks on woman suffrage, the state Republican party had forced Sam Wood out of the canvass, and the local equal rights organization had collapsed. Lecture commitments could not be met and funds were exhausted. "The campaign was left to run itself and of course it ran into the ground," Blackwell reported when he returned to the state in October.[41] Stanton and Anthony arrived in September, and did everything they could to revive the canvass. Anthony, at first unable to find a male escort, remained in Lawrence to organize the forces. Stanton began a tour of the state in the company of former Governor Charles Robinson. They traveled from village to town in his open carriage and spoke at least once every day from early September until the election on November 7.[42]

To offset the Republican attacks, Stanton and Anthony concentrated their efforts on Democrats, who were one-quarter of the Kansas electorate. Although the Democratic State Committee had come out against both black and woman suffrage, the Equal Rights Association found many rebel Democrats willing to cooperate with it. In Lawrence County, Democrats and woman suffrage Republicans cosponsored a ticket in opposition to the regular Republican slate. In Leavenworth, local Democrats had their ballots printed up for woman suffrage. Stanton and Robinson stumped the border towns, where Democrats were strong.[43] Although equal rights organizers had quietly sought Democratic votes since the beginning of the canvass, they now concentrated

40. *HWS,* II, 248.
41. Henry Blackwell to Lucy Stone, October 25, 1867, Blackwell Family Collection, LC. Also see Noun, *Strong-Minded Women,* p. 70.
42. Harper, *Life and Work of Susan B. Anthony,* I, 283.
43. George Francis Train, *The Great Epigram Campaign in Kansas: Championship of Women* (Leavenworth, 1867), pp. 54–55; Robinson to Stanton, November 20, 1867, Elizabeth Cady Stanton Papers, LC; Stanton, *Eighty Years and More,* p. 245.

on this tactic to the exclusion of others.[44] Their appeals to Democrats became more open and much more partisan. Provoked by Republican antifeminism, Stanton and Anthony took an important step away from the high-minded political campaign they had believed appropriate to Reconstruction and had intended the Equal Rights Association to conduct. They yielded to the partisanship around them, and as a result, their faith in popular politics was never again quite so strong as it had been before they went into Kansas.

The significance of the decision to appeal to Democrats was symbolized and heightened by the entrance of one particular Democrat, George Francis Train, into the campaign. Train was a nationally known Copperhead, as well as financier, eccentric, railroad promoter, Fenian, and woman suffrage man. His name occasionally surfaces in histories of the postwar period. He was one of the organizers of the most ambitious financial scheme of the era, the Credit Mobilier. He was also the first man, although not the first person, to be arrested under the Comstock law for sending obscene materials through the mails. Most significant for the Equal Rights Association, he was a flamboyant racist, and attacks on the intelligence and integrity of black people were basic to his political arsenal.[45] Although he was very much the individualist, his politics represented one wing of the Democratic party, which was willing to affiliate white supremacy with the democratic aspirations of woman suffragists, the labor movement, and others, in order to challenge the popularity of the Republican party at the polls.[46]

In 1867 Train was on a one-man campaign for the presidency and knew a good source of publicity when he saw one, which he

44. See Henry Blackwell to Olympia Brown, June 12, 1867, Olympia Brown Willis Papers, SL.

45. Victoria Woodhull was the first person arrested under the Comstock law. For information on Train, see Willis Thornton, *The Nine Lives of Citizen Train* (New York, 1948).

46. Lawrence Grossman, *The Democratic Party and the Negro: Northern and National Politics, 1868–1872* (Urbana, Ill., 1976), p. 4.

did in Kansas. In July he volunteered his services to solicit Democratic, especially Irish, votes on behalf of the woman suffrage referendum. After considering his offer for several weeks, Anthony accepted. "Come to Kansas and stump the State for equal rights and female suffrage," the State Impartial Suffrage Association telegraphed him.[47] Beginning on October 21, Train stumped the border towns for the last two and a half weeks of the campaign. He advocated much besides woman suffrage—currency reform, Fenianism, his own presidential campaign. Often he seemed to be touring more on behalf of himself than of the enfranchisement of women. His rhetorical style was a combination of excessive sentimentalism and barroom humor, neither of which was particularly compatible with woman suffrage agitation. He delighted in bawdiness and entertained his audiences with casual suggestions of how he and Anthony, who were traveling together, spent the nights.[48]

Most of all, it was Train's racism that violated the historical traditions and political principles of women's rights. Train slandered the freedmen whenever he could and anchored his advocacy of woman suffrage to his racism. Without quite calling for the defeat of black suffrage, he offered women's votes as a weapon to be used against the specter of black supremacy he portrayed. He taught his audiences that racial conflict was a fact of nature, not a phenomenon of history, and that increased power for blacks must always be at whites' expense. At Olathe, he put his analysis into verse:

> Woman votes the black to save,
> The black he votes to make the woman slave,
> Hence when blacks and 'Rads' unite to enslave the whites,
> 'Tis time the Democrats championed woman's rights.

47. For Train's offer, see Mrs. W. L. Hazard to Anthony, August 20, 1867, Olympia Brown Willis Papers, SL. The telegram to Train was dated October 2, 1867, and signed by Wood, Robinson, Stanton, Anthony, M. W. Reynolds, and Mrs. J. H. Land; it is printed in *The Great Epigram Campaign*, p. 5.
48. Train, *Great Epigram Campaign*, pp. 37, 54–55, and 59. The Kansas campaign does not seem to have loomed very large for Train in comparison

He often cloaked his racism in the principle of a literate electorate, and dared his audiences to choose "Muscle, and Color
and Ignorance," over "Beauty, Virtue and Intelligence."[49] In this
apocalyptic vision of black men against white women, he completely ignored black women.

Anthony's willingness to violate twenty years of women's rights
history and connect the Equal Rights Association with Train's
racism astonished her contemporaries. It was a measure of her
political desperation, not just in Kansas, but for the future of the
woman suffrage movement. In explaining and defending Train's
participation in the canvass, Stanton was openly vengeful. "So
long as opposition to slavery is the only test for a free pass to your
platform . . . , and you do not shut out all persons opposed to
woman suffrage," she challenged abolitionists, "why should we
not accept all in favor of woman suffrage to our platform and
association, even though they be rabid pro-slavery Democrats?"[50]
By contrast, Anthony simply seemed disoriented by the treachery
of those she had thought were her allies. After her initial hesi-
tancy about him, the usually sober Anthony was excessive in her
praise of Train, whom she portrayed as the savior of woman suffrage. She believed him "a *man terribly* in *earnest*—one who
never fails—who takes *woman* . . . as the only salvation for
man." "No other man I ever saw could *move mountains*," she
told Anna Dickinson.[51]

By collaborating with Train, Stanton and Anthony were react-
ing to and intensifying antagonisms they had not been able to
control. Equal rights organizers had begun the Kansas campaign
by trying to forge a joint voting bloc in favor of suffrage for
blacks and women, but Republicans had sabotaged their efforts.
By turning to Train, they gave substance to the charges of antifeminist Republicans that the woman suffrage movement was a

---

with his other escapades. He does not mention it in his autobiography, *My
Life in Many States and in Foreign Lands* (New York, 1902).
    49. Train, *Great Epigram Campaign*, pp. 32 and 7.
    50. *HWS*, II, 264.
    51. Anthony to Dickinson, November 28, 1867, Anna Dickinson Papers,
LC.

tool that the Democratic party used against the freedmen. Blacks and women did not begin the campaign as enemies of each other's enfranchisement. To the degree they ended it that way, they were victims of the Republicans' policy of dividing them. Yet, the swiftness and energy with which Stanton and Anthony turned from their own abolitionist traditions to Train's racism remains remarkable. At this point, their racism was opportunist and superficial, an artifact of their anti-Republicanism and their alienation from abolitionists. However, it drew on and strengthened a much deeper strain within their feminism, a tendency to envision women's emancipation in exclusively white terms. They learned from Train how to transform white women's racism into a kind of sex pride, a technique to which they were later to turn in building the woman suffrage movement.

"I believe both propositions would have been carried," Stanton wrote of the Kansas campaign; "but with a narrow policy, playing off one against the other, both were defeated."[52] Black suffrage was rejected in Kansas by a vote of three to one; it had been defeated a month before in referenda in Pennsylvania and Ohio as well. Woman suffrage polled two thousand votes less than black suffrage, for a total of 9,000.[53] "With all the obstacles which the dominant party could throw in our way; without organization, without money, without political rewards to offer, without any of the means by which elections are usually carried, we gained one-third of all the votes cast!" Olympia Brown marveled. "Surely it was a great triumph of principle."[54] Salvaging optimism from their defeat, feminists incorrectly predicted that they would build on their 9,000 votes to win woman suffrage in Kansas in the near future.[55]

In the wake of their defeat, equal rights leaders disagreed sharply about Train's impact on the election. Stanton and An-

52. Stanton, *Eighty Years and More,* p. 254.
53. Flexner, *Century of Struggle,* p. 147.
54. Brown to Anthony, March 16, 1882, as reprinted in *HWS,* II, 261.
55. Lucy Stone to Olympia Brown, January 6, 1867, Olympia Brown Willis Papers, SL.

thony believed that he was responsible for the surprisingly large number of votes woman suffrage received. Stanton contended that defeat would have been much more severe if Train had not "galvanized the Democrats into their duty." Anthony claimed that the woman suffrage referendum would have won if he could have campaigned longer.[56] On the other side there were those who thought that Train's participation had alienated more Republicans than it had attracted Democrats. Lucy Stone thought that "if Susan had done differently we should have had a much larger vote," and was "utterly disgusted and vexed" by Train. Governor Robinson agreed with Stone. "The large vote against us at Lawrence and Topeka was largely due to the Train-Anthony movement . . . ," he wrote to Olympia Brown. "There being no Democrats of any account in those localities, but nearly all Republicans, it had the effect to drive all the latter against the movement, except such as were actuated by conviction of duty."[57]

Train's actual impact on the Kansas election was less than either side contended. A comparison of returns from those counties where he campaigned and those where he did not indicates that he can only be credited with increasing the woman suffrage vote very slightly. The state-wide average for woman suffrage was 32 percent; the average vote cast in favor of it in the counties visited by Train was only two percent higher. Moreover, the black suffrage vote in the same counties was also two percent higher than the statewide average of 37.5. To the degree that Train can possibly be credited with increasing the vote for woman suffrage, he must be credited with the same impact on black suffrage. Indeed, although Train's participation does not correlate significantly with the woman suffrage vote, the black suffrage vote does.[58] Despite Republican attacks on woman suffrage, and the

56. Stanton, "Kansas," *Revolution*, January 8, 1868, p. 1; Anthony to Olympia Brown, November 7, 1867, Olympia Brown Willis Papers, SL.

57. Stone to Olympia Brown, undated, Olympia Brown Willis Papers, SL: Robinson to Stone, December 23, 1867, *ibid*.

58. This statistical analysis is taken directly from an excellent unpub-

Equal Rights Association's willingness to turn to racist arguments, those who were favorably inclined to black suffrage were most likely to support enfranchisement for women. This suggests that the original equal rights strategy of uniting the two issues may have been well received among some portion of Kansas voters.

The long-term effect that Train's participation had on woman suffrage is somewhat harder to assess. Stanton and Anthony seem to have been nearly alone among the friends and supporters of equal rights in their unqualified praise for his contribution. Other equal rights workers in Kansas either had not wanted to accept Train in the first place or were ashamed of the racist turn the campaign took after he joined it. In any case, no one else would defend him publicly. Governor Robinson claimed that the "more earnest workers" in Kansas were "very much mortified" by Train. Veteran feminists back east like Martha Wright and Lucretia Mott also disapproved.[59] However, most of these people were willing to consider Train an isolated incident, and remained committed to the woman suffrage movement; nor did they repudiate Stanton and Anthony because of their decision to work with him. Clarina Nichols resumed her political correspondence with Anthony within a few months of the election and never mentioned Train. Governor Robinson, who was very harsh in his criticism of the Train episode, manifested a continued belief in the political sincerity and leadership of Stanton and Anthony.[60] Olym-

_____

lished study, "The 1867 Woman Suffrage Referendum in Kansas: A Case Study in Voting Analysis," by Charles E. Halm, Jr., (Johns Hopkins University, 1973). Allen, Lyon, Riley, Wabansee, Cherokee, Ottawa, and Woodson counties gave a majority for black suffrage; Train's canvass included the first three of these. Cherokee, Riley, and Woodson went for woman suffrage; Stanton's report in the first issue of the *Revolution*, that Leavenworth County also did so was incorrect; the measure was defeated there, 53 percent to 47.

59. Robinson to Stanton, December 5, 1867, Elizabeth Cady Stanton Papers, LC; Stanton to Wright, January 8, 1869, *Stanton Letters*, pp. 119–120; Stanton, "Editorial Correspondence," *Revolution*, September 24, 1868, pp. 177–179. Also see William Lloyd Garrison to Alfred Love, December 18, 1867, Boston Public Library, and Samuel J. May to Lucy Stone, March 10, 1868, NAWSA Collection, LC.

60. Nichols to Anthony, April 14, 1868, "Papers of Clarina Nichols,"

pia Brown is particularly interesting in this regard. Her judgment was so respected that everyone associated with the Kansas canvass tried to convince her to take her or his side on Train. Brown was critical of Train and thought "the course of action pursued by Mrs. Stanton and Miss Anthony in Kansas" a serious mistake. Yet she remained politically affiliated with them, refused to focus her analysis of the Kansas defeat on Train, and considered Republican policy the major factor in the failure of the referendum there.[61]

The most important aspect of the Train episode was the breach it created in the leadership of the movement between Stanton and Anthony on the one hand, and Stone and Henry Blackwell on the other. Stone and Blackwell charged that Anthony had acted unilaterally in associating the Equal Rights Association with Train.[62] Moreover, despite the criticism leveled at them, Stanton and Anthony continued to cooperate with Train after the election. They traveled east with him on a woman suffrage speaking tour that he sponsored, and announced the imminent publication of a feminist journal that he was to finance.[63] These actions further fueled the conflict with Stone and Blackwell. "We are now in the midst of a serious quarrel with Miss Anthony and Mrs. Stanton and the Train admixture," Stone wrote to Olympia Brown in January.[64] The claim that Anthony had acted undemocratically by inviting Train into the Kansas campaign was translated into the charge that she had mismanaged equal rights funds there. Stone and Blackwell contended that Anthony had squandered money in Kansas, spending enormous amounts on Train

---

p. 549; Charles Robinson to Olympia Brown, December 22, 1867, Olympia Brown Willis Papers, SL.

61. Lucy Stone to Brown, undated, Olympia Brown Willis Papers, SL; Brown to Stone and Henry Blackwell, November 8, 1869, ibid.; Brown to Anthony, March 16, 1882, as reprinted in HWS, II, 260. Also see Brown to Mrs. Weston, January 21, 1871, Olympia Brown Willis Papers, SL.

62. Stone to William Lloyd Garrison, March 6, 1868, Boston Public Library.

63. Flexner, Century of Struggle, p. 150.

64. Stone to Brown, January 6, 1868, Olympia Brown Willis Papers, SL.

at the expense of regular equal rights speakers like Brown and themselves.[65] Anthony's reputation for scrupulous financial honesty in the conduct of reform activity was very dear to her, and these charges must have produced enormous bitterness. The intense personal animosities were only the most obvious aspect of a growing political split in the leadership.

Many years later, Blackwell explained that he had strongly opposed Train because, "so soon after the war, an alliance with a pro-slavery democrat was extremely shocking to the friends of woman suffrage, almost all of whom were abolitionists."[66] Yet Blackwell himself had appealed both to Democrats and racists to support woman suffrage. In Kansas, he advised Olympia Brown to pursue "Democrats to offset the votes of those Republicans who think a negro *better* than a woman." In connection with the Fourteenth Amendment debates, he had written an open letter to southern legislatures, proposing woman suffrage as a counter to black suffrage and a way to maintain "the political supremacy of your white race."[67]

More than Train's Copperhead politics, or his racism, it was his overt anti-Republicanism that was at issue within the Equal Rights Association. William Lloyd Garrison could think of nothing worse to say about a man he considered a "semi-lunatic" than that he went about "denouncing Republicanism."[68] Train made no secret of his hope of inflicting a humiliating blow to the Republican party's progressive image by associating himself publicly with woman suffrage. "Having split the Radical party here . . . ," he explained to his Kansas audiences, "the Demo-

65. *Ibid.,* and E. A. Studwell, Equal Rights Association treasurer, to Henry Blackwell, January 16, 1869, Blackwell Family Papers, SL. These financial animosities lingered for well over a year.
66. Henry Blackwell, unpublished reminiscences of Lucy Stone, written c. 1898, Blackwell Family Collection, LC.
67. Blackwell to Brown, June 12, 1867, Olympia Brown Willis Papers, SL; Blackwell, "What Can the South Do?" January 15, 1867, reprinted in *HWS,* II, 929–931.
68. Garrison to Alfred Love, December 8, 1867, Boston Public Library.

crats are carrying off the honors of going solidly for woman suffrage."[69]

While Stone and Blackwell opposed Train for his public attacks on the Republican party, Stanton and Anthony were drawn to him on precisely that basis. They had entered the Kansas campaign hostile to Republicans and emerged from it even more convinced that the party was the enemy of woman suffrage. "The Kansas Republican treatment of our movement disgusted me . . . ," Anthony wrote to Anna Dickinson. "Not one leading politician—living one—stood by us in the deadly breach—they all mean to delude us into silence and use us to serve party ends—who can trust the Republican leaders after this?"[70] Her repeated claim that Train was responsible for the 9,000 votes that woman suffrage did get was a way of underlining the charge that Republicans had, in Olympia Brown's words, "selfishly and meanly defeated the woman suffrage amendment."[71] Moreover, suffragists fixed the blame less on local Republicans than on national leaders. "Do not suppose that such men or such arguments had the power to defeat a righteous cause . . . ," Olympia Brown wrote of the antifeminist Republicans in Kansas. "It is rather to the cowardly and suicidal policy of the Republican leaders that the defeat of both woman and negro suffrage is due."[72] Republican treachery in Kansas convinced Anthony that the party was "a sinking ship" and that "rats—that is female rats ought to know enough to leave."[73]

The growing split in the leadership of the American Equal Rights Association also turned on the advisability of maintaining the connection of woman suffrage with abolitionism. To An-

69. Train, *Great Epigram Campaign*, p. 29.
70. Anthony to Dickinson, November 28, 1867, Anna Dickinson Papers, LC.
71. Brown to Anthony, March 16, 1882, as reprinted in *HWS*, II, 260.
72. Brown, unpublished manuscript account of Kansas campaign, 1868, Olympia Brown Willis Papers, SL.
73. Anthony to Anna Dickinson, November 28, 1867, Anna Dickinson Papers, LC.

thony, Stanton, and the feminists who gathered around them, Kansas proved that abolitionists would never respond to their appeals to act in the interest of woman suffrage. They concluded that organized abolitionism, having accepted the Republican party as the framework for protecting the freedman, had nothing to offer woman suffrage except repeated counsels to defer to the black man's greater need. "This is where Wendell Phillips failed," Stanton wrote some months after Kansas. "He should have passed, when slavery was abolished, from the abolitionist to the statesman, instead of falling back to the Republican platform."[74] The official histories of suffragism agree in portraying this disillusionment with abolitionists in Kansas as a major turning point in the movement. However, the explanations they give for the break do not focus on abolitionists' position with respect to the Republican party, but on "the stolid incapacity of all men to understand that woman feels the invidious distinction of sex exactly as the black man does that of color."[75] Achieved by abstracting the Kansas episode from its particular historical setting, this generalization cannot explain why men sometimes act to support feminist demands and sometimes do not, why feminists felt compelled to break away from abolitionists in 1867 and not twenty years before. The answer lies instead in the shifting political situation, which brought the two movements together before the Civil War and drove them apart in 1867.

In the wake of their political disillusionment in Kansas, Stanton, Anthony, and the feminists who followed their leadership began to extricate the woman suffrage movement from its deep dependence on abolitionists. They turned away from the Equal Rights Association as the center of their efforts to advance the enfranchisement of women. The association survived for another year and a half, and Stanton and Anthony remained in it, but it was more a forum for fighting out the differences that had been

74. Stanton to Thomas Wentworth Higginson, January 13, 1868, *Stanton Letters,* pp. 120–121.
75. *HWS,* II, 265. See also Stanton, *Eighty Years and More,* p. 254.

exposed among its leaders than a locale for serious woman suffrage agitation. Disaffiliation from organized abolitionism deprived these suffragists of the political framework through which they had worked since Seneca Falls and left them isolated as they had never been before. "All the old friends, with scarce an exception, are sure we are wrong," Anthony wrote in her diary on the first day of 1868.[76] If their movement was to continue to grow, they would have to find other bases for it. The break with abolitionists forced Stanton's and Anthony's wing of the woman suffrage movement to explore new alliances, new constituencies, and new strategies.

Ultimately, the most important result of the Kansas experience was that it led Stanton and Anthony to reorganize woman suffrage as an autonomous feminist movement. They recalled their political coming of age in the *History of Woman Suffrage:*

Our liberal men counseled us to silence . . . in Kansas and New York, . . . and threatened if we were not, we might fight the battle alone. We chose the latter, and were defeated. But standing alone we learned our power; . . . We would point for [the young women of the coming generation] the moral of our experiences: that woman must lead the way to her own enfranchisement, and work out her own salvation with a hopeful courage and determination that knows no fear nor trembling.[77]

The newspaper that Train helped them start, the *Revolution,* was both symbol and vehicle of this independence. Soon after the first issue appeared, in January 1868, Train departed for Ireland. Stanton and Anthony were left with the entire financial burden, but also with the sole editorial direction of the paper. Its motto, "Principle, Not Policy—Justice, Not Favors—Men Their Rights and Nothing More—Women Their Rights and Nothing Less," was a public declaration of the movement's independence from abolitionist and Republican priorities. "That is

76. Diary entry, January 1, 1868, as reprinted in Harper, *Life and Work of Susan B. Anthony,* I, 295.
77. *HWS,* II, 266–267.

why the *Revolution* is thrown upon the world at this hour," wrote Anthony. "We must have a paper through which we can make our claim in our own way and time."[78]

The *Revolution* was not the first American periodical dedicated to the improvement of women's status; Stanton herself had been associated with the *Lily*, a temperance, women's rights, and dress reform journal of the 1850's. However, the *Revolution* was certainly the least trammeled and most daring feminist paper that had yet—and perhaps has ever—appeared. In its pages, the editors—Stanton, Anthony, and Parker Pillsbury, formerly of the *Standard*—tried to convey a complex sense of women's oppression and a rich vision of their emancipation. "Take the *Revolution*," Stanton advised, "in which not only the ballot, but bread and babies will be discussed."[79] The *Revolution* reported on female farmers, inventors, sailors, and thieves, on any woman who disproved that "nature contended them all for the one mission of housekeepers."[80] The editors wrote and reprinted articles on prostitution, infanticide, the need for sex education, cooperative housekeeping, and the nonmonogamous practices of Oneida communitarians and Utah Mormons. They published the writings of Frances Wright and Mary Wollstonecraft and discovered a feminist heritage that was many centuries old. Friends advised them to change the paper's name to something more in keeping with the genteel tradition of women's journalism, but only the *Revolution* would suit them. It indicated their goal of building woman suffrage into a movement that promised women total revolution in every aspect of their lives.

78. Anthony to Anna Dickinson, November 28, 1867, Anna Dickinson Papers, LC.
79. *Revolution,* January 22, 1868, as quoted in Lutz, *Created Equal,* p. 160.
80. *Revolution,* January 29, 1868, p. 59.

Chapter Four

The Search for Allies:
The Democratic Party
and the
National Labor Union

Although Stanton, Anthony, and the feminists who joined them in the search for an alternate political context exulted in their newly independent position, they needed both allies and a general vision of social reform to replace the abolitionist/Republican framework they had abandoned. For a brief period, suffragists continued in the direction that Train had indicated for them, trying to establish connections with others on the fringes of the Democratic party to formulate a challenge to Republicans that could attract northern voters and would include woman suffrage. However, the resistance of the Democrats to a new departure in general, and to the franchise for women in particular, quickly terminated this effort. Instead, feminists found a much more congenial political atmosphere among labor reformers, who shared with them a desire to seize the reform initiative from Republicans. Moreover, while a relationship with the Democrats involved considerable opportunism for the suffragists, labor politics, in contrast, offered an egalitarian ideology that was very attractive to them. By the summer of 1868, they had begun to establish connections with the National Labor Union, the political arm of the postwar labor reform movement. This budding strategic alliance helped to draw feminists' attention to working women, with whom any possibility for a labor framework for woman suffrage ultimately rested.

"I never felt so wholly, so deeply involved in pushing our claims," Anthony wrote to Olympia Brown as she prepared the premiere issue of the *Revolution.* "We must and will be heard now."[1] Stanton also surveyed the future with unbounded optimism. "Our 'pathway' is straight to the ballot box, with no variableness nor shadow of turning," she declared to Thomas Wentworth Higginson.[2] Yet suffragists' decision to sever their ties with abolitionists did not encourage or even permit them to isolate themselves politically from other reformers. Precisely because they had developed within and been dependent on Garrisonian abolitionism for several decades, suffragists needed to identify an alternate reform context in which to situate themselves now. The feminist movement was small and had to have allies to make its impact felt, particularly as it represented a disfranchised class demanding political rights without any of the traditional political weapons. "We must look for our support to new men," Olympia Brown wrote to the *Revolution.*[3]

Nor was suffragists' need to establish new political connections only tactical, a search for co-petitioners in their appeals to Congress. The break with abolitionism had also deprived them of the ideological framework within which they had understood and argued the necessity of women's emancipation. In an early issue of the *Revolution,* Stanton charged that the greatest treachery of Radicals and abolitionists was that they had been able to lay claim to the only democratic ideology suffragists knew, the Garrisonian philosophy of universal moral equality, and had built a political program on it that excluded woman suffrage.[4] This was a serious matter for the woman suffrage movement. It literally deprived feminists of a political language in which to make their case. By 1868, for instance, Radicals and abolitionists had succeeded in equating the terms "impartial" and "universal suf-

1. Anthony to Brown, January 1, 1868, Olympia Brown Willis Papers, SL.
2. Stanton to Higginson, January 13, 1868, Boston Public Library.
3. "What the People Say to Us," *Revolution,* February 5, 1868, p. 67.
4. Stanton, "William Lloyd Garrison," *Revolution,* January 29, 1868, p. 50.

frage" with their own demand for adult manhood suffrage, thereby obscuring the disfranchisement of women.[5] Feminists needed a new ideological framework, both to argue for the importance of enfranchising women and to connect woman suffrage to the total transformation of society, which had always been the scope of their reforming ambitions.

The first and most obvious place to turn, especially for political allies, was the Democratic party. Suffragists had cooperated with individual Democrats ever since Republicans refused their petitions in 1865. By 1868, Stanton's and Anthony's intensified anti-Republicanism, their extreme political isolation, and Democrats' own disorganization encouraged them to try for formal Democratic support. From the founding of the *Revolution,* in January 1868, until the Democratic presidential convention in July, feminists worked to make woman suffrage part of the Democratic platform. Sometimes they were defensive and claimed abolitionists and Republicans had driven them to political expediency. "The party out of power is always in a position to carry principles to their logical conclusions," the editors of the *Revolution* explained to an audience no doubt astonished by the frequency of their appeals to Democrats.[6] At other times, they argued that the Democrats had a consistent and principled record of support for women's rights and franchise reform. Elizabeth Cady Stanton, whose family traditions were strongly Democratic, often made this claim and seemed especially enthusiastic about the prospect of bringing woman suffrage into the Democratic camp.[7]

To suffragists, the most appealing characteristic of the Demo-

5. See, for instance, "Fourth of July," *Standard,* June 1, 1866, p. 3. At the 1867 convention of the Equal Rights Association, a resolution was passed, "That the present claim for 'manhood suffrage,' marked with the words 'equal,' 'impartial,' 'universal,' is a cruel abandonment of the slave women of the South, a fraud on the tax-paying women of the North, and an insult to the civilization of the nineteenth century" (*HWS,* II, 190–191).
6. "Who are Our Friends?" *Revolution,* January 15, 1868, p. 24.
7. Stanton, "To Our Radical Friends," *Revolution,* May 14, 1868, p. 296, and Stanton, "What is a Democrat?" *Revolution,* September 30, 1868, p. 138.

cratic party in early 1868 was its extreme state of disorganization. The various elements within it—Copperhead and Peace Democrats, bankers and labor leaders—were searching about for a platform that could move the party beyond the issues of antebellum politics and allow it to challenge postwar Republican power. The revival of the women's rights movement directly after the war had occurred in a similar context of party confusion and jockeying for leadership among Republicans. Out of that confusion, Republicans had established a fairly clear strategy that centered around manhood suffrage and preservation of northern victory. Woman suffrage had proved incompatible with the Republicans' political program; perhaps it could win the support of Democrats. However, the racism at the heart of the Democratic party made it difficult for feminists to find a place for themselves within it. Even though the *Revolution* adopted some of Train's racist arguments, frequently contending that the intelligence and morality of white women were necessary to counter the alleged corruption and ignorance of black men, its politics were still too problack for most Democrats.[8]

Therefore, when a group of Democrats was daring enough to advance the name of Salmon P. Chase, chief justice of the Supreme Court and a longtime abolitionist, as the Democratic candidate for president, the suffragists of the *Revolution* responded immediately.[9] Chase seemed to offer the possibility of an equal

8. See, for instance, Stanton, "William Lloyd Garrison," *Revolution,* January 29, 1868, p. 50. Stanton wrote to the Democratic vice-presidential candidate, "In the name of the educated women of this country, I protest against the enfranchisement of another man of any race or clime until the daughters of Jefferson, Hancock, and Adams are crowned with all their rights" (Stanton to Frank P. Blair, October 1, 1868, Elizabeth Cady Stanton Papers, LC). Parker Pillsbury also wrote articles in this vein. See, for example, "Educated Suffrage," *Revolution,* June 18, 1868, pp. 376–377. This argument came close to the educated suffrage position simultaneously being developed by liberals such as Edwin Godkin, although generally the *Revolution* did not call for an actual literacy test for the suffrage. For more on this kind of reasoning, see below, Chap. 6.

9. For details on the Chase candidacy, see Charles H. Coleman, *The Election of 1868: The Democratic Effort to Regain Control* (New York, 1933), and Grossman, *The Democratic Party and the Negro.*

rights campaign at the heart of the Democratic party. Feminists not only appreciated Chase's friendship for the freedmen. He had a record of concrete support for women's rights as well.[10] Pillsbury wrote several editorials urging the Democrats to nominate Chase, abandon their nostalgia for slavery, and take up the standard of universal suffrage that the Republicans had jetisoned.[11] "If the democratic party were wise, they would exalt the divine idea of equality . . . ," Stanton wrote. "With the broader platform of 'Universal Suffrage' and 'Woman's Rights' inscribed in their banners, they would sweep the country from Maine to California in the coming election."[12]

By early June, however, the Chase movement had disintegrated, victim of the Democrats' stubborn determination to make political decisions as if the Civil War had not happened. "The Democrats will be *fools* & blind ones as usual," Anthony wrote to Anna Dickinson, "so *won't* vault over the heads of the Republicans to Universal Suffrage & Chase."[13] But despite their increasing conviction that the Democrats would not adopt any forward-looking positions, Stanton and Anthony went ahead with plans they had made to memorialize the Democratic convention on behalf of woman suffrage. They were encouraged to do so by New York Democrats who had supported Chase, and especially by Horatio Seymour, former governor of the state and a personal friend of Stanton's.[14] Seymour's support and last-minute enthusiasm overshadowed the suffragists' more dispassionate evaluation of what they might expect from the Democrats. By the time Anthony actually presented their petition to the convention, suffra-

10. As governor of Ohio, Chase had supported the passage of a married women's property act, and as secretary of the Treasury during the war, he had been responsible for the introduction of female clerks into U.S. government service (*HWS*, I, 167 and *HWS*, III, 808).

11. See, for example, "The Standard of Morality," *Revolution,* May 28, 1868, p. 329.

12. "To Our Radical Friends," *Revolution,* May 14, 1868, p. 296.

13. Anthony to Dickinson, June 3, 1868, Anna Dickinson Papers, LC.

14. Anthony to Dickinson, June 29, 1868, *ibid.* Seymour sponsored the suffragists' memorial to the Democratic convention. He was, of course, the man that the Democrats ultimately chose as their presidential candidate.

gists had lost what little ideological ground they had ever had for appealing for the party's support. Their memorial was a pastiche of arguments directed at all the contradictory elements in the party, from those who might be outraged at the specter of "white women—their own mothers and sisters . . . cast . . . under the heel of the lowest order of manhood," to those who wanted to finish the work of enthroning "Democracy" over "Aristocracy."[15] The Democrats ignored the memorial, pausing only long enough to ridicule it. "One more opportunity has been given the Democratic party, which it has ignominiously spurned," Pillsbury wrote in the *Revolution* after Anthony's humiliation at the convention. "We wash our hands of any further complicity in such folly and criminality."[16]

Even before the convention in July, however, the *Revolution*'s editors had begun to identify the labor reform movement as a much more likely political ally. Like woman suffrage, that movement was an emerging force with ambitions for social change that the Republican party could not contain. In particular, feminists were drawn to the National Labor Union, a labor reform organization founded in 1866 to be the national political voice of working people. As early as April 1868 the *Revolution* declared, "The principles of the National Labor Union are our principles. We see on the surface of this great movement the dawn of brighter days."[17] Like other middle-class veterans of antebellum reform, feminists were attracted by the political vitality and egalitarian premises of labor reform. As independent reform movements, woman suffrage and labor reform had a great deal in common—the ambition to perfect American democracy, a belief in the supreme power of law, and the desire to go beyond the Republican party's program of black suffrage. Feminists

15. For suffragists' 1868 memorial to the Democrats, see *Proceedings of the Democratic National Convention, held at New York, July 4–9, 1868* (Boston, 1868), pp. 27–28.
16. Pillsbury, "Democracy Restored," *Revolution*, July 16, 1868, p. 24.
17. "The National Labor Union and U.S. Bonds," *Revolution*, April 9, 1868, p. 213.

began to lay the groundwork for an alliance with the National Labor Union, and to project a third party that would work for woman suffrage as well as labor's demands.

Unlike other friends of labor, however, feminists claimed to speak for women, and this affected the National Labor Union's response to them. While its reform ambitions made it receptive to feminists and the political alliance they proposed, its trade union roots led in the opposite direction. The skilled white working men with whom it was most closely connected considered women a competitive labor force, and were hostile to the politics of sexual equality that feminists espoused. It soon became clear that the prospects for an alliance between labor reform and woman suffrage relied on working women.

The labor reform movement was a result of the Civil War's impact on working people.[18] Working men and women were affected by the ideological currents of the war, especially the enthusiastic nationalism and the belief in the superiority of a free-labor society over slavery. Simultaneously, they were subjected to particular economic pressures—wage cuts and extreme inflation—even while their employers were enjoying high profits. The result was a sharp wartime rise in both political and economic protest among working people. This upsurge involved the range of mid-nineteenth century wage-earners, from the skilled white working men of the trade unions, to the male and female factory hands in the textile and shoe industries. There were many wartime strikes aimed at maintaining wages in the face of rising prices, among which those of the skilled working men were the most successful. On the political level, a distinct working-class perspective began to emerge in reaction to the efforts of both Republicans and Democrats to direct popular political energies into their own partisan channels. While the form and tactics of the labor reform movement varied considerably from place to

18. See Montgomery, *Beyond Equality,* chap. 3, "The War and the Worker." Montgomery's achievement is to identify the dimensions of this labor reform movement, and situate the National Labor Union within it.

place, the elements that were common to all aspects of it were the claim to speak for working people and the demand that eight hours be established as the legal limit for a wage-earning day.

This was the context in which the National Labor Union was formed in August 1866.[19] Its goal was to draw the movement together and to articulate its political position on the national level. Although it aimed to speak for the broad range of people who worked for their living, it most closely reflected the perspective of skilled white working men, who were a minority of the working population but its most well organized sector. The organization primarily took the form of annual labor congresses, attended by representatives of trade unions and trade assemblies and by individual labor reformers. It demanded federal legislation on various reforms intended to benefit working people— changes in the currency and credit systems and in the distribution of federal lands, and above all the establishment of the eight-hour day. However, it never succeeded in becoming the focus of the actual political activity of the labor reform movement, which remained concentrated on the state level. Instead, the significance of the National Labor Union stemmed from the clarity with which it expressed labor reform goals and programs and the national attention it gained for them.

The men who formed the National Labor Union were veteran trade unionists who turned to political strategies out of a sense of the serious limitations of the economic weapons available to them, particularly trade unionism. William Sylvis, the single most commanding figure in the organization, was representative of this process. He had founded the Iron Moulders International Union, and built it into one of the strongest trade unions in the country. Although he never abandoned his belief in the importance of trade unions, he considered them too defensive a strategy, inade-

19. For more information on the National Labor Union, see *ibid., passim.;* Gerald Grob, "Reform Unionism in the National Labor Union," *Journal of Economic History,* 14 (1954), pp. 126–142; and Philip Foner, *History of the Labor Movement in the United States,* (New York: International Publishers, 1947), I, chaps. 18–20.

quate to counter capitalists' power over workers.[20] Sylvis was a major force behind the National Labor Union's declaration, at its founding convention, that it eventually intended to form a National Labor Party.[21] The labor movement had traditions of independent political activity reaching back to the local working men's parties of the 1820's. The political aspirations of the National Labor Union were distinguished from these by being national in scope. Like feminists, labor reformers had been awakened to the importance of reform legislation at the federal level by the examples of the Thirteenth Amendment and of Radical Republicans' fight for black suffrage in Congress.

Much about the seven-year history of the National Labor Union can be understood in terms of the tension between its political aspirations and its trade union roots. Although it aimed to unite all working people in a single national force, the National Labor Union remained dependent for its influence on the allegiance of the trade unions. Trade unionists were a minority of the working population, and sometimes saw their economic interests as conflicting with those of other workers. Trade unionism was a relatively powerful form of economic defense in the nineteenth century, but one that was available only to skilled workers, who used their monopoly over a craft as leverage against their employers. Moreover, the preservation of that monopoly often set union members against other workers, whom they saw as threatening to take some part of the craft away from the union's control. Trade unionists were particularly suspicious of black men and white women.[22] Craft solidarity was the mainstay of trade

20. Jonathan Grossman, *William Sylvis: Pioneer of American Labor* (New York, 1945), pp. 98–99.

21. "Resolutions of the Founding Convention of the National Labor Union," 1866, *Documentary History of American Industrial Society,* ed. John R. Commons et al., (Cleveland, 1910–1911), IX, 135.

22. This is not to imply that black women were not objects of suspicion, but only that they did not compete directly with white male trade unionists for jobs. Most historical analyses of the connection between racism and sexism, and trade unionism begin about 1890, with the American Federation of Labor. See, for instance, Alice Kessler-Harris, "Where Are the Organized Women Workers?'" *Feminist Studies* 3 (1975), pp. 92–110. An

unionism, but it was a narrow, inward-turning impulse. To the degree that it was carried into the National Labor Union, it pointed away from labor politics and broad electoral constituencies.[23]

The political aspirations of the National Labor Union were closely connected to its desire to expand labor's constituency beyond the skilled white men who were already organized into trade unions. The men who founded the National Labor Union believed that the domination of capital could only be overcome by the united forces of a group much larger than trade unionists or even urban wage-earners. The desire for greater labor unity was at the very center of the new organization. Its leaders wanted to reach out to farmers, women, and black people, and this too led to conflict with the traditions of trade unionism. Their most ambitious step in this direction was toward black workers. In the face of the racist traditions and exclusionary practices of trade unions, the leaders of the National Labor Union urged white working men to admit blacks into their organizations on the basis of their common membership in "the class that labors." In an address to the National Labor Union in 1867, Andrew Cameron, editor of the nation's foremost labor paper, argued that maintaining racial barriers would "inflict greater injury upon the cause of labor reform than the combined efforts of capital."[24] At its annual meetings, the organization moved very slowly in this direction, prodded by its leaders and by the pressure of black workers. However, the trade unions connected to it remained adamant in their racism, and would concede to blacks only the right to organize their own segregated local unions.[25]

---

examination of this relationship in the earlier period, when trade unions were establishing themselves and women were first entering the industrial labor force, would be a valuable undertaking.

23. Trade unions frequently avoided consideration of political issues as dangerously divisive (Foner, *History of the Labor Movement,* I, 423). At the first congress of the National Labor Union, a minority of delegates argued for the rejection of the proposal for a labor party on these grounds (*ibid.,* p. 373).

24. As quoted in Richard O. Boyer and Herbert M. Morais, *Labor's Untold Story* (New York, 1955), p. 32.

25. See Foner, *History of the Labor Movement,* I, 395–402.

Similarly, the commitment of the National Labor Union to greater labor unity allowed it to reach out to include working women, who had been regarded with unflinching hostility by male unionists and uniformly excluded from their organizations. The traditional barriers to women in the trade unions were less fierce and more elusive than those against blacks. Despite the pioneering role women workers played in the first factory strikes of the 1820's and 1830's, trade union men considered them a competitive labor force, ready to undersell male labor at a minute's notice. Like the use of machinery, the introduction of women workers into an industry was associated with the loss of craft-control over the work process, and in some industries, such as printing, women were considered strikebreakers by nature.[26] In contrast to these traditions of hostility, the founding convention of the National Labor Union passed a friendly although vague resolution offering "our individual and undivided support to the sewing women and daughters of toil in this land," and inviting women's cooperation in the work of labor reform.[27] The organization's leaders pushed for an even bolder position on sexual solidarity. In his 1867 address, Andrew Cameron endorsed the principle of equal pay for equal work, whenever women proved themselves "capable to fill the positions now occupied by the stronger sex—and in many instances they are eminently qualified to do so."[28]

Particularly in light of its relatively hospitable attitude to women workers, the National Labor Union's vision of political reorganization was very close to feminists' own. To suffragists, the National Labor Union seemed to have inherited the reform impulse which abolitionists had abandoned by becoming mere Republican politicians. It had wide reform ambitions that went well beyond the programs of either existing party. Moreover, it

26. See Elizabeth Baker, *Technology and Women's Work* (New York, 1964), pp. 39ff. Also see Chap. 5 below.
27. As quoted in Flexner, *Century of Struggle,* p. 132.
28. "Address to Workingmen," 1866, in Commons, ed., *Documentary History of American Industrial Society,* IX, 156–157.

was willing to establish a third national party, to create its own political framework, in order to work for its goals. It saw itself as the basis of a new reform force in national politics, which was precisely what suffragists were searching for. "The one bow of promise we see in the midst of this general political demoralization that all our thinking men deplore today," Stanton wrote, "is the determined, defiant position of the laboring classes, and the restless craving of women for nobler and more serious purposes in life."[29]

The similarities of the political positions in which labor reformers and woman suffragists found themselves were underlined by the circumstances of their meeting. Although the *Revolution* had given very favorable notice to the National Labor Union earlier, it was in conjunction with the Democratic national convention in July that the two groups of reformers actually met. Stanton and Anthony were among the middle-class friends of labor who were invited to the "Special Council" that the National Labor Union called on the eve of the convention to consider its political course.[30] It resolved to invite either national party—"we care not which"—to meet its demands, and made plans to petition the Democrats on behalf of the eight-hour day and currency reform. After the Special Council, Stanton, Anthony, and the president of the National Labor Union met with influential New York Democrats to coordinate their petitions to the convention.[31] Anthony was very taken by the National Labor Union's militant approach to the Democrats and its willingness to go an independent political route if necessary. "The *Workingmen's Union* held a grand meeting Thursday night," she wrote to Anna Dickinson. "They mean to make the Democrats go their plank, or smash them—so they say."[32]

29. Stanton, "Watch Your Rulers," *Revolution,* November 26, 1868, p. 329.

30. Montgomery, *Beyond Equality,* p. 395. For more information on the Special Council, see "National Labor Union—A Consultation Meeting," *New York Times,* July 3, 1868, p. 5, and "Proceedings of the Special Council," *Workingman's Advocate,* August 22, 1868, p. 4.

31. Harper, *Life and Work of Susan B. Anthony,* I, 305.

32. Anthony to Dickinson, June 28, 1868, Anna Dickinson Papers, LC.

The Democratic convention rejected both petitions, although it treated the woman suffragists more rudely than it did the labor reformers. By the time the Democrats had repudiated them, however, feminists were thoroughly enthusiastic about the prospects of an independent alliance with the National Labor Union. Beginning in July 1868, the editors of the *Revolution* began to call for a new political party built around the combined programs of the labor reform and woman suffrage movements. "Let us call a national convention of all those outside party trammels," Stanton proclaimed, "and make a platform worthy of the eventful times in which we live."[33] The *Revolution* printed a biography of and articles by National Labor Union founder, William Sylvis, began a series on labor's proposals for financial reform, and solicited letters of encouragement from labor reformers around the country.[34] A representative response from "F. S. C." in Pennsylvania urged the formation of "a new party in the interests of labor which is really in the interests of all."[35] A spokesman for the National Labor Union responded warmly to suffragists' enthusiasm. "There is no doubt that the great labor movement . . . will gather to it many of the reforms of the age," he wrote to them, "the most prominent of which are those advocated in the columns of the *Revolution*."[36]

By calling for a new party of labor reform and suffrage, feminists were able to reassert their fidelity to the egalitarian impulses of women's rights, which the circumstances of their break with the abolitionists had done much to weaken. Their elitist tendency to contrast the intelligence and morality of women like themselves with the ignorance of black and immigrant men, which

33. "The People's Party," *Revolution,* July 16, 1868, p. 28.
34. For an article written by Sylvis, see *Revolution,* November 5, 1868, p. 285. A biographical sketch of him appeared in the July 2, 1868 issue. Mary Kellogg Putnam, daughter of the currency reformer, Edward Kellogg, became associated with the *Revolution* in this period: see a letter from her, November 12, 1868, p. 297. For letters from labor reformers, see: W. F. C., "Industrial and Social Democracy," August 27, 1868, p. 117, and T. W. Ewing, "A New Political Party," August 13, 1868, p. 87.
35. "A New Political Party," *Revolution,* July 30, 1868, p. 51.
36. *Revolution,* July 9, 1868, p. 9.

had surfaced in the suffragists' arguments in the first months after Kansas, disappeared during this period. Instead, they reproclaimed their democratic faith in the sovereignty of the people, the unlimited possibilities for reform, and the coming of the social millennium. "Until every citizen shall be cloaked with all his rights, and feel a personal responsibility for the nation's welfare," Stanton wrote, "our republicanism, our democracy, is a sham, and our boasted experiment of self-government remains untried."[37] Their independent stance allowed them to charge abolitionists with abandoning true reform for a place in the Republican camp, and revolutionary aspirations for narrow goals. "We differ from our [pro-Republican] friends just at this point," Stanton wrote. "We think our national life does not depend on any party but on the safety, sobriety and education of its citizens."[38]

As their exposure to the National Labor Union continued, the feminists of the *Revolution* adopted many of the labor reformers' ideas. They came to understand why the labor movement equated wage slavery with chattel slavery, and they went beyond the abolitionist critique of the ownership of persons to the labor movement's critique of the effective ownership, or appropriation, of labor. "I find that the same principle degrades labor as upheld slavery," Stanton observed. "The great motive for making a man a slave was to get his labor, or its results, for nothing." They readily accepted the working-class belief that labor was the source of all wealth; they learned to criticize the very rich, not simply because they had more than the poor, but because they had stolen their wealth from those who had created it. Suffragists adopted labor reformers' assessment of what posed the greatest danger to the future of democracy—the centralization of land and money in the hands of a few monopolists. They even came to understand the importance of strikes "as a link in the chain of [the laboring classes'] final triumph."[39]

37. "The People's Party," *Revolution*, July 16, 1868, p. 28.
38. "Look Up Higher," *Revolution*, September 17, 1868, p. 168.
39. All quotes from Stanton, "On Labor," manuscript of speech, Elizabeth

Feminists and other middle-class sympathizers differed from labor reformers, however, in their actual distance from the poor and working people whose cause they espoused. They were not workers—despite Anthony's career as a teacher or Pillsbury's nostalgia for his brief experience as an agricultural wage-earner—and they did not move among working people. Their commitment to and faith in the poor tended to be idealized and romantic. "The poor man does the labor of the world, then starves and dies, while crafty villians feast and clothe themselves in royal robes," Stanton wrote in the excessively lyrical style she used when she was treading politically unfamiliar ground.[40] When it came to actual efforts to improve the situation of the poor, they could not quite imagine working people as the agents of their own emancipation. "There is no hope of any general self-assertion among the masses," Stanton believed. "The first steps for their improvement must be taken by those who have tasted the blessings of liberty and education."[41] Similarly, they tended to identify class antagonism, rather than class itself, as the problem against which they fought. Their goal was the reconciliation, not the abolition, of capital and labor. Stanton expressed this idealistic conviction in a particularly feminist way. "Until capital and labor are linked together by the higher law of affection, which is woman," she wrote, "craft and cunning will subordinate strength and activity, and the few will monopolize the wealth of the world."[42]

On one issue, however, suffragists were in a position to have a much more profound understanding than labor leaders—the sexual division of labor, and the barriers to sexual solidarity among workers. The labor movement, trade unionism and labor reform both, reflected primarily the experience of male workers. The National Labor Union's tentative friendliness to women was a significant advance over the sexual hostility that predominated

Cady Stanton Papers, LC. This speech has been published in *Signs: Journal of Women in Culture and Society*, 1 (1975), 260–263.
40. "Capital and Labor," *Revolution*, April 30, 1868, p. 264.
41. Stanton, "On Labor."
42. "The Wealth of the World," *Revolution*, May 28, 1868, p. 321.

in the trade unions, but it was still a limited position. Sylvis and other labor pioneers appealed for an end to sexual conflict, which they understood was detrimental to male and female workers alike, but they did not challenge the sexual division of labor on which that conflict was based. They accepted as natural and desirable the categorization of wage labor into "women's work" and "men's work," and even more basically, the sexually determined division between waged work as a whole and the unwaged labor that most women did in the home. They believed that once relations between labor and capital had been revolutionized, women would leave wage labor and return to their "natural" place in the home. Even as he championed woman's rights as a worker, Sylvis believed that "she was created to be the presiding deity of the home circle, the instructor of our children . . . [to] make us glad in the days of adversity and . . . console us in our declining years."[43]

While nineteenth-century feminists did not develop a comprehensive critique of the sexual division of labor, they chipped away at its edges and heightened its contradictions. Because the situation of women was always at the center of their concerns, they challenged the labor movement to expand its definition of workers and their needs beyond men. They began to insist that what women did in their homes was work, but that it differed from the work that most men did because it was unpaid, unsocialized, and unrelenting.[44] Faced with the problem of reconciling feminism and the male-dominated labor movement, they noticed that the characteristic demands of organized labor—decent wages and an eight-hour day, for instance—were irrele-

43. 1864 speech by Sylvis, as quoted in Israel Kugler, "The Women's Rights Movement and the National Labor Union (1866–1872)," (doctoral diss., New York University, 1954), pp. 416–417.
44. Pillsbury, "Woman's Work," *Revolution*, August 27, 1868, pp. 120–121. See also Elizabeth Cady Stanton, "Housework," *Revolution*, December 24, 1868, p. 393. This article contains more information about the actual labor involved in domestic work than Pillsbury's but is nonetheless marred as an analysis of housework by the fact that it is written from the perspective of an employer of domestic labor.

vant to most women, whose labor was domestic. Women are "not generally recognized as any part of the labor interest," Pillsbury wrote in a brilliant analysis of the impact that women might have on the labor movement. "It will be discovered, however, that they are not only part of the laboring class, but so terribly of it as to be beyond the reach of the eight hour law."[45] Moreover, he argued, the reconciliation of male and female workers would be complicated by the fact that men depended on women's unpaid work as well as their own wages to survive. "How many of us must go supperless to bed if housewives claimed the eight hour demand as their own?" he asked.[46] "It is to be regretted that the Working Men's Unions do not more readily grasp the idea that all their efforts for self-extrication and elevation are vain," the *Revolution* editorialized, "until the claims of the more oppressed working women are recognized."[47]

Suffragists' hope for an alliance with labor reform came to focus on the third annual congress of the National Labor Union, scheduled for September 1868. Anthony was particularly determined that women participate in the congress—"She who would be free, herself must strike the first blow," she exhorted—and was able to get several feminists to attend.[48] Their reception was mixed. The majority of delegates received them warmly, and seemed open to a political alliance between woman suffrage and labor reform. The women had the strong support of most of the officers, including William Sylvis, the newly elected president. However, a minority of delegates, reflecting the traditional trade union perspective on women, vigorously opposed any connection with woman suffrage and the feminist politics it represented. The experience served to demonstrate that, when it came to an alliance with labor reform, the political choices of the feminist

45. "The Largest Store in the World," *Revolution*, September 3, 1868, p. 136.
46. "Work and Workers," *Revolution*, August 27, 1868, p. 104.
47. "Women's Work and Wages," *Revolution*, July 23, 1868, p. 33.
48. Anthony, "The Workingman's National Congress," *Revolution*, September 17, 1868, p. 169.

movement were bound up with the economic position of women and working men's attitudes toward them.

In general, suffragists had many reasons to be pleased with the 1868 National Labor Congress. In his opening address, retiring president J. C. C. Whaley spoke at length about the depressing impact of sexual competition in the labor force on both men and women. "The question of female labor is one of paramount importance to the industrial classes and merits the attention of trade organizations, local and national," he insisted. He urged working men to respond to the use of working women to undersell their labor, not by excluding women from their unions, but by cooperating with them to elevate their wages and overcome their exploitation.[49] Following Whaley's lead, the congress appointed a committee on female labor, which called for a special effort to form labor organizations among working women and to win federal and state laws for equal pay for equal work among government employees.[50] The most substantial achievement for women at the congress was that, for the first time, four of them—Susan B. Anthony, Elizabeth Cady Stanton, Mary Kellogg Putnam, and Mary Macdonald—were awarded regular delegate status.[51] All four were suffragists, connected with the *Revolution*. Their admission as delegates gave substance to the willingness of Sylvis and other labor leaders to bring women workers into the National Labor Union.

A fifth woman, Kate Mullhaney, also played a prominent role at the congress. She was nominated for second vice-president, and appointed special assistant secretary, with responsibility for working women, the first, and only, woman ever to hold office in the National Labor Union. She was not, however, at the congress, having stayed away "under the idea that female delegates

49. *Proceedings of the Second Session of the National Labor Union, in Convention Assembled at New York City, September 21, 1868* (Philadelphia, 1868), pp. 5–6.

50. *Ibid.*, pp. 24–25.

51. "National Labor Congress," *New York World*, September 23, 1868, p. 4.

would not be admitted."[52] Mullhaney, founder and leader of a union of women collar laundry workers in Troy, New York, was one of the rare female leaders to emerge in the labor movement during this period. A friend and protégé of Sylvis, who was also from Troy, Mullhaney was dependent on him and other male labor leaders, and in a weak position to test the extent of male support for women workers. The push to have women received as equals at the National Labor Congress came instead from women outside the labor movement.

Although the National Labor Congress gave women a warm reception, a minority of delegates had strong objections to associating the labor movement with anything that suggested formal recognition of the demand for woman suffrage. On the first day of the congress, Stanton's application for delegate status was challenged on the grounds that she represented a woman suffrage society and not a labor organization. Even though the other three women delegates were suffragists, carried credentials from organizations that had only been formed a short time before, and were not working women, Stanton alone was challenged, because she presented credentials from a suffragist organization.[53] The challenge provoked heated debate, but considerable support for Stanton, and she was seated by a vote of forty-four to nineteen.[54] The next day, the delegates who had voted against her,

52. *New York Times,* September 25, 1868, p. 2. There is very little information on Mullhaney. See John B. Andrews and W. D. P. Bliss, *History of Women in Trade Unions* (Washington, D.C., 1911), pp. 106–107.

53. "National Labor Congress," *New York World,* September 23, 1868, p. 4. Stanton presented credentials from the Woman Suffrage Association of America, a nonexistent organization. (The first real national woman suffrage organization was not formed until 1869; see Chap. 6 below.) Susan B. Anthony represented the Working Women's Association, an organization she had formed just days before, which eventually became very important; see Chap. 5. Mary Kellogg Putnam presented credentials from the same organization. Mary Macdonald represented the Mt. Vernon Women's Protective Labor Union. Despite its name, it was an organization of taxpaying women, fighting to win political rights in their town. For more on this organization, see "Women in Council," *New York World,* September 17, 1868, p. 4.

54. *Proceedings of the Second Session of the National Labor Union,* p. 19.

mostly representatives of the building trades, threatened to withdraw from the congress unless her credentials were revoked.[55]
Although they did not succeed in unseating her, they were able
to get the labor congress to forswear woman suffrage. It passed
a resolution that "by the admission of Mrs. Stanton as a delegate
to this body, the National Labor Congress does not regard itself
as endorsing her particular ideas or committing itself to the question of Female Suffrage."[56] A second debate on woman suffrage
was stimulated by the report of the committee on female labor,
which Anthony chaired. The committee included women's enfranchisement along with trade unions and vocational education
in its list of "honorable means to force employers to do justice to
women." The same delegates who had opposed the seating of
Stanton objected to the "wedge" this granted woman suffrage.
"You know that women have very fertile imaginations . . . ,"
Henry Keating of the New York Bricklayers, insisted. "They will
say that the Congress approves of the ballot." Another delegate,
the influential labor journalist Jonathan Fincher, declared that
"this 'ism' of Woman's Suffrage will never be endorsed by the
trades unions." Their arguments prevailed, and the delegates
voted to remove all mention of woman suffrage from the report.[57]

The demand for woman suffrage drew the fire of trade unionists because of its implications for real feminist power. Unlike the
demands for vocational education, female trade unions and protective associations, and even equal pay for equal work, the
demand for woman suffrage was beginning to generate an independent feminist movement. It was not simply a call for justice,
with only the power of its own righteousness behind it, but the

55. "National Labor Congress," *New York World,* September 23, 1868,
p. 4. For the claim that Stanton's opponents were from the building trades,
see Kugler, "The Women's Rights Movement and the National Labor
Union," p. 93.
56. "National Labor Congress," *New York World,* September 24, 1868,
p. 4.
57. "National Labor Congress," *New York World,* September 23, 1868,
p. 4. Fincher's comment was reported in "National Labor Congress," *Revolution,* October 1, 1868, p. 204.

basis of a growing force of women, making and pressing for their own demands. With their history of hostility to women workers, male trade unionists were particularly reluctant to become involved with an independent women's movement, which could set its own terms for cooperation between the sexes.

Despite the National Labor Union's refusal to offer formal recognition to woman suffrage, the feminist delegates considered the congress a great success and were optimistic about a future alliance with labor. Stanton saw the congress's two major achievements as the historic recognition it had accorded women and the substantial steps it had taken toward the formation of a national labor party: "They have inaugurated the grandest movement of the century, proved themselves wise in reading the signs of the times, and cunning in securing the only element of faith and enthusiasm that will make the NEW NATIONAL PARTY OF AMERICA . . . triumphant in 1872." She imagined blacks deserting the Republican party and joining women and working people, to form "a triple power that shall speedily wrest the sceptre of government from the non-producers—the land-monopolists, the bondholders, the politicians."[58]

Missing from her revolutionary vision, as from the 1868 labor congress in general, was the working woman. Her involvement was unavoidable, however, once the labor and feminist movements began to explore their common ground. Indeed, wage-earning women were already beginning to intrude on the scene, through the Working Women's Association that Anthony had helped to form days before the congress to earn her credentials as a delegate. Within a year, the presence and activity of working women themselves would completely revise suffragists' political calculations.

58. Stanton, "National Labor Congress," *Revolution,* October 1, 1868, p. 200.

Chapter Five

The Search
for a Constituency:
The Working Women's
Association

The possibilities for an alliance with the National Labor Union, and especially their experience at the 1868 National Labor Congress, helped to draw suffragists' attention to working women and the part sexual inequality played in their lives. The determined opposition of a minority of trade unionists to any affiliation with the woman suffrage movement served to demonstrate that the relations between men and women in the labor force, particularly trade unions' hostility to women, were a barrier that must be confronted before workers' and feminist reforms could be linked. Furthermore, suffragists' claim that the enfranchisement of women was compatible with the aims of labor reform led them to women in the labor force to find support for their position among working people themselves. The focus of this effort was the Working Women's Association, which Anthony and a group of wage-earning women formed in September 1868, initially to provide Anthony with delegate credentials for the 1868 National Labor Congress. The association existed for almost a year. During that time, it was the focus of suffragists' efforts to organize women to demand their own enfranchisement and emancipation.

Two interconnected sets of historical relationships shaped the experiences and political responses of working women. One was the sexual division of labor, the systematic inequality that trapped women in a few underpaid occupations and often denied them paid employment altogether, and was supported by both male

workers and employers. The other was the class relations of industrial capitalism, which centered on the growing group of
workers who sold their labor for wages, increasingly distinguished
their interests from those of others in the society, and produced
a heightened level of conflict between wage-earners and their
employers. Under the leadership of the suffragists, the Working
Women's Association began to do what no labor organization
had done before—bring together wage-earning women to challenge the organized power of men over them. However, its ability
to penetrate to the core of the sexual division of labor was limited
by the middle-class perspective of its leaders. Despite their moral
and political sympathies with working people, suffragists never
learned to see the problems of women in the labor force from the
perspective of wage-earners themselves. Their own middle-class
experience remained their standard for feminism, and, when a
strike intensified class antagonisms, they found themselves on the
opposite side from the workers, female as well as male. Within
a year, the unavoidable realities of class conflict had shattered
the Working Women's Association and with it all possibilities of
an alliance between woman suffrage and labor reform. Subse-
quently, suffragists turned back to middle-class women as their
primary constituency. Nonetheless, the Working Women's Association stands as a pioneering attempt to build a working wom-
en's feminism that could address economic grievances as well as
political ones.

The approach that suffragists took in the Working Women's
Association and the obstacles that they faced were closely related
to the particular working women who joined the organization.
Most of the charter members of the association were newspaper
typesetters. Their perspective on the sexual division of labor was
unusual. Unlike most wage-earning women, who were trapped
on the women's side of the division, the typesetters were a female
minority in a male-dominated trade. They had firsthand experience with the pressures male workers and employers used to keep
women in an economically subordinate and vulnerable position.

Moreover, they were skilled workers, a fact that exposed them to the sharp class conflict that existed between the skilled men of the trade unions and their employers. But partly because their position differed from that of most women workers, it revealed in an unusually clear way the pressures to which all were subject.

The sexual division of labor, and women's inferior place in it was the central fact of nineteenth-century working women's economic lives. Women comprised about one-quarter of the non-agricultural wage-earners. The overwhelming majority of workers were in sexually segregated occupations. Men and women labored in different industries, in different capacities, according to different wage scales. In general, men's discontent with the sexual division of labor was limited to their fear that women would undersell male labor and displace men from their jobs. Women experienced the division differently and more pervasively. For them, it meant being forced to find work in a very few industries and occupations, primarily domestic service, the needle trades, and the shoe industry. In 1870 there were approximately 1,300,000 nonagricultural wage-earning women, of whom 70 percent were domestic servants and another 24 percent were operatives in textile, clothing, and shoe factories. In addition, this sexual segregation of occupations created a situation in which women's labor was priced independently from and much lower than men's. Finally, traditions of craft unionism and labor politics, which encouraged workers to cooperate to improve their employment conditions, were almost unknown among women.[1]

The women printers who formed the Working Women's Association were the elite of the female wage-earning force. Women had worked as newspaper printers since the eighteenth century, when they assisted their husbands and fathers in family establishments and occasionally became proprietors in their own right. As

1. The statistics are from Montgomery, *Beyond Equality*, pp. 453–454. For a general overview of the sexual division of labor, see Heidi Hartman, "Capitalism, Patriarchy, and Job Segregation by Sex: The Historical Roots of Occupational Segregation," *Signs: Journal of Women in Culture and Society*, 1 (1975), 137–169.

newspaper printing changed from a family to an industrial enterprise, women remained an important element in it, but as wage-earners rather than wives and daughters. It has been estimated that in 1850 there were 1,400 women employed as newspaper compositors, 16 percent of the total work force in the industry.[2] Their working conditions were far superior to those of most other mid-nineteenth century women in the labor force. A good compositor could earn between $15 and $20 a week for about eight hours' work a day, while sewing women and domestics worked far longer for much less. A survey of New York City working women indicated that female typesetters earned more than any other group, except professionals and the self-employed.[3] Much like the profession of medicine in this same period, the trade of printing had a strong attraction for women who aspired to a more profitable and honorable field for their labor. Moreover, typesetting was a skill. Unlike most other jobs that women could hold, typesetting permitted them a certain degree of the craft-pride that was the nineteenth-century male worker's primary source of dignity. Like the pioneering factory operatives at Lowell in the 1830's, female typesetters took from their work a sense of dignity and autonomy distinctive in a society that praised dependence in women.

Despite their relative advantages, however, women typesetters still could not escape the depressing impact of the sexual division of labor. Their position compared well to that of other working women, but not to that of men in their trade. Their wages were far lower than men's. This in turn reflected their much more limited skills. Most women printers could only set type and could not perform any of the other tasks involved in newspaper printing. They never learned the whole range of printing skills because the union barred them from its apprenticeship program, through which men learned the entire trade. Instead, women

2. Baker, *Technology and Women's Work*, pp. 37–49.

3. "Working Women's Association," *Revolution*, October 8, 1868, pp. 214–215. "Our Working Classes," *New York Times*, March 17, 1869, p. 12.

learned on the job or in the brief training sessions run by their employers. In addition, women's hold on their jobs was terribly insecure. Whereas male printers enjoyed the protection of the National Typographical Union, the union excluded women and worked to drive them out of the industry. As a result, women were hired and fired with great frequency.[4]

This process of systematic sex discrimination was shaped by the intense labor conflict that characterized the printing industry. Employers and union men struggled with each other for the power to manipulate the sexual division of labor in their own interests. Printing was among the more highly unionized crafts in the mid-nineteenth century. The National Typographical Union was the oldest and one of the most powerful national trade unions in the country. Its strongest local was No. 6, in New York City, which conducted frequent and successful strikes to maintain high wages for its members. As early as 1853, New York City newspaper owners tried to break the union's power during a strike by hiring women and training them to set type. Over the years, most women entered the industry in this fashion. The newspaper owners portrayed themselves as philanthropists. They claimed that they hired women because they wanted to relieve their suffering and increase their wage-earning opportunities.[5]

The National Typographical Union's response to the use of women as strikebreakers was to try to keep them out of the printing industry altogether. The union refused to organize women, hoping that this policy would drive them, if not back to their

4. On apprenticeship requirements in printing in New York City, see George A. Stevens, *New York Typographical Union No. 6: Study of a Modern Trade Union and its Predecessors* (Albany, 1913), chap. 25. In *Technology and Women's Work,* Elizabeth Baker mistakenly criticizes women printers for being "reluctant" to take four-year apprenticeships (p. 37). On the contrary, there is no indication that male printers ever considered women as apprentices.

5. Stevens, *New York Typographical Union No. 6,* is a superb study of this local. Chapter 21 surveys the position of women in printing extensively but from a perspective essentially favorable to the union, and therefore inadequate from the perspective of woman workers.

kitchens, at least out of the composing room. The National Typographical Union first considered the question of women workers at its 1854 national convention. Two resolutions were presented to the delegates, both urging that local unions have the option to decide policy "with regard to women in the printing business." The only difference between the two was that one included a set of introductory clauses declaring the union's "lively interest in" and "warmest desires" for working women. The real intent of both resolutions was to protect the union's public image, not unorganized women in the printing industry. The printers were concerned that their employers had succeeded in depicting themselves as friends of the working woman, and the union as her enemy. The option being considered was not whether local unions would admit women into membership, but whether local unions would work to drive them from the industry. The convention rejected both local option resolutions because they granted too much to women. Instead, it adopted a national policy stating that the union "will not encourage . . . the employment of females as compositors."[6]

A sharp increase in the number of women in printing during the Civil War led the union to reexamine its position at its 1867 national convention. It considered a report, coauthored by a member of Local 6, which argued that the union should reverse its policy and actively work to organize women printers. "Female labor will never cease injuring male labor until . . . [men and women] assume that position of identity which is their normal condition," the report asserted. It urged that the male printers "throw around their sisters the protecting power of their organizations." The report's strong stand in favor of sexual equality represents one of the high points in the history of nineteenth-century trade unionists' attitudes toward women workers, and probably reflects both the pressure of women in the printing trade and the growth of feminist sentiment in society at large. Nonethe-

6. *Ibid.,* pp. 423–424.

less, it was still a minority position within the printers' union, and was defeated by a vote of twenty-nine to seventeen.[7] Instead, the national union adopted a resolution that permitted locals the option of organizing women printers. This represented the most evasive, weakest position it could have taken on the issue by that time.[8]

The particular situation that drove women typesetters to seek the help of suffragists resulted from a strike that Local 6 called in December 1867 against the *New York World*. To fight the union, the owners of the *World* had hired women and trained them on the job to set type. Women responded in large numbers to this opportunity to learn a skill. The *World* claimed that it trained over one hundred women during the strike. In September 1868, ten months after the strike had begun, the *World* and Local 6 reached a settlement. As part of their agreement, the women typesetters were dismissed. They protested, but the employers piously claimed that they had been forced to fire them because their work had not proved as good as the men's. Mindful of the public image they had cultivated as friends of the working woman, the employers reported that they had found jobs for as many of the women as they could, in good conscience, recommend. They placed them in the book and job printing sector of the industry, where wage scales were much lower than in newspaper work.[9]

The *Revolution* followed the progress of the *World* strike and the fate of the women typesetters. During the strike, it published an article, purportedly written by one of the female compositors, describing the use of women as strikebreakers and urging them to hold on to their jobs and learn as many skills as they

7. *Ibid.*, pp. 428–429.
8. *Proceedings of the Fifteenth Annual Session of the National Typographical Union, held in the City of Memphis, Tennessee, June 5–7, 1867* (New York, 1867), p. 4.
9. On the strike, see Stevens, *New York Typographical Union No. 6*, p. 402. The *World*'s owners explained their reasons for firing the women in a letter, September 20, 1868, quoted in *ibid.*, pp. 431–432.

could.[10] After the strike was settled and the women fired, the *Revolution* charged the printers' union with deliberately excluding women from the trade, and colluding with their employers to discharge them from the positions they held. As always, the *Revolution* related the unjust treatment of women to their disfranchisement. "This is the case all over the country both with women and negroes, ignored everywhere by the 'printers' unions,' " the editors argued. "Now what is the reason? Only this, they are disfranchised classes, hence degraded in the world of work."[11]

Within a few weeks, the Working Women's Association was formed at the offices of the *Revolution*.[12] Although it was formally an organization open to all women in the labor force, female printers predominated in its membership and held most of its offices. Eventually the organization claimed over one hundred wage-earning members.[13] The president, Mrs. Anna Tobbitt, embodied the role that women had played in the rapidly fading family print shop. She was the wife of a small, independent printer, and worked in her husband's shop. Susie Johns, Augusta Lewis, and Emily Peers, the organization's vice-presidents, were much more representative of women in the newspaper industry of the day. All three were young, unmarried, and wage-earning typesetters. Peers and Lewis soon emerged as the leading spokespeople in the Working Women's Association for the wage-earners' point of view. Both had been employed at the *World* during the strike. Lewis, about whom there is an unusual amount of biographical information available, began in the newspaper industry as a writer. She claimed she sought work as a printer "as an educating factor in helping me in writing."[14] After she

10. M. C. B., "Female Compositors," *Revolution*, March 19, 1868, p. 164.
11. "California Ahead Again," *Revolution*, September 10, 1868, p. 149.
12. "Working Women's Association," *Revolution*, September 24, 1868, p. 181.
13. "National Labor Congress," *Workingman's Advocate*, September 4, 1868, p. 1. Compare this to Anthony's estimate that there were two hundred women printers in New York in 1868 ("Women's Typographical Union," *Revolution*, October 15, 1868, p. 231).
14. Augusta Lewis, as quoted in Stevens, *New York Typographical*

was fired, she got a job demonstrating the new Alden typesetting
machine. Peers was working as forewoman in the nonunion shop
of the *National Anti-Slavery Standard*. Elizabeth and Julia
Brown, sisters who worked as clerks at the *Revolution*, were
elected secretary and treasurer of the association. The membership's mixture of wage-earning women, their female employers,
and self-employed women printers illustrates its leaders' tendency
to emphasize the common experiences women had with sexual
barriers in the work force, and to ignore the divisions of class
position.

From the beginning, the typesetters and suffragists disagreed
over the place of the suffrage demand in the Working Women's
Association. Stanton and Anthony thought that enfranchisement
"was at the bottom of all reforms for the material welfare of
women," and should be the association's foremost goal. The
typesetters, however, disagreed, and rejected Stanton's suggestion
that they name their organization the Working Women's Suffrage Association.[15] This was not because the working women
were against suffrage. Augusta Lewis, for one, thought that the
association might eventually work actively for it.[16] What they
objected to was the priority that suffragists wanted to give the
vote. In part, they disagreed with the suffragists because they
were more skeptical of the vote's limitations as a political tool.
Stanton argued that the economic position of working women
would be vastly improved when they were enfranchised, but she
could not convince the typesetters that their wages would rise and
their labor would become more respected once they had the vote.

Union No. 6, p. 432. For more information on Lewis, see Eleanor Flexner,
"Augusta Lewis Troup," *NAW*, III, 478–479. Much is known about Lewis
because she married Alexander Troup, an officer and important figure in
the printers' union. By contrast, almost nothing is known about Emily Peers,
who like most nineteenth-century women labor leaders briefly rose into
prominence and then disappeared into the masses of working women.

15. "Working Women's Association," *Revolution,* September 24, 1868,
p. 181.

16. "Working Women in Council," *New York World,* September 18, 1868,
p. 2.

Emily Peers did not think that the suffrage was "the great pana-
cea for the correction of all existing evils." At most, she thought,
"by it we might gain some point otherwise doubtful."[17] In addition, typesetters were uneasy with the radical changes in women's
status and sexual relations that the vote had come to symbolize.
Lewis argued that working women, like most women in the
1860's, were afraid of being labeled "strong-minded." "The word
'suffrage' would couple the association in the minds of many
with short hair and bloomers and other vagaries," she explained,
and thought the organization should hold off suffrage agitation
until it was better established.[18]

Yet the disagreement between typesetters and middle-class
suffragists over the importance of the vote did not prevent them
from being able to form an organization and work together in it.
Their differences were subsumed within their common commitment to sexual equality. In particular, both groups believed in
the eradication of economic discrimination against women and
the achievement of sexual equality in the labor force. The ground
they shared was feminism, not suffragism. "You and I may hold
an entirely different opinion," Peers said to Stanton and Anthony,
after she had criticized their faith in the ballot, "but waiving
what is problematical, there is a broad common ground upon
which we can stand, agreeing fully and entirely. We can reach
out, one to another—the highest to the lowest—the hand of
fellowship. We can make theory and practice go hand in hand,
. . . working closely up to our convictions."[19] The convictions
that suffragists and typesetters shared were that women as a sex

17. For Stanton's comments, see "Working Women's Association," *Revolution,* September 24, 1868, p. 181. For Peers's comments, see "Working
Women's Association #1," *Revolution,* October 1, 1868, p. 197.
18. "Working Women's Association," *Revolution,* September 24, 1868,
p. 181. Similarly, a group of San Francisco typesetters, writing to the
Revolution, apologized for their aversion to politics and their "lack of
strongmindedness" ("California Ahead Again," *Revolution,* September 10,
1868, p. 149).
19. "Working Women's Association #1," *Revolution,* October 1, 1868,
p. 197.

were unjustly treated, that men, acting collectively to defend their
sexual privileges, were to blame for women's current degraded
status, and that sexual equality was the desirable condition of
human society. In short, they shared the rudiments of a feminist
politics.

The core of the suffragists' feminism was their belief that
women had the capacity and the right to reach out beyond the
dependence that characterized their domestic lives, to establish
some kind of independent position in the world outside the home.
The major route that they advocated to female independence
and equality was enfranchisement. They believed that as citizens,
women would be acting along with men as individual members of
the community, not as part of their families. The other way that
they recognized for women to emancipate themselves from their
domestic isolation and dependent status was to work outside the
home. Unlike housework, labor done outside the home enabled
women to earn money, which was the basis for economic independence. Money was also the symbol of community recognition
of work that had social significance. Whereas domestic work
seemed, even to feminists, in part an expression of women's nature,
work outside the home established women along with men as individuals whose labor contributed to the community's wealth.
This was the feminist framework within which suffragists were
attracted to the typesetters in particular, and to working women
in general.

Suffragists were certainly not the only people who devoted special attention to the working woman in the late 1860's. Newspaper and magazine journalists, charity workers, novelists, and
labor leaders regularly deplored the exploitation and misery of
the working woman's life, her low wages, oppressive working
conditions, economic marginality, and vulnerability to prostitution. In fact, the degraded working woman can be said to have
replaced the degraded slave woman in the post–Civil War period
as a staple of popular imagery and superficial social criticism.
Yet there was an important distinction between this general advocacy of the working woman and the suffragists' position. Most

of the female worker's defenders were outraged because her situation violated woman's natural right to be protected, to be sheltered from the brutalities of the marketplace by the strong arm of man. Their championship of working women was essentially philanthropic and assumed woman's inherent weakness.[20]

Although suffragists drew on these same popular images of economic and sexual exploitation, their premises and goals were different. They believed that the entry of women into the labor force was a positive development and that the problem was not that women had to work outside their homes, but that they confronted the barriers of sexual prejudice when they did so. Their response to the suffering of working women was to attack sexual inequality in the labor force. They argued that as long as women were "crowded" into a few occupations, they could never demand decent wages for their labor, and insisted that women be permitted to enter "new and more profitable employments."[21] Suffragists championed the woman in the labor force on the basis of what they perceived as her strengths—her independent manner, craftsmanship, competence, and productive capacities. Whereas others saw the female worker solely as the symbol of women's victimization, the feminists also saw her as the symbol of women's potential power, an indication of the direction that women should develop in the future to achieve emancipation. To most of suffragists' contemporaries, the representative working woman was the sewing woman. The workers in the needle trades were deemed typical less because there were so many of them than because, in their miserable garrets, they revealed the suffering to which women were believed to be condemned when forced out of their homes to support themselves. For suffragists, however, the representative working woman was the statistically insignificant skilled worker, whose craft opened up to her the possibility of honorable independence and equality with men.

20. See, for instance, "The Chances for Women to Work," *New York Times*, February 18, 1868, p. 4.
21. Stanton, "Working Women's Association," *Revolution*, November 5, 1868, p. 280; "Working Women," *Revolution*, October 1, 1868, p. 200.

The feminist character of the Working Women's Association was not widely appreciated. When the association was first formed, it was received with the expectation that it was within the benevolent tradition of female philanthropy, an indication that the women's rights movement had given up its strident rhetoric and illusory aims—its feminism—for more ladylike goals. The *New York Times* believed that the women's rights movement was "more practical" and "less visionary" and "much better directed at this time than formerly. . . . It is now very formidable where it was a few years ago simply ridiculous." Similarly, the *New York Herald* thought that the Working Women's Association was a decided advance over "women's rights spouting conventions."[22] Anthony was amused by the absurdity of the assumption that, in forming the Working Women's Association, she was departing from her feminist goals. Speaking to an audience of several hundred working women at a lecture sponsored by the association, she claimed the event had been "the doings of Women's Rights." "Excuse me, audience, I beg your pardon," she said, with uncharacteristic humor. "No one would believe it that the cloven foot of Woman's Rights was stamped upon the undertaking, if I had not stated so."[23]

As for the typesetters, their position within the printing industry led them to develop a similar feminist perspective. Caught between their employers and the union, they identified the sexual division of labor as their primary economic grievance and sexual equality in the labor force as their goal. They believed in equal pay for equal work, because they were among the small minority of women workers who were in a position to imagine men and women doing the same job. As Emily Peers said, in her eloquent exposition of the common feminism that linked typesetters and suffragists, "We know that for the same labor, capably, conscientiously performed, there should be the same compensa-

22. "Professional and Working Women," *New York Times,* October 14, 1868, p. 4; the article from the *New York Herald* was reprinted in the *Revolution,* November 5, 1868, p. 299.
23. "A Struggle for Life," *New York Times,* November 16, 1868, p. 5.

tion."[24] However, men and women did not do equal work within the newspaper industry, primarily because women had been excluded from union apprenticeship programs. The women typesetters were aware of this structural inequality and its impact on their wages. They "did not expect that they would be paid the same price as men, as a general rule," explained Christina Baker, who worked at the nonunion *Brooklyn Eagle*, "because they had not had the same chance to learn as the men."[25] Therefore, along with equal pay, they wanted equal training, admission into union apprenticeship programs, and the right to do equal work.

The female typesetters' demands for sexual equality distinguished their position from that of their erstwhile defenders among their employers, who insisted that the sexual division of labor benefited women. The newspaper owners, claiming that they had women's best interests at heart, encouraged them to enter the industry but wanted to see them remain in an inferior position within it. An editorial in the *New York Times* ridiculed the Working Women's Association's preoccupations with equality and "the fancied rights of women," against which it contrasted "real workers . . . and the plain unvarnished tales of real wrongs." The *Times* urged working women to recognize that their chief attraction was the cheapness of their labor, and that they were making a grievous error by demanding equal pay for equal work.[26]

The employers elaborated their case by arguing that women were incapable of doing equal work, even when they had the same opportunities as men. The *World* had justified its firing of the women typesetters on the grounds that their work had been inadequate, despite equal treatment with men.[27] The women

24. "Working Women's Association, #1" *Revolution*, October 1, 1868, p. 197.
25. "Working Women's Association," *New York World*, September 29, 1868, p. 7.
26. "The Lady Reformers at Fault," *New York Times*, January 10, 1869, p. 4; "The Chances for Women to Work," *New York Times*, February 18, 1868, p. 4.
27. Letter to the *New York World*, September 20, 1868, as quoted in Stevens, *New York Typographical Union No. 6*, pp. 431–432.

denied that they had been treated fairly, and defended their abilities against the *World*'s assertions. Peers denied that female typesetters were lazy and would not work complete shifts. "She did not shirk her work in the office;" she explained, "no matter what time of night it was that she would be required to stop, she did it cheerfully." Christina Baker quoted her earnings with considerable pride, despite the fact that she worked at a low rate and "does not come very early to the office." "She had been at the business six months," Baker insisted, "and would say that she was as good as any man who had worked the same length of time."[28]

Although the typesetters rejected the employers' claims to be their staunchest allies, their greatest hostility was reserved for the union. While the newspaper owners gave them training and jobs, albeit inferior ones, the union excluded them from membership and from the shops that it controlled. The experience of Agnes Peterson, a San Francisco typesetter, was typical. "I found the proprietors of all the offices quite willing to give me employment," she wrote to the *Revolution,* "but the Typographical Union refused to permit me to work, the members threatening to leave any office where a lady might be employed. . . . I did not wish to work for any less but asked for an exception to be made in my case or to admit me into the Union. My request was treated with contempt."[29] Hostility to the union was a major theme during the early months of the Working Women's Association. At the first meeting, Augusta Lewis complained of "the decided prejudice in the Union against women setting type among men."[30] Christina Baker reported that women who worked with her at the *Brooklyn Eagle* would not come to the association because they suspected that it was sponsored by the union, "were bitterly opposed to the Union," and feared that it

28. "Working Women's Association #1," *Revolution,* October 1, 1868, pp. 196–197; "Working Women's Association," *Revolution,* October 8, 1868, pp. 214–215.
29. "California Ahead Again," *Revolution,* September 10, 1868, p. 149.
30. "Working Women's Association, #1," *Revolution,* October 1, 1868, pp. 196–197.

was trying to take over their jobs.[31] When a representative of Local 6 suggested that the president of the National Typographical Union attend a meeting of the Working Women's Association, the women typesetters rejected his offer. "I think the women can organize without the help of the men," Peers said sharply.[32]

The typesetters' feminism and their collaboration with suffragists reflected their antagonistic experiences with the union and male workers. Female typesetters saw their interests as lying with other women and not with their male co-workers. From their perspective, the National Typographical Union was an organization for the protection of male workers against women, as much as against employers. Peers characterized the union as an association committed to "the exclusion of women from the hardly-earned avenues of labor she has entered."[33] Moreover, the history of the labor movement provided few models to suggest that it could be otherwise, that trade unions might protect workers, not just men. In the face of the printers' historic commitment to excluding women from their trade, the women typesetters saw their male co-workers as the enemy. They turned for help to the suffragists, who advanced the interests of women as a sex.

Once the Working Women's Association had been formed, its members focused their attention on specific proposals for elevating women and raising the value of their labor. Anthony reported that women printers in San Francisco had responded to the union's exclusionary policies by forming their own cooperative printing office. She proposed that the New York typesetters follow their example.[34] The prospect of a shop cooperatively operated by women attracted both suffragists and typesetters. It united the end of independence with the means of collective ac-

31. "Working Women's Association," *Revolution,* October 8, 1868, pp. 214–215.
32. "Working Women's Association, #1," *Revolution,* October 1, 1868, pp. 196–197.
33. *Ibid.*
34. "Working Women's Association," *New York World,* September 29, 1868, p. 7; "What the People Say to Us," *Revolution,* October 22, 1868, p. 244.

tion among women for their own elevation. The typesetters took up Anthony's proposal, formed themselves into a new organization called the Women's Typographical Union, and appointed a committee to begin to set up a women's print shop.[35] The Women's Typographical Union was organized for the particular purpose of establishing a producers' cooperative, and was not meant to replace the Working Women's Association, which was to remain open to all working women and receptive to other strategies for their elevation.

The women typesetters' success at self-organization drove the National Typographical Union to action. Signaling their intention to deal aggressively with the sexual discrimination they suffered, their move to organize independently threatened the printers' union and convinced it, as nothing else could, to include women.[36] Even by the second meeting of the Working Women's Association, representatives of Local 6 were present, anxious to defend themselves against charges of hostility to the women, to assure the typesetters of the union's interest in their welfare, and to challenge their decision to work with suffragists. Alexander Troup, secretary of Local 6, promised that "if the female compositors will work together with the members of the Union, they will get an equal remuneration for their labor." The women typesetters remained suspicious of such vague assurances of cooperation. "Will the Union allow ladies to join their ranks as members?" Peers challenged Troup, who had not come to offer the women membership. Although Troup equivocated, Peers continued to take the offensive, insisted that he propose her for membership, and gave him her dollar initiation fee.[37]

35. "Working Women's Association #1," *Revolution*, October 1, 1868, pp. 196–197; "Working Women's Association," *Revolution*, October 8, 1868, pp. 214–215.

36. Most of the histories of women in the printers' union credit Local 6 with initiating the unionization of women printers, and overlook the prior activity of the women themselves. See, for instance, Stevens, *New York Typographical Union No. 6*, p. 422, and Baker, *Technology and Women's Work*, p. 41.

37. "Working Women's Association," *Revolution*, October 8, 1868, pp. 213–214: "Working Women's Association #1," *Revolution*, October 1, 1868, pp. 196–197.

After the women formed the Women's Typographical Union, Local 6 representatives returned, with much more extensive offers of aid. "Knowing that your interests are identical with our own," they proposed to the women that the men's local "hire a hall for your meetings, furnish you with books, stationery, etc., and assume all other expenses which it may be necessary for you to incur in getting your Association into working order, and to continue to do so until your Union shall be in a condition to support itself." They described the procedure for the Women's Typographical Union to apply for a charter as a local of the National Typographical Union. Anthony saw Local 6's offer as a great victory in the battle for sexual equality. "You have established a union and for the first time in women's history in the United States you are placed, and by your own efforts, on a level with men, as far as possible, to obtain wages for your labor," she said to the women typesetters. "I need not say that you have taken a great, a momentous step forward in the path to success."[38]

Suffragists were optimistic that the apparent successes of the Working Women's Association, and especially the idea of producers' cooperatives, could be extended from typesetting to other sorts of work. "Out of the present Association will be formed cooperative unions in every branch of industry," Stanton proclaimed. "As the gods help those who help themselves, we urge on all workingwomen to rouse up from the lethargy of despair and make one combined, determined effort to secure for themselves an equal chance with men in the whole world of work."[39] Anthony organized a meeting at the Working Women's Home, a charity boarding house for working girls, to form a second division of the Working Women's Association. Over a hundred women attended, the majority of them sewing machine operators. They reported their wages, which averaged five to seven dollars a week, their eleven-hour days, and their deplorable working con-

38. "Women's Typographical Union," *Revolution,* October 15, 1868, p. 231.
39. Stanton, "Working Women's Association," *Revolution,* November 5, 1868, p. 280.

ditions. Anthony concluded the meeting by exhorting them to cultivate "a wholesome discontent," hold mass meetings, and "get the ballot." Then, "the men of the Trade Unions will sustain you with money and assistance," she assured them. At a small second meeting a week later, Anthony announced the formation of a "sewing machine operators union," that would establish a co-operative garment shop.[40]

The second Working Women's Association and the Sewing Machine Operators Union were both stillborn, however. Unlike the typesetters, the women at the Working Women's Home had not come to the suffragists on their own. They were simply an available audience and did not respond when Anthony brought them her formula for their advancement. Nor did the Working Women's Association generate any other cooperative shops. The typesetters' experience could not be generalized. Their position as skilled women in a male-dominated trade, which lay at the center of their impulse to organize, set them too far apart from the masses of working women. The Working Women's Association's goals of independence and equality had little meaning for women who had no male workers with whom to compete and all they could do to earn a subsistence wage. The needlewomen at the Working Women's Home wanted higher wages and, as they explained to Anthony, the assurance of steady work.[41] Nothing in their present situation made the control of all the profits of their own industry seem a reasonable goal, or attracted them to the suffragists' vision of opening up more trades and professions to women. Moreover, the union men of printers' Local 6 had been a critical factor in the female typesetters' self-organization, first by trying to exclude them from the industry and then by offering significant support to the organization the women formed to protect themselves. Trade union men had no immediate interest in aiding most working women, particularly those in the needle trades, and would not have any for another half-century.

40. "Working Women's Association #2," *Revolution,* October 1, 1868, pp. 197–198.
41. "Working Women," *New York World,* October 7, 1868, p. 7.

Unable to establish more self-help organizations, the Working Women's Association searched for other practical ways of elevating female workers. In particular it began to investigate and publicize the living and working conditions of women wage-earners. Eleanor Kirk, an aspiring journalist who became active in the association, wrote a series of articles called "Heart Aching Facts" for the *Revolution,* "to place these Facts before the public, in order that they may fully comprehend the dire necessities of New York's working women." In November, small committees were formed to gather information on women in different industries.[42]

The case of Hester Vaughn, a young English immigrant accused of infanticide, was the high point of the Working Women's Association's investigative efforts. Vaughn was a domestic servant who had been seduced by her employer, became pregnant, and was dismissed from her position. She gave birth unattended and was found three days later with her dead infant by her side. She was tried, found guilty of infanticide, and sentenced to death. When the presiding judge passed sentence, he said that the crime of infanticide had become so prevalent, that "some woman must be made an example of."[43]

The Working Women's Association mobilized to defend Vaughn. In speeches and articles, its members gained wide publicity for the case and their interpretation of it. Speaking on behalf of the association, Anna Dickinson, the most famous woman orator in the country, and herself a former wage-earner, described Hester Vaughn as an example of the horrors to which working women were subjected.[44] The association sent a delegation that included a feminist doctor to Moyamensing Prison outside Phila-

42. Eleanor Kirk, "Another Dose of Facts," *Revolution,* October 29, 1868, pp. 261–262, and "Heart Aching Facts," *Revolution,* November 12, 1868, p. 294. On the committees, see "Working Women's Association," *Revolution,* December 24, 1868, p. 395, and Sarah F. Norton, "Working Women's Association," *Revolution,* December 31, 1868, pp. 406–407.
43. "The Case of Hester Vaughn," *Revolution,* December 10, 1868, pp. 357–358.
44. "A Struggle for Life," *New York Times,* November 6, 1868, p. 5. See also Stanton, "Hester Vaughn," *Revolution,* November 19, 1868, p. 312.

delphia to meet Vaughn. Activities in Vaughn's behalf culminated at a mass meeting of working women in New York to
protest her sentence. The meeting passed a memorial to the
governor of Pennsylvania demanding her retrial or pardon, and
collected three hundred dollars for her use once she was re-
leased.[45] Following the meeting Stanton and her cousin, Elizabeth
Smith Miller, went to Pennsylvania, met with the governor, and
presented the petition.[46] When Vaughn was quietly pardoned
and deported to England six months later, no mention was made
of the Working Women's Association, but its efforts were no
doubt critical to her release.[47]

The Vaughn case permitted the association to raise a whole
series of issues about the oppression of working women. The economic limitations on them, specifically Vaughn's inability to find
any work other than domestic service, lay at the center of her
sexual vulnerability.[48] In addition, the association attacked the
sexual double standard that fixed all blame on Vaughn, first for
her pregnancy, and then for the death of her infant. It argued
that Vaughn was not a criminal, but the victim of a social system that forced women, especially poor women, to murder their
illegitimate children or face social ostracism. "What a holocaust
of women and children we offer annually to the barbarous customs of our present type of civilization, to the unjust laws that
make crimes for women that are not crimes for men!" Stanton
wrote.[49] Finally, the association claimed that the injustices suffered by Vaughn reflected women's political powerlessness. They
challenged the entire judicial proceeding which had found her

45. "The Case of Hester Vaughn," *Revolution*, December 10, 1868, pp.
357–358. See also "Hester Vaughn," *New York World*, December 1, 1868,
p. 1, and "Hester Vaughn," *New York World*, December 2, 1868, p. 1.

46. Stanton, "Editorial Correspondence," *Revolution*, December 10, 1868,
p. 360.

47. Pillsbury, "Hester Vaughn Once More," *Revolution*, August 19, 1869,
p. 105, and "Hester Vaughn," *New York World*, May 21, 1869, p. 4.

48. Pillsbury, "The Hester Vaughn Meeting at Cooper Institute," *Revolution*, December 10, 1868, p. 361.

49. Stanton, "Hester Vaughn," *Revolution*, November 19, 1868, p. 312.

guilty, because women had been excluded from it, and only men permitted to sit in judgment.[50]

Despite its strength and success, the Vaughn protest indicated the inability of the Working Women's Association to sustain a truly working woman's feminism. The association had initially raised the prospect of female workers as the agents of their own emancipation. The typesetters' path to the organization of the Women's Typographical Union embodied this approach, but the efforts to defend Hester Vaughn two months later did not. Originally Anthony had envisioned the association as an organization for women to help themselves, but at the protest meeting she characterized it as a way for women to replace men as the protectors of "the defenceless of their own sex."[51] The suffragists' middle-class perspective and distance from wage-earners contradicted their feminist faith in working women and eventually led them back to the benevolent model they had seemed to transcend. The wage-earning woman remained the object of the association's attentions, but the suffragists did not look to her as the active element in the organization. Instead they focused on prominent and philanthropic women, whose responsibility to their own sex they wanted to awaken. Although many working women attended the Vaughn meeting, voted to petition the governor of Pennsylvania, and contributed money on Vaughn's behalf, Stanton was most impressed with the "importance [of] women of wealth, education and leisure study[ing] the laws under which they live, that they may defend the unfortunate of their sex in our courts of justice."[52]

This change in emphasis reflected a shift in the active membership of the Working Women's Association. The typesetters who had begun the organization came from the tiny stratum of skilled workers who were the elite among wage-earning women. Instead of growing beyond the typesetters to include the unskilled

50. "Hester Vaughn," *New York World,* December 2, 1868, p. 1.
51. *Ibid.*
52. Stanton, "Hester Vaughn," *Revolution,* December 10, 1868, p. 360.

workers who dominated the female labor force, the association developed outside the working class, among a group that might be called middle-class working women. These were usually women in occupations that involved intellectual rather than manual labor and conditions that gave them considerable control over their work. Frequently, they were self-employed people or entrepreneurs. Free-lance authors, independent business women, and female professionals, they responded to the association's approach to women workers. Because the kind of work they did was socially respectable and relatively well paid, it provided them with a sense of autonomy and individual achievement and some degree of economic independence. They worked out of choice as much as out of necessity. They appreciated the Working Women's Association's identification of working women as a model for female emancipation. In a later era, similar people would be distinguished from the masses of women in the labor force by the label "career women," an acknowledgment not merely of their middle-class status, but also of the fact that they were middle-aged working women who had not retired to their homes because of marriage.

Celia Burleigh, who joined the association two months after its founding, was one such middle-class working woman. She had been a teacher in Syracuse, personal secretary to pioneer educator Emma Willard in Troy, and then one of the first women in the Universalist ministry. After she married abolitionist William Burleigh in 1865, she continued to pursue her ministerial career.[53] Another member of the association and a particularly interesting representative of this group was Dr. Clemence Lozier, an important figure in the history of women in medicine. Like Burleigh, Lozier had begun her working life as a teacher. She had suffered through a bad marriage until she heard a lecture by Elizabeth Cady Stanton on divorce and decided to get one.[54] At

53. I am indebted to Anne Firor Scott for the information on Burleigh's relationship to Emma Willard.
54. *In Memoriam: Clemence S. Lozier* (New York, 1889), pp. 37–38.

the age of thirty-seven, she began training for medicine, and by the 1860's had a flourishing obstetrical practice. She was a middle-aged woman with a vocation, and working was a way of life for her, not a premarital episode. Her income was very large—as high as $25,000 a year—and with it she established the New York Medical College and Hospital for Women in 1863, and also made substantial contributions to the *Revolution*. Through such activities, as well as the kind of medicine she practiced, she demonstrated her commitment to the elevation of her sex. However, she did not become a consistent and serious feminist activist until she joined the Working Women's Association in 1868. For the rest of her life she was dedicated to women's rights, and was the president of the New York City Woman Suffrage Association for fifteen years. The connection that the Working Women's Association made between women's economic lives and their political and social rights attracted women such as Lozier, much as the connection between abolitionism and women's rights had drawn an earlier generation of women.

Other middle-class women who joined the Working Women's Association were in the process of building similar careers or becoming professionals. Perhaps because of its connection with the newspaper industry, the association seems to have attracted an unusual number of writers and journalists. Eleanor Kirk, who became one of its most active members, was beginning to experience some success as a journalist at the time she joined. She had begun by writing for the *Revolution* and within a year was a regular contributor to *Packard's Monthly*. She specialized in descriptions of the economic pressures and moral temptations on New York City working women. As is the case even with women who achieved considerably greater prominence than Kirk did, it is difficult to retrieve the details of her personal life, but there is

---

For general information on Lozier, see Mary Ormsbee Whitton, *These Were the Women, U.S.A., 1776–1860* (New York, 1954) and Milton Cantor, "Clemence Lozier," *NAW*, II, 440–442.

some evidence that she, like Lozier, was divorced.[55] Sarah Norton
was also building a modest career as a journalist and lecturer
when she joined the Working Women's Association.[56] Another
member was Ellen Louise Demorest, a pioneering business
woman who was on her way to becoming the chief arbiter of
Parisian fashion for middle-class American women. She too was
involved in journalism and along with her husband published the
popular women's magazine, *Demorest's Monthly*.[57] Many of these
same women were simultaneously members of Sorosis, the New
York women's organization that is generally credited with initiating the women's club movement. Like the Working Women's
Association, Sorosis held up the working woman as a model for
female emancipation. Jennie June Croly, its founder and president, criticized those who saw women who worked only as objects of pity. "I think on the contrary," she asserted, "that the
working woman is to be congratulated; that it is the idle women
who are more truly objects of sympathy."[58]

Suffragists welcomed such middle-class women into the Working Women's Association. Their definition of a working woman
was someone who labored outside the home, had the capacity for
self-support, and was socially productive. Although most such
women were wage-earners, the suffragists did not distinguish
between those who sold their labor as a commodity and those
who did not. Thus, Anthony believed that she and the women

55. Kirk's articles began to appear in *Packard's Monthly* in September
1869. For the comment about her divorce, see Kirk, "To My Friends in
Rhode Island," *Revolution*, August 6, 1868, p. 77.
56. I have been unable to find any biographical information on Norton.
After writing in the *Revolution*, she was a contributor to *Woodhull and
Claflin's Weekly* in 1870 and 1871.
57. Ishbel Ross, "Ellen Louise Demorest," *NAW*, I, 459–460; Ross,
*Crusades and Crinolines: The Life and Times of Ellen Curtis Demorest and
William Jennings Demorest* (New York, 1963).
58. Croly, "Working Women and How to Help Them," *Demorest's
Monthly*, August, 1869, pp. 310–311. For more information on Sorosis, see
Marguerite Dawson Winant, *A Century of Sorosis, 1868–1968* (Uniondale,
New York, 1968), and Karen Blair, "The Clubwoman as Feminist: The
Woman's Culture Club Movement in the United States, 1868–1914" (doc-
toral diss., State University of New York at Buffalo, 1976).

typesetters shared the same status because she supported herself as a newspaper editor and free-lance lecturer. Suffragists were more comfortable with the middle-class working women than with wage-earners because the former moved in the same circles as they, shared values, tastes, and associates with them, and conferred a kind of social acceptability on their efforts. Moreover, suffragists inclined to believe that social changes, especially the kind of ideological changes they wanted to see in woman's sphere and woman's image, came from the top down in society, rather than from the bottom up.[59] Celia Burleigh offered the "observation . . . that when one class was raised, that class in turn raised the class below them."[60] Given this framework, suffragists considered middle-class working women strategically important as well as socially desirable, and a critical constituency to attract.

The influx of this group helped to drive working-class women out of the Working Women's Association. By late spring, 1869, the regular membership was entirely middle-class. When Kate Mullhaney visited the association to raise funds for her striking Troy Collar Laundry Union, she was amazed at what she found. She had understood, the *World* reported, "that they were an association of working women, and that was the reason she had come among them . . . , but as she looked around upon them, they were not the working women she had been accustomed to see. She had to work all day in the shop, and this she did not think, judging from their appearances, that they did."[61] In some cases working-class women were driven out of the association in an open and malicious manner. Elizabeth Brown, the *Revolution* clerk who had been the organization's first treasurer, was deliberately removed from office. More often, poor working women were pushed out in a less overt fashion.[62] The meetings

59. For instance, see Sarah Norton's comments in "Women's Rights," *New York World,* December 18, 1868, p. 7, and also Anna Dickinson's analysis in "Struggle for Life," *New York Times,* November 6, 1868, p. 55.
60. "The Woman's Bureau," *New York World,* May 21, 1869, p. 2.
61. "Working Women's Association," *New York World,* July 2, 1869, p. 5.
62. "Working Women's Association," *New York World,* May 6, 1869, p. 5.

were moved from Cooper Union, downtown, to the Women's Bureau, a recently opened uptown mansion. Dues were raised from ten cents to twenty-five cents a month, despite the protests of a few that most wage-earning women could not afford such rates.[63] Anthony, who was very much taken with the kind of middle-class women who were joining the association, supported both changes.[64] Augusta Lewis later described how the class character of the Working Women's Association changed. She claimed that the "society at one time comprised over one hundred working women, but as there was nothing practical done to ameliorate their condition, they gradually withdrew." She also cited "literary" and "suffrage" discussions, and middle-class monopoly of the association's offices as serious problems. "As a society," she concluded, "either the want of knowledge or the want of sense renders them, as a working-women's association, very inefficient."[65]

The association floundered under middle-class control. The only options opened to its middle-class members were either benevolent activities on behalf of their "downtrodden" sisters, or the kind of literary and intellectual self-improvement for which Sorosis and other women's clubs were being established. At one point the organization contemplated the establishment of a sort of glorified Working Women's Home, where poor working women could room and board at reasonable rates, but the project was never implemented.[66] Instead the members spent most of their time debating such questions as "who are the most systematic in business—men or women?" and "women's equal right with men to applaud."[67] The result was programmatic paralysis

63. "Women's Bureau," *New York World,* May 21, 1869, p. 2; "Working Women's Association," *New York World,* May 20, 1869, p. 5.

64. "Working Women's Association," *New York World,* April 8, 1869, p. 5.

65. "National Labor Congress," *Workingman's Advocate,* September 4, 1869, p. 1.

66. "Working Women's Association," *New York World,* February 11, 1869, p. 5.

67. "Working Women's Association," *New York World,* May 6, 1869, p. 5.

and membership demoralization. When the association met to prepare a report of its accomplishments for its first year, no one but Anthony had any idea of what to say. Eleanor Kirk spoke for them all: "I quite agree with the newspapers that we should begin to do something practical. . . . I'm so tired of being called impractical."[68]

The transformation of the Working Women's Association into a middle-class organization was greatly accelerated by the collapse of the suffragists' alliance with the women typesetters during the spring of 1869. The original impulse to the alliance had been the hostility between male unionists and women in the printing industry, but that hostility was beginning to disappear. Ever since the women had formed their own typographical union in October, 1868, their ties with Local 6 had been growing stronger and their connections with suffragists proportionately weaker; the women typesetters had begun to see their position more as trade unionists, committed to protecting their craft, and less as feminists, committed to eradicating sexual discrimination. Among the results of this altered perspective was their decision to cooperate with union printers in keeping other women out of the trade. The female typesetters' détente with the union also had an effect on the suffragists. Without the influence of politically conscious wage-earning women like the typesetters, suffragists were more reluctant than ever to acknowledge the class antagonisms that underlay all labor politics. The women typesetters came to side openly with organized labor while the suffragists, unwilling to admit that sides must be taken, found themselves the allies of employers.

The specific situation in which this change became obvious was a second printers' strike in the winter of 1869 during which suffragists and women typesetters took opposite sides. In January 1869, Local 6 declared a strike in the book and job printing sector of the industry, to raise wages there to union scale. In contrast to the *World* strike of the previous fall, woman compositors and male unionists cooperated on this occasion. The

68. *Ibid.*

Women's Typographical Union labored earnestly to prevent the
use of women as strikebreakers. Augusta Lewis took the leading
role in this effort.[69] She advertised for women to contact her
before taking jobs as typesetters in book and job printing firms.
The majority of the women who responded to her had been
hired and fired during the *World* strike, were loathe to repeat
the experience, and were willing to cooperate with the union.
With the Women's Typographical Union's aid, Local 6 conducted a fairly successful strike that was settled after eleven
weeks.[70]

In return for the women's help, the 1869 convention of the
National Typographical Union admitted the Women's Typographical Union as its first all-female local. In addition, the
national constitution was revised to permit the chartering of other
such locals, provided that the women did not work below union
rates and had the support of local union men. Augusta Lewis
thanked the delegates "for your just decision, in granting protection and a charter to us, not as women, but as workers, and
extending to us your aid and protection, not as men, but as an
organization seeking to elevate labor."[71] The National Typographical Union was the second national trade union to admit
women into membership, preceded only by the Cigarmakers
Union. This was, of course, an important victory for women in
the labor movement. The deciding factor in it had been the
efforts of woman printers themselves. Because of the organization
and activity of the Women's Typographical Union, the kind of
pro-woman position that the union had rejected at its 1867 na-

69. There is no further mention of Emily Peers after the Women's Typographical Union became involved with the National Typographical Union.
Lewis replaced her as the group's spokesperson. The reasons for Peers's
withdrawal are impossible to establish, but she had certainly been the most
articulate feminist among the typesetters.
70. Stevens, *New York Typographical Union No. 6*, p. 433.
71. *Report of the Proceedings of the Seventeenth Annual Session of the
National Typographical Union, Held in Albany, New York, June 7–11,
1869* (Cincinnati, 1869), p. 7; Stevens, *New York Typographical Union
No. 6*, pp. 435–436.

tional convention was acceptable to a majority of delegates two years later.

Anthony also saw opportunities for working women in the book and job printing strike, but from the opposite perspective. Her actions revealed her essential ignorance of trade union principles as well as the dangers inherent in her middle-class approach to working women's problems. Early in the strike, she petitioned the book and job printing employers' association to contribute money for the establishment of a training school to teach women to set type. She appealed on behalf of "women who are stitching with their needles at starving prices" and who had come to the Working Women's Association looking for more skilled and better paying jobs. The circumstances surrounding her appeal suggest that the employers' association may have manipulated her into making it. Her petition was written only the day before their first scheduled meeting to deal with the strike. She was also invited to make her proposal in person at the meeting.[72] Her presentation seems to have been weak and confused. "She said she hardly knew how she came there, but she had been informed that they were in consultation on the strike, and she thought it would be a good time for her to . . . advocate the cause of women," the *World* reported.[73]

Within a few days, the employers' association responded to Anthony's petition by announcing that it intended to train women to set type and place them in shops. In particular, the firm of Gray and Green announced the establishment of a six-week training program for female typesetters.[74] For all intents and purposes, this "training program" was another example of what employers had always done to defend themselves against the printers' union—hire women, train them on the job, and employ them for the length of a strike. Anthony's petition merely helped the employers once again to portray their strikebreaking

72. *Ibid.,* pp. 433–434.
73. "Labor Movements," *New York World,* January 30, 1869, p. 4.
74. "Our Working Classes," *New York Times,* March 17, 1869, p. 12.

efforts as philanthropic, rather than self-interested. The employers and their allies insisted on describing their use of women strikebreakers as the "training school" that Anthony had requested. The *Nation* congratulated Gray and Green and the "ladies of the *Revolution*" on their "training school." "In this practical side of the woman question, the public will always sympathize with employers however much craftsmen grumble."[75]

The labor movement criticized Anthony for siding with employers during the strike. Yet most of the criticism was surprisingly fraternal. The major exception, of course, was Local 6, which condemned her petition as "an infamous measure."[76] Other labor critics were somewhat less severe. The *Workingman's Advocate,* its editorial said, was "very much pained to see our good friend Miss Susan B. Anthony take the step which she did," and considered the petition "to say the least . . . ill-timed."[77] The corresponding secretary of the National Labor Union, John Vincent, published an open letter to Anthony. He granted that she may have been "actuated by the best wishes for her sex," but criticized her for violating the basic trade union principle of labor solidarity during a strike.[78] Although she apologized for her mistake, Anthony could not grasp the essence of Vincent's criticism. She responded that she continued to advise all women printers to join the National Typographical Union, that she supported the coalition between Local 6 and the female typesetters, that she did not think that women should work for less than men, and that she continued to believe that "in union alone there is strength."[79] She did not really understand that, by appealing to the employers during the strike, she had weakened the union's position.

The printers' strike and its repercussions not only clarified

75. "The Printers' Strike," *Nation,* February 11, 1869, pp. 108–109.

76. *Workingman's Advocate,* February 13, 1869, p. 3.

77. "Small Potatoes," *Workingman's Advocate,* February 13, 1869, p. 2.

78. "Miss Anthony and the Printers," *New York World,* February 1, 1869, p. 5.

79. Anthony to Vincent, February 3, 1869, quoted in Alice Henry, *The Trade Union Woman* (New York, 1915), p. 252.

suffragists' inability to operate within the context of working-class politics. It also highlighted the conflict between the suffragists' feminism and the sexist traditions that were deeply entrenched in nineteenth-century trade unionism. The year before, at the 1868 National Labor Congress, this conflict had taken the form of the delegates' reluctance to be associated with the demand for woman suffrage. At the 1869 congress, it was more open, and much more serious.

Local 6 brought its charges against Anthony to the 1869 National Labor Congress to resolve. It asserted that the Working Women's Association was not a "bona fide labor organization," and that Anthony had "striven to procure situations for girls from which men had been discharged." Local 6 substantiated its case with details of the book and job printing strike, and a letter from Augusta Lewis describing how inhospitable the Working Women's Association had become to wage-earning women. The printers demanded that Anthony's delegate credentials be revoked. The debate that ensued was long and so heated that the first sergeant at arms in the National Labor Union's history was appointed to keep order.[80]

Anthony responded at length to the charges against her. Her basic defense was that the Working Women's Association, although not a trade union, was nonetheless a labor organization whose specific commitment was to "equalizing the rights of laboring women with men." In defense of her decision to petition the printing employers' association for assistance, Anthony argued that the printers' union had been unwilling to join with the Working Women's Association to open up new occupations to women or increase the number of skilled women in the labor force. "I want to ask the Cooperative printers' union of New York how many girls they have taken to learn the type-setting business? How many women have you ordered each department

80. "National Labor Congress," *Workingman's Advocate,* September 4, 1869, p. 1. This is the only account of the congress, and all quotes are from it.

or establishment to take as apprentices and to train in the art of
typesetting?"

The spokesman for Local 6 could not understand Anthony's
point. Just as Anthony's class bias prevented her from understanding the class forces represented by a strike, his craft unionism left him incapable of understanding the feminist demand to
lower those barriers around his trade directed against women.
His answer revealed the central role trade unions played in
maintaining both the racial and the sexual divisions of the labor
force. "If a girl is a member of our union, we will give her
work . . . ," he explained, "but we do not go outside of our
organization. You might as well ask why we don't send for the
colored men or the chinese to learn the trade. There are too
many in it now." The efforts of craft unions to protect their
monopolies over the skilled trades had always been one of the
basic elements of the sexual division of labor and women's inferior place within it. The concessions that the women typesetters
had won from the National Typographical Union had not really
changed this situation. The union remained committed to pre-
venting the dissemination of printing skills and to keeping new
workers out of the trade. What it had been forced to do was to
extend its protection to women who were already working in the
industry. This was by no means the same as a commitment to
increase the number of women in the trade. The union was not
about to lower the barriers it had raised against women entering
the industry in the first place. Still the only ways they could
break into printing itself remained serving as strikebreakers or
working at below union wages in nonunion shops.

Most of the congress delegates did not like the prospect of
having to decide between the principles and power of trade
unionists, who were the National Labor Union's strength, and
the possibilities of a broad political alliance with feminists. Some
of Anthony's friends among the leaders of the National Labor
Union convinced her to withdraw voluntarily so that the congress
would not have to "disgrace itself" by revoking her credentials.

The printers, however, were committed to a confrontation and insisted on a vote. When the question was called, Anthony was seated by a narrow margin of fifty-five to fifty-two. The next day, Local 6 announced that it would withdraw from the congress if Anthony remained seated. The congress's leaders tried to engineer a temporary adjournment and a permanent compromise, but they failed, and Anthony's credentials were resubmitted to a vote. Faced with the threatened loss of an important group of unionists, many trade union delegates who had supported Anthony the first time switched their votes or abstained the second, and she was unseated by a vote of sixty-three to twenty-eight.[81]

The corollary of male unionists' refusal to bring any more women into their trades was their belief that women's natural place was not in the labor force, but in the home, doing unpaid work for their husbands and children. "The lady goes in for taking women away from the wash tub, and in the name of heaven who is going there if they don't?" the spokesman for Local 6 asked indignantly, early in the debate over Anthony's credentials. "I believe in woman doing her work and men marrying them, and supporting them." His was not an incidental prejudice, inadvertently revealed, but an important part of trade unionists' criticism of Anthony and the feminist politics she represented.[82] Somewhat reluctantly, Anthony acknowledged at the congress what the male unionists feared: her goal was to emancipate women from domestic isolation into the public world of citizenship and socialized labor, to release them from their dependence on and subservience to men. "All women are in the power of men," she said, near the end of the debate. "We ask for a change, and we demand a change." What she wanted for working women, for all women, was at once obvious in its justice, and

81. On the first vote, Anthony received twenty-eight of the sixty-six trade union votes; on the second, she received only eight. I am indebted to David Montgomery for these figures.

82. This is the position taken by Montgomery in *Beyond Equality*, p. 319, and Foner in *History of the Labor Movement*, I, 387.

revolutionary in its implications for the relations between men and women: "to give them a chance to earn an honest living . . . not merely a pittance, enough to keep body and soul together, but sufficient to enable them to invest in building societies, and have houses and homes of their own, and make them just as independent as anybody in the country."

Anthony's expulsion from the 1869 National Labor Congress confirmed the collapse of the Working Women's Association.[83] Although the suffragists continued to emphasize the emancipating possibilities of nondomestic labor for women, they made no more deliberate attempts to organize a constituency of working women. The end of their active interest in working-class women had an especially negative effect on the typesetters with whom it had begun. Without an organized and independent feminist movement behind them, women could not win any more victories in the National Typographical Union and soon lost what ground they had gained. The support they had received from male unionists had always been very tentative, and without outside pressure it disappeared. By 1871 Augusta Lewis, who had a deep personal loyalty to the union, saw little reason for other women to support it. "We refuse to take the men's situations when they are on strike, and when there is no strike if we ask for work in union offices we are told by union foremen 'that there are no conveniences for us,' " she explained at the 1871 printers' convention. "It is the general opinion of female compositors that they are more justly treated by what is termed 'rat' foremen, printers and employers than they are by union men." The provision in the National Typographical Union's constitution under which the Women's Typographical Union had been chartered

83. For a brief period after the National Labor Congress, Sarah Norton tried to revive the association, but had no more success with it than Anthony. The organization's last recorded act before its formal dissolution was the decision to drop the adjective "working" from its title ("Women's Mutual Aid Association," *New York World*, December 24, 1869, p. 3).

was revoked in 1878.[84] By the end of the century, the position of women compositors was essentially what it had been in 1867. They were isolated from male printers, in the unorganized sectors of the industry, underskilled, underpaid, and hostile to the union.[85] Women did not make significant gains in the trade union movement again until the early twentieth century, when middle-class feminists once more worked to build a women's movement to which they could belong.[86]

Ironically, the failure of the Working Women's Association alerted suffragists to an entirely different constituency, a middle-class one. They saw how strongly middle-class working women and other renegades from genteel ladydom were drawn to the ideology of female autonomy and equality that underlay both the Working Women's Association and the infant suffrage movement. Such women, organized on behalf of their own emancipation and not the uplift of their less fortunate sisters, were the people around whom an independent feminist movement would be built. Even before the 1869 labor congress voted to expel Anthony, she and Stanton had joined with several middle-class veterans of the Working Women's Association and other women like them to form the National Woman Suffrage Association. Unlike the Equal Rights Association and the Working Women's Association, it proved capable of sustaining a viable political movement.

84. Stevens, *New York Typographical Union No. 6,* pp. 437–439.
85. Andrews and Bliss, *History of Women in Trade Unions,* p. 189.
86. See: Alice Kessler-Harris, "Where Are the Organized Women Workers?"; Nancy Schrom Dye, "Feminism or Unionism? The New York Women's Trade Union League and the Labor Movement"; and Robin Miller Jacoby, "The Women's Trade Union League and American Feminism," all in *Feminist Studies,* 3 (1975), 92–110, 111–125, and 126–140.

Chapter Six

The Fifteenth Amendment
and the
Emergence of
Independent Suffragism

The revival of congressional debate on the suffrage provisions of the Constitution in the winter of 1869 coincided with the collapse of the Working Women's Association and reinforced the impact of that collapse on suffragists. It helped to draw their attention away from the kind of economic demands that were at the center of working women's concerns, and to give suffragists renewed confidence that political equality was the key to women's emancipation.[1] The focus of their attention was the Fifteenth Amendment, proposed by Radical Republicans to strengthen Constitutional protection for the freedmen's political rights. The Fifteenth Amendment was intended to do what the Fourteenth Amendment did not—explicitly prohibit disfranchisement on the grounds of race and commit the federal government to enforce that prohibition. Radicals introduced it once Grant had secured the presidency for the Republican party and the Fourteenth Amendment, after two years of struggle, was finally ratified.

1. After February 1869, the *Revolution* editors increasingly confronted and rejected the argument that economic rather than political demands were the key to women's emancipation. For instance: "Much is said, written and printed of women's work and wages and stupid men ask, why not dwell on this theme altogether, and mend the matter, instead of talking forever about Woman Suffrage. And no form of answer, argument or illustration can ding it into such skulls that the surest way to remedy the work and wages evil is to get hold of the ballot for women" (Parker Pillsbury, "Women's Working and Wages," *Revolution*, April 22, 1869, pp. 249–250). Often, such arguments were directed explicitly at working women. See, for instance, "Labor Reform," *Revolution*, November 4, 1869, p. 282.

While the Fifteenth Amendment debates stimulated woman suffrage from the outside, conflict among suffragists powered the movement from within. Differences that had appeared in the aftermath of the Equal Rights Association's defeat in Kansas continued to grow through 1868, even while Stanton and Anthony were busy within the Working Women's Association, until there were full-fledged factions among suffrage leaders. On one side were Stanton, Parker Pillsbury, Anthony, and a few others, who were determined to challenge Republican plans for Reconstruction because the party so obviously refused to support woman suffrage. On the other side were Lucy Stone, Henry Blackwell, Thomas Wentworth Higginson, and other equal rights leaders, who disagreed strongly with the *Revolution*'s anti-Republicanism, although they too were disappointed by Republicans' refusal to support the enfranchisement of women. They believed that the woman suffrage movement had no alternative but to continue to solicit the help of Republicans. They came to this conclusion because they considered the party the most powerful force in postwar politics, because they trusted in its commitment to egalitarian principles, and because they believed that most woman suffrage supporters were pro-Republican and would desert the movement if it repudiated Republicanism.[2]

This difference over the role of the Republican party became a difference over the Fifteenth Amendment, which represented the party's final program for Reconstruction. Stanton and Anthony denounced it for excluding women, while the pro-Republican suffragists accepted and supported it in exchange for the promise of future Republican support for votes for women. Both

2. Alice Stone Blackwell, *Lucy Stone,* p. 210. "Woman Suffrage Journals," *Woman's Advocate* (New York), February, 1870, pp. 3–4. "Suffrage Amendments," *Standard,* December 12, 1868, p. 2.

The *Woman's Advocate* (New York) was published monthly for a year from the New York offices of the *Standard.* In January 1870 it was replaced as the organ of pro-Republican suffragism by the *Woman's Journal,* published by Stone and Blackwell in Boston. Another journal with the same title was published in 1869 from Dayton, Ohio, and will be designated below as *Woman's Advocate* (Dayton).

factions tried to sustain their rival claims to leadership by drawing people who already supported woman suffrage to them and finding new women to join the movement. This competitive organizing process led to the formation of two national organizations, the National Woman Suffrage Association and the American Woman Suffrage Association. Although their founding institutionalized the split among suffragists, it also advanced the woman suffrage movement as a whole by providing it with a much firmer basis for sustained growth and with a sustained political program, which it had always lacked.

Throughout this process, the anti-Republican faction led by Stanton and Anthony took the lead. Their decision to break with abolitionists and the Republican party brought them to the recognition that only the activity of women would lead to their emancipation and enfranchisement. Therefore, they worked to shift feminist political demands from the edges of other reform movements to an organized body of women themselves. The creation of this independent women's movement was the greatest achievement of feminists in the postwar period, and its significance continued to be felt well after Reconstruction and the reform pretensions of the Republican party had passed into history.

In November 1868 a group of pro-Republican suffragists formed the New England Woman Suffrage Association. Their object was to counter political initiatives being made by Stanton and Anthony. "The strength of Mrs. Stanton and Miss Anthony's position is that they are acting zealously & constantly . . . ," one of the pro-Republican suffragists, Thomas Wentworth Higginson, wrote. "What we ought to do . . . is 'criticize by superior action.' "[3] The events leading up to the formation of the New England Woman Suffrage Association illustrate the degree to which it was a direct reaction to the *Revolution*'s suffrage

3. Higginson to William Lloyd Garrison, October 11, 1868, Boston Public Library.

politics. The idea for a regional suffrage society had originated several months before with Olympia Brown, a supporter of Stanton and Anthony. Brown had concluded from her experience in Kansas that the Equal Rights Association's strategy of linking woman suffrage and black suffrage would lead to "work for the Negro more than for the woman" until woman suffrage became a "clear-cut, separate and single question."[4] She proposed that a society be organized, dedicated to that single goal. By May 1868, however, Brown had lost control of the proposal to a group from the New England Anti-Slavery Society, including Abby Kelley Foster, Stephen Foster, and Higginson. They did not share her basic premise that the woman suffrage movement needed to pursue an aggressive, independent strategy.[5] The first decision of the new planning group was to postpone the founding convention until November 1868, to avoid interfering with the Republican presidential campaign.[6] They also made deliberate efforts to exclude their political rivals. When Stanton inadvertently received an invitation, Stephen Foster wrote to her to ask her not to attend.[7]

At the founding convention of the New England Woman Suffrage Association, Republican leaders were prominently involved. In particular, several members of the Bird Club, the small but powerful group of antislavery politicians who controlled the Massachusetts Republican party, attended. Henry Wilson, senator from Massachusetts, and Francis Bird, whom

4. Gwendolen B. Willis, ed., "Olympia Brown, An Autobiography," *Annual Journal of Universalist Historical Society*, 4 (1963), 38.
5. Abby Kelley Foster to Brown, May 20, 1868, Olympia Brown Willis Papers, SL, and Higginson to William Lloyd Garrison, October 11, 1868, Boston Public Library. Blackwell and Stone, who had not yet moved from New Jersey to Boston, were not deeply involved in the planning, although they did attend the organization's founding convention.
6. Abby Kelley Foster to Brown, May 20, 1868, Olympia Brown Willis Papers, SL; Brown, "Formation of the New England Woman Suffrage Association," unpublished manuscript, *ibid*.
7. Foster's request that Stanton not attend is mentioned in Stanton's letter to him, November 4, 1868, Boston Public Library.

the *Independent* described as the "leading Republican politician in Massachusetts," sat on the platform.[8] Republican leaders had good reason to support those who were willing to challenge Stanton and Anthony for leadership of the woman suffrage movement. The ideological underpinnings of the party's stature, basic to its political dominance in the Reconstruction period, were its claims to be the party of progress. The suffragists of the *Revolution* were the first major group of postwar reformers to defect publicly from the Republican camp and to challenge the party's reform pretensions. "The Republican party is a party and cares for nothing but party!" Olympia Brown insisted.[9] In light of the mass defection, four years later, of former abolitionists to the Liberal Republican insurgency, the nature of the threat posed in 1868 by the independent stance of Stanton and Anthony becomes clearer. It was an early indication of what the Republican party would eventually have to confront, the loss of control over the direction of American reform.

Inasmuch as the Republican party had clearly rejected the equal rights strategy of advancing the enfranchisement of blacks and women together, the New England suffragists' dependence on the party forced them to grant black suffrage strategic priority over woman suffrage, even on their own platform. The abolitionists who participated in the New England Suffrage Association, such as Frederick Douglass and the Fosters, embraced this constraint enthusiastically. In fact their involvement in the New England Woman Suffrage Association can best be understood as part of their efforts on behalf of black suffrage, an attempt to keep women's rights from interfering with it. They contended that the freedmen were in a much more precarious position than women and thus demanded reformers' undivided attention. "If the elective franchise is not extended to the negro, he dies," Douglass argued at the founding convention. "Woman has a

8. "The Next Great Question," *Independent,* November 12, 1868, p. 4. Also see "The Disfranchised Class," *New York World,* November 11, 1868, p. 1.
9. *HWS,* II, 311.

thousand ways by which she can attach herself to the ruling power of the land that we have not."[10] Others, most notably Lucy Stone, used the New England association's platform to argue with great sincerity, passion and militance, for women's right to political power. Stone objected strenuously to Douglass's claim that "the cause of the negro was more pressing than that of woman's."[11] Yet her protest was deprived of any real force because she remained politically dependent on Republicans and abolitionists, who refused to give women's enfranchisement their concrete support. Senator Henry Wilson, who sat on the platform with her, was helping at about that time to shape the Fifteenth Amendment, and made no attempt to include woman suffrage in it.[12] Stone urged women to press their claims vigorously, but she had no way to induce Republicans to accept them. In effect, her position was the same as Douglass's: she could do no more than offer woman suffrage to the Republican party as a trust, to be redeemed after the work of Reconstruction had been completed.

New England suffragists' desire to attract and hold Republican support led to a dominant role for men at the founding convention. The organizing committee made special efforts to locate "prominent and able men," particularly ministers, to sign the call to the meeting.[13] Higginson occupied the chair most of the time, men were the majority of the speakers, and fourteen of the convention's twenty honorary vice-presidents were men.[14] But while men took a very active part, many women were present as well. Abolitionists such as Abby Kelley Foster and Paulina Wright Davis, who had integrated women's rights agitation into their antislavery work for years, attended. There were also some

10. "Woman Suffrage," *New York World*, November 19, 1868, p. 5.
11. "The Disfranchised Class," *New York World*, November 11, 1868, p. 1.
12. DuBois, *Black Reconstruction*, p. 378.
13. Brown, "Formation of the New England Woman Suffrage Association," Olympia Brown Willis Papers, SL.
14. "The Disfranchised Class," *New York World*, November 11, 1868, p. 1.

new faces, women not previously connected with women's rights. Several of these were relatives of prominent reformers and intellectuals, for instance Lydia Emerson and Isabella Beecher Hooker, who were seated on the platform. Harriet Hanson Robinson, a former Lowell textile operative and wife of the influential antislavery journalist and Bird Club member, William Robinson, came with her husband. It was her first women's rights convention, and although initially apprehensive, she soon became enthusiastic. "Good meetings and good speeches, I thought. I felt good about it," she wrote in her diary. "The audience was remarkable . . . thoughtful, sincere, and earnest-looking (as if they meant something)."[15] There were several prominent literary women, notably Louisa May Alcott, who had just published the first installment of *Little Women*. The most celebrated of the new faces at the convention was Julia Ward Howe, wife of another Bird Club member, Samuel Gridley Howe. Mrs. Howe was a successful author and the very personification of New England ladydom. Like many other literary women, she had not identified herself with the women's rights movement before the war. Higginson persuaded her to attend the New England Woman Suffrage Convention, where she confessed that the women's rights movement had become so prominent that she could no longer look on it with disdain.[16]

The major order of business was the formation of the New England Woman Suffrage Association. Julia Ward Howe was selected to be its president, and Lucy Stone was a member of its executive committee.[17] The New England Woman Suffrage Association was the first major political society that proclaimed votes for women as its goal, anticipating by six months the National Woman Suffrage Association, organized by Stanton and Anthony. There was considerable irony in its position as ground-

15. Diary entry, November 11, 1868, Harriet Hanson Robinson Papers, SL.
16. Julia Ward Howe, *Reminiscences, 1819–1899* (Boston, 1900), p. 372.
17. "Boston Women's Rights Convention," *Woman's Advocate* (New York), January, 1869, pp. 54–59.

breaker; indeed, speaker after speaker at the convention insisted on the necessity of delaying efforts for women's enfranchisement until black suffrage was firmly secured. Francis Bird declared, "Negro suffrage, being a paramount question, would have to be settled before woman suffrage could receive the attention it deserved," and Frederick Douglass and Henry Wilson said much the same thing.[18] Julia Ward Howe announced that she was unwilling to demand the vote for herself until it was secured to blacks.[19]

Once formed, the association inclined to tactics that did not place woman suffrage in conflict with black suffrage. Because congressional debates on the extension of the national franchise focused on the freedmen, the organization directed most of its efforts to state legislatures. The most substantial campaign it conducted was in Massachusetts, where its support among Republicans was the strongest. More than 7,500 petitions were collected and sent to the state legislature, which appointed a special committee on woman suffrage to consider them.[20] Lucy Stone was very optimistic. "You will be glad to know that we stand a fair chance in Massachusetts of getting the word 'male' (what shall I say?) squelched," she wrote to a friend. "The legislature is largely Republican and temperance, and from such material much is to be hoped."[21] The Massachusetts legislators voted twenty-two to nine against woman suffrage, however. Susan B. Anthony was quick to comment that this proved that New England suffragists had struck a bad bargain in cooperating with Republicans.[22]

18. "Women's Rights Convention, *New York Times,* November 20, 1868, p. 1; "Women's Rights—Boston Convention," *New York Times,* November 19, 1868, p. 1; "The Boston Women's Convention," *Independent,* November 26, 1868, p. 4.
19. "Woman Suffrage," *New York World,* November 21, 1868, p. 5.
20. *New York Times,* March 31, 1869, p. 10, and April 17, 1869, p. 1.
21. Stone to Samuel J. May, April 9, 1869, Blackwell Family Collection, LC.
22. Anthony, "Who Killed Cock Robin," *Revolution,* June 10, 1869, p. 353.

The political differences between the New England Woman Suffrage Association and the *Revolution* suffragists were most obvious when it came to the Fifteenth Amendment. Because the New England group accepted the necessity of a constitutional amendment that focused exclusively on black enfranchisement, they did not work to have woman suffrage included in the debates. Instead, they developed an alternate proposal for congressional action and pressed for legislation that would enfranchise women in the District of Columbia and the territories, to be followed by a constitutional amendment at some unspecified time in the future.[23] This strategy was clearly patterned after the history of congressional action on black suffrage, which had proceeded from legislation directed at the District and territories, to a constitutional amendment that affected all American citizens. However, the timing of the New England association's proposal for legislation enfranchising women in the District suggests that it was also motivated by a desire to divert woman suffrage efforts away from the Fifteenth Amendment debates. In January 1869 Henry Wilson introduced a District woman suffrage bill into the Senate, and Blackwell and Stone came to Washington to lobby for it, just as congressional debates on the Fifteenth Amendment were at their height.[24] Once the Fifteenth Amendment was passed in late February, agitation for a District woman suffrage bill seems to have ceased.

Stanton and Anthony disagreed with the New England association's approach. "To leave [woman suffrage] to the States and the partial acts of Congress, is to defer indefinitely its settlement," Stanton argued.[25] While the New England group carefully avoided any interference with the drive for black suffrage, Stanton and Anthony courted conflict with abolitionists and Radicals by insisting that woman suffrage be included with black suffrage in the process of constitutional amendment. At first, they

23. Aaron Powell, "Woman as Voter," *Woman's Advocate* (New York), January, 1869, pp. 36–39.
24. "Notes," *Woman's Advocate* (New York), February, 1869, p. 110.
25. *HWS*, II, 350.

tried to influence the wording of the Fifteenth Amendment so that it would enfranchise women as well as the freedmen. Immediately after the presidential elections, the *Revolution* announced a petition drive, and Stanton went to Washington to lobby for an amendment that included woman suffrage.[26] Probably as a result of her efforts, Samuel Pomeroy of Kansas submitted a proposal to the Senate for an amendment that defined suffrage as a right of citizenship and enfranchised women as well as black men. "Now let the work of petitioning and agitating . . . be prosecuted with a vigor unknown before," the *Revolution* urged. "And let Senator Pomeroy be honored with receiving and presenting to the Senate such a deluge of names as shall . . . convince Congress and the whole government that we can be trifled with no longer."[27]

The *Revolution*'s demand that the amendment include woman suffrage rested on a political analysis quite different from that of the New England Woman Suffrage Association. New England suffragists believed that Reconstruction issues—the political status of the freedmen and the conditions for readmission of the southern states—must be resolved before Republicans would move to support votes for women.[28] Stanton and Anthony believed that woman suffrage could only be achieved while congressional Reconstruction was still under way. The Republican party had inaugurated the process of constitutional revision in order to protect its military and political victory over the southern ruling class, and they contended that woman suffrage must be won before that process was completed. Once Reconstruction issues, particularly black suffrage, were settled, the tense partisanship and political polarization they had generated would disappear, and with them any strategic possibilities for the enactment of

26. "Appeal for Equal Suffrage," *Revolution*, November 19, 1868, p. 305. "Washington—Proceedings of Congress," *New York World,* December 10, 1868, p. 5.
27. "Now Is the Hour," *Revolution,* December 10, 1868, p. 360.
28. See comments of Giles Stebbins, "Woman Suffrage Convention," *New York Times,* January 21, 1869, p. 5.

woman suffrage. "The few who had the prescience to see the long years of apathy that always follow a great conflict, strained every nerve to settle the broad question of suffrage on its true basis while the people were still awake to its importance," Stanton wrote in retrospect.[29] Years later, a Wisconsin suffragist and doctor, Laura Ross Wolcott, remembered that Stanton and Anthony had "warned . . . that the debate once closed on negro suffrage, and the amendments passed, the question would not be opened again for another generation." History, Dr. Wolcott pointed out, had vindicated Stanton and Anthony; "the fair promises of Republicans and Abolitionists that, the negro question settled, they would devote themselves to woman's enfranchisement" were never redeemed.[30] From an even longer perspective, it is clear that, after Reconstruction, suffragists did not have another substantial chance to secure the franchise for women in the Constitution until the decade following 1910. Like the 1860's, this was a period characterized by considerable constitutional revision and the struggle of a major party to retain the political allegiance of reformers who were threatening to bolt it.

In February 1869 Congress finally passed a version of the Fifteenth Amendment that enfranchised black men but ignored the demand for woman suffrage. The passage of the amendment intensified the differences within the woman suffrage movement. The New England Woman Suffrage Association supported the amendment and urged its ratification.[31] The *Revolution* suffragists did not. Still committed to getting woman suffrage into the Constitution, they refused to support the Fifteenth Amendment unless it was "redeemed" by a sixteenth amendment that would enfranchise women and be submitted simultaneously for ratification. Congressman George W. Julian of Indiana introduced a bill for a sixteenth amendment and the *Revolution* pressed for

29. *HWS,* II, 367–368.
30. *HWS,* III, 641.
31. Henry B. Blackwell, "The Era of Reconstruction," *Woman's Advocate* (New York), January, 1869, pp. 7–12.

its passage.[32] Of greater concern to New England suffragists even than the *Revolution*'s refusal to join the chorus of support for the Fifteenth Amendment was the paper's open criticism of it for its betrayal of women. Stanton argued:

So long as there is a disfranchised class in this country, and that class its women, a man's government is worse than a white man's government with suffrage limited by property and educational qualifications, because in proportion as you multiply the rulers, the condition of the politically estranged is more hopeless and degraded. . . . It is an open, deliberate insult to American womanhood to be cast down under the iron-heeled peasantry of the Old World and the slaves of the New, as we shall be in the practical working of the Fifteenth Amendment, and the only atonement the Republican party can make is now to complete its work by enfranchising the women of the nation.[33]

The refusal of the *Revolution* suffragists to support the Fifteenth Amendment inflamed already severe conflicts among reformers. More than a century has passed, and still historians become partisans in the hostilities that their opposition created.[34] Supporters of black suffrage were infuriated by the *Revolution*'s criticisms of the amendment, and especially by its callous disregard for the perilous position of the freedmen. Many woman suffragists would not join in the *Revolution*'s opposition. "Could I with breath defeat the Fifteenth Amendment I would not do

32. Stanton, "The Sixteenth Amendment," *Revolution,* April 29, 1869, p. 266.

33. *HWS,* II, 348–355. The quote is from Stanton's speech at a suffrage convention which she and others organized in Washington, D.C., in late January 1869. As early as December, the *Revolution* declared that it would oppose any amendment that excluded women from its provisions. See "Manhood Suffrage," December 24, 1868, p. 392. Also see "Paulina Wright Davis on the Fifteenth Amendment," *Revolution,* June 7, 1869, reprinted in *HWS,* II, 336–337.

34. The most recent example of this is Philip S. Foner, ed., *Frederick Douglass on Women's Rights* (Westport, Conn., 1976), which very much takes the anti-*Revolution* position on the conflict over the Fifteenth Amendment.

it," Frances Dana Gage wrote. "Keeping [the colored men] out, suffering as now, would not let me in all the sooner, then in God's name why stand in the way?"[35] On the other hand, there were those who were thrilled by Stanton's and Anthony's insistence that a revolution that omitted women was no revolution at all, and were inspired by them to new levels of womanly self-respect. Long-time abolitionist-feminist Paulina Wright Davis agreed with the *Revolution*'s criticisms of the Fifteenth Amendment, even though she wanted to see the black man have all the freedoms that the white man had. "But I should like to see the black woman remembered. . . . When will women realize that they are slaves, and with one mind and one heart, strike the blow which will set them free?"[36]

The position Stanton and Anthony took against the Fifteenth Amendment reveals much about their political development after the Civil War and especially after their 1867 break with abolitionists. Their objections to the amendment were simultaneously feminist and racist. On the one hand, their commitment to an independent women's movement was intensifying the feminism that underlay their demand for woman suffrage. Although they acknowledged the similarities between the inferior position women held with respect to men and the status of other oppressed groups, they believed that women's grievances were part of a distinct system of sexual inequality, which had its own roots and required its own solutions. This led them to repudiate the Fifteenth Amendment, not only because women were omitted from its provisions, but because they believed that its ratification would intensify sexual inequality. They argued that the doctrine of universal manhood suffrage it embodied gave constitutional authority to men's claims that they were women's social and political superiors. On the other hand, this feminism was increasingly racist and elitist. The women among whom it was growing

35. *Woman's Advocate* (New York), August, 1869, as cited in Foner, ed., *Frederick Douglass*, p. 36.
36. Davis, "The New England Anti-Slavery Convention," *Revolution*, July 1, 1869, pp. 417–418.

were white and middle-class and believed themselves the social and cultural superiors of the freedmen. The anti-Republican suffragists chose to encourage these women to feel that the Fifteenth Amendment meant a loss of status for them, and to try to transform their outraged elitism into an increased demand for their enfranchisement. New England suffragists also had racist arguments for woman suffrage in their rhetorical arsenal, but the political decision to maintain abolitionist allies and to court Republican support kept them from using these weapons.[37] By contrast, the *Revolution*'s militant anti-Republicanism permitted and even encouraged Stanton and Anthony to approach woman suffrage by way of attacks on the freedmen.

The anti-Republican suffragists' basic objection to the Fifteenth Amendment was that it would leave sex the only legitimate qualification on the federal suffrage.[38] The amendment's supporters proudly proclaimed that it would make universal manhood suffrage the law of the land and bring the country that much closer to a true democracy. From a feminist perspective, however, this exclusively masculine definition of democracy was a step backward for freedom. In response to the democratic claims that its sponsors made, Stanton argued that the ratification of the Fifteenth Amendment would establish an "aristocracy of sex," because all men would be enfranchised, while all women remained without political privileges.[39] "If the Fifteenth article of Constitutional amendment ever gets ratified and becomes the rule of suffrage, it will have one good effect," she wrote in the *Revolution*. "Woman will then know with what power she has to contend. It will be male versus female, the land over. All manhood will vote not because of intelligence, patriotism, property or white skin, but because it is male, not female."[40] Phoebe Couzins, a St. Louis law student who was an associate of Stanton and

37. See Chap. 3 above, note 67 for an early example of Blackwell's racism.
38. Stanton, "Women and Black Men," *Revolution*, February 11, 1869, p. 88. Stanton, "A Pronunciamento," *Revolution*, July 15, 1869, p. 24.
39. "Manhood Suffrage," *Revolution*, December 24, 1868, p. 392.
40. Stanton, "Drawing the Lines," *Revolution*, March 11, 1869, p. 153.

Anthony, agreed. "I repudiate the Fifteenth Amendment, because it asks me to acquiesce in an assertion to which I utterly refuse to assent, i.e. the inferiority of women."[41]

New England suffragists, on the other hand, argued that the establishment of universal manhood suffrage was a step on the road to the enfranchisement of women. Henry Blackwell wrote that the Fifteenth Amendment would introduce the principle that the suffrage was "a personal right inherent in the human nature of the citizen" into the Constitution, and this would make it easier to secure woman suffrage.[42] Unlike the *Revolution,* which saw woman suffrage in terms of its effect on the sexual distribution of power and privilege, Blackwell approached women's right to vote as one case of the general principle that *all* human beings had an inherent right to self-determination and individual liberty. This theory of the universality of democratic rights was women's rights' ideological inheritance from prewar abolitionism and had powered the movement through its first decade. By the 1860's, however, it was beginning to harden into a dogma, a set of ideological abstractions that resisted any connection with political and social reality. New England suffragists habitually criticized Stanton and Anthony for being "low" and "political," meaning in part that they were willing to cooperate with racists and Copperheads, but also that they were attempting to link woman suffrage and the sexual and economic dimensions of women's oppression. By contrast, New England suffragism prided itself on the moral purity of its convictions and considered it a virtue that its commitment to absolute justice superseded the vagaries of history and the details of women's condition. A partisan of the New England association praised its approach to suffragism because "it leaves the consequences to God, and says this is wrong and this is right; I must refrain from the one and do the other regardless of effect." To this he opposed the approach of

41. "Speech of Phoebe Couzins," *Revolution,* July 9, 1869, pp. 12–13.
42. Blackwell, "The Era of Reconstruction," *Woman's Advocate* (New York), January, 1869, pp. 7–12.

the *Revolution* which was "uneasy and anxious as to results. . . . It wants facts and will be content with nothing less."[43] Compared to the politics of the *Revolution*, New England suffragism was deeply principled, but it was also abstract and did not strive to connect women's political status with other aspects of their oppression. In contrast to the *Revolution*'s multifaceted feminism, it encouraged the advance of woman suffrage as an isolated demand, rather than as one element in a program for the emancipation of women.

New England suffragists' charge that the *Revolution*'s opposition to the Fifteenth Amendment was racist, however, is an accusation that warrants serious consideration. There are at least two elements to this charge, which must be examined separately. To many supporters of black suffrage, feminists' decision to agitate for the constitutional enfranchisement of women while the freedmen were still fighting for their political rights demonstrated a disregard for the suffering of black people which was itself racist. They argued that the freedmen had an overwhelming claim on reformers' energies because they needed the suffrage to protect their lives and liberty from former slave-owners.[44] This was an unacceptable strategic standard for feminists to apply to themselves because it essentially precluded any serious political activity on their part. Those who considered woman suffrage agitation itself a betrayal of the ex-slave, for instance Phillips and Douglass, sometimes ignored or minimized women's grievances to make their position. Stone, Stanton, and others recognized and criticized this antifeminist tendency.[45]

What was true, however, was that the tactics the *Revolution*

43. F. A. Hinckley, "Justice Vs. Expediency," *Woman's Advocate* (New York), March, 1870, pp. 107–108. See also "Salutory," *Woman's Advocate* (New York), January, 1869, p. 49.

44. See comments of Catherine Stebbins, *Woman's Advocate* (New York), March, 1869, pp. 172–173. See also Frederick Douglass to Josephine S. Griffing, September 27, 1868, published in "Two Letters," ed. Joseph Borome, *Journal of Negro History*, 33 (1948), 469–471.

45. See exchange between Wendell Phillips (*Standard*, July 3, 1869, p. 1) and Stanton ("A Pronunciamento," *Revolution*, July 15, 1869, p. 24).

suffragists developed for advancing the feminist movement in this period were often racist. In particular, they began to use arguments that exploited white women's fear and hatred of black people. To challenge the Fifteenth Amendment, Stanton argued the position that it was wrong to elevate an ignorant and politically irresponsible class of men over the heads of women of wealth and culture, whose fitness for citizenship was obvious. "American women of wealth, education, virtue and refinement," she wrote in behalf of a sixteenth amendment, "if you do not wish the lower orders of Chinese, Africans, Germans and Irish, with their low ideas of womanhood to make laws for you and your daughters, . . . to dictate not only the civil, but moral codes by which you shall be governed, awake to the danger of your present position and demand that woman, too, shall be represented in the government!"[46] Such arguments slandered the freedmen by implying that poor black men were more responsible for women's disfranchisement than rich white ones. They also narrowed the focus and appeal of the suffrage movement. While ostensibly defending the rights of all women, Stanton spoke only on behalf of those of the white middle and upper classes. This elitist approach was suffragists' response to the fact that the women who were drawn to woman suffrage were likely to be white, Anglo-Saxon, and from propertied families. The political direction that the *Revolution* gave them, the way it tried to develop their suffragism, was to encourage them to feel that their social and economic status entitled them to political power, even if their sex did not.

In no one was the relationship between feminism and an elite class position clearer than in Elizabeth Cady Stanton, who formulated some of the most antidemocratic arguments for woman suffrage during this period. Stanton was from an exceptionally privileged background, more so than any other first-generation suffragist. Her family was among the wealthiest in

46. Stanton, "The Sixteenth Amendment," *Revolution*, April 29, 1869, pp. 264–265. See also: Stanton, "A Constitutional Patchwork," *Revolution*, February 18, 1869, pp. 104–105, and Paulina Wright Davis' and Stanton's comments to the 1869 Equal Rights Association convention, *HWS*, II, 391 and 359.

upstate New York, and its political and economic power reached back into pre-Revolutionary days. She moved comfortably in the world of the powerful and had a tendency to use her personal connections with highly placed men to advance woman suffrage.[47] Usually her elitism was overshadowed by her awareness of the common sexual oppression that linked her situation with that of less privileged women, but there were times when she could not control her rage at being denied privileges that by class position should have been hers. "In the Old World . . . , women of rank have certain hereditary rights which raise them above a majority of men, certain honors and privileges not granted to serfs and peasants . . . ," she said in response to the Fifteenth Amendment. "But here, in this boasted Northern civilization, women of wealth and education, who pay taxes and obey the laws, who in morals and intellect are the peers of their proudest rulers, are thrust outside the pale of political consideration."[48]

On the basis of their different approaches to woman suffrage and to the political situation the Fifteenth Amendment had produced, Stanton and Anthony and the New England suffragists organized support for their respective positions. Although competing with each other for adherents, they began to consolidate suffrage sentiment into a stronger, more coherent political force. Both factions tried to get veteran women reformers as well as women new to political activity to group behind them. Because New England suffragists accepted the power of the Republican party and the primacy of black suffrage as their own strategic framework, they were able to rely heavily on former abolitionists for support. Conversely, Stanton and Anthony concentrated on women relatively new to political agitation and less troubled by divided reform loyalties.

47. The major biography of Stanton is Lutz, *Created Equal.* Examples of Stanton's habit of appealing personally to highly placed men were her audience with Governor John W. Geary of Pennsylvania in November 1868 on behalf of Hester Vaughn, and her successful efforts to get former governor Horatio Seymour of New York, a personal friend, to present the suffragists' memorial to the 1868 Democratic National Convention.

48. *HWS,* II, 355.

New England suffragists began to augment their forces immediately after the founding convention of the New England Woman Suffrage Association. The organization of state affiliates was specifically mandated by the convention and was crucial to the success of the New England association's bid for leadership of woman suffrage forces.[49] Affiliated state societies gave weight to its claim that its politics were more representative of general suffrage sentiment than those of Stanton and Anthony. Over the winter of 1868–1869, Stone, Blackwell, Higginson, and other New England leaders traveled all over New England to address woman suffrage conventions and state legislatures. "I am much gratified in the promptness you have shown in this matter of State Associations," Stephen Foster wrote to Elizabeth Buffum Chace, who was planning a woman suffrage convention for Rhode Island, "and sincerely hope that other New England states will imitate your noble example."[50] Within a month of the New England woman suffrage convention, state suffrage societies had been formed in Rhode Island and New Hampshire. Veteran abolitionists were the leaders in both. No state society was organized in Massachusetts because the New England association itself filled that function, but woman suffrage conventions and societies were organized in several Massachusetts counties. There were also suffrage activities in Maine and Vermont.[51] A historian of the New England Woman Suffrage Association notes that between 1868 and 1873 societies were formed in all the New England states and, with the exception of the Connecticut society, were organized by the New England association.[52]

Stanton and Anthony began their organizing efforts as soon as Congress had passed a Fifteenth Amendment that did not include women. In mid-February they went to Chicago and during

49. "Women's Rights Convention," *New York Times,* November 20, 1868, p. 1.
50. Foster to Chace, as quoted in Lillie B. C. Wyman and Arthur C. Wyman, *Elizabeth Buffum Chace,* I (Boston, 1914), p. 310.
51. *HWS,* III, 368, 340, 270, 382, and 352.
52. Lois B. Merk, "Massachusetts and the Woman-Suffrage Movement" (doctoral diss., Radcliffe College, 1958), p. 200.

the next six weeks met with local suffragists in Missouri, Wisconsin, and Ohio. Many of the women whom they contacted, particularly in the larger cities, were like the middle-class women they had come to know in the Working Women's Association. In Chicago they met Myra Bradwell, a trained lawyer and legal journalist fighting for admission to the Illinois Bar, and Mrs. J. F. Willing, author, later to become professor of English at Illinois Wesleyan University. In Wisconsin Stanton and Anthony made contact with Lillie Peckham, a promising young law student, Dr. Laura Wolcott, and Augusta Chapin, a Universalist minister. In St. Louis they worked with Adaline Couzins, a Civil War nurse whose daughter, Phoebe, had just become the first woman admitted to Washington University Law School. In Bloomington Stanton met three women who were successfully managing their own businesses, and she was very impressed by them.[53]

Of the approximately two dozen women who arranged meetings for Stanton and Anthony during their midwestern tour, only two seem to have been involved in prewar reform and they were only marginally active: Ellen Fray of Toledo had attended the 1848 women's rights convention in Rochester and Mary Livermore had done some antislavery work in Chicago.[54] Instead, many of those women had been active in the Sanitary Commission and other home-front support efforts during the war. Livermore was the most prominent and had gained national recognition as a leader of the Sanitary Commission, but Couzins, Bradwell, and others had been active on the local level.[55] They exemplified the large numbers of women who first recognized themselves as public people and citizens when they mobilized for war and represented a promising field for the expansion of the woman suffrage movement.

53. Stanton's weekly letters to the *Revolution* about her midwestern trip are reprinted in *HWS*, II, 368–378.

54. Robert E. Riegel, "Mary Livermore," *NAW*, II, 410–413. On Fray, see *HWS*, I, 809.

55. Frances Willard and Mary Livermore, eds., *The American Woman: Fifteen Hundred Biographies* (New York, 1897), pp. 115, 211, and 367–368; Riegel, "Mary Livermore," *NAW*, II, 410–413; *HWS*, III, 596–598.

These midwestern women were ready to be organized into the movement and for political activity, and they responded immediately to Stanton and Anthony. Sarah Williams explained how the women of Toledo reacted: "A large circle of intelligent and earnest women were longing and waiting to do something to speed the movement for woman suffrage, when the coming of these pioneers of reform roused them to action. It was like the match to the fire all ready for kindling, and an organization was speedily effected."[56] Four months later, Williams and other Toledo suffragists embarked on their first political activity, forcing the local library association to permit women to vote and hold office along with the male members.[57] Their choice of target reveals simultaneously how tentatively these new converts moved into the public arena and how important the *Revolution*'s message of political equality for women was for them. In Galena Stanton and Anthony met another group of women who had traveled from Iowa to hear them speak. These women, on their return home, formed the Northern Iowa Woman Suffrage Association. Their first political activities were equally hesitant. They organized a women's Fourth of July celebration and sponsored a feminist lecture by Phoebe Couzins.[58]

The organizing efforts that Stanton and Anthony undertook, somewhat accidentally with New York women in the Working Women's Association, and more deliberately on their midwestern tour, marked an important departure for the woman suffrage movement. Previously suffragists had concentrated their energies on agitation, not organizing. They had used propaganda techniques learned in the abolitionist movement—petition-gathering, article-writing and speech-making. They communicated with large numbers of women who signed their petitions and listened to their speeches, but the contact was brief and the impact, for

56. *HWS*, III, 503. Williams went on to become owner and editor of the *National Citizen and Ballot Box,* a major suffrage journal in the 1870's and 1880's.
57. *Revolution,* June 10, 1869, reprinted in *HWS*, III, 503–504.
58. Noun, *Strong-Minded Women,* pp. 112–113 and 118.

both parties, minimal. More recently they had begun to lobby among politicians, but still they had not deliberately sought out new women to join them in the work. Some new women had come into the ranks, but the recruitment process was incidental to the growth of the movement. These political techniques were suitable for abolitionists, because the people they tried to convince were not the people they sought to liberate. They were much less appropriate for a feminist movement, in which the goal of emancipation ultimately depended on the mobilization of women themselves.

The switch from agitation to organizing forced suffragists to make important changes in their political style and content. As Garrisonian ultraists, they had been trained to express their ideas in the most radical form possible. Yet this approach was rarely the best way to organize new women into active involvement in the suffrage movement. Instead, they learned that they were successful as organizers to the degree they communicated their ideas in terms that their audiences could understand and on which they could act. In Bloomington Stanton faced an audience of women who had just been reminded by a local clergyman of their inferiority to men. Although Stanton was a militant anticleric, she avoided a direct attack on clerical tyranny, which would have been of little use to women as vulnerable to clerical pronouncements on their proper sphere as these. Rather, she took a gentler approach. As she later described it, "Finding the ladies of Bloomington somewhat scarified and nervous under the Reverend's firing, I tried to pour oil and wine on their wounded spirits, by exalting intuition and . . . deploring the slowness, the obtuseness, the materialism of most of the sons of Adam. It had its effect. They soon dried their tears, and with returning self-respect, told me of all the wonderful things women were doing in that town."[59] Stanton and Anthony had to modify their political style because they were no longer dealing with women who had already placed themselves outside the feminine pale by becoming

59. *HWS,* II, 372.

abolitionists. Their new converts faced serious social disapproval
for the first time when they committed themselves to woman
suffrage. Dubuque women were labeled "extremely Radical" and
"freethinkers," just for forming a woman suffrage society.[60]

The turn to organizing pushed Stanton and Anthony in a direction that ran counter to other aspects of their hard-won political independence. Their break with abolitionists had freed them
to investigate new aspects of the oppression and emancipation of
women. As a result, their feminism was becoming much more
radical, especially with respect to sexual and economic issues.
Organizing, on the other hand, acted as a brake on their radicalism. Many of their new converts were particularly uncomfort-
able with Stanton's bold attacks on marriage. Livermore explained that midwestern suffragists were hampered in their work
by "innuendoes" of sexual radicalism.[61] Stanton had to deny that
she intended to challenge the sanctity of the family, which is
precisely what she intended to do. "I am opposed to the
PRESENT legalized marriage, and the marriage and divorce
laws . . . ," she explained. "But so far from abolishing the in-
stitution of marriage, I would have it more pure and holy than it
is today by making woman the dictator in the whole social
realm."[62] Such disclaimers were hard on Stanton, who was tem-
peramentally inclined toward following ideas to their ultimate
conclusions; her ability to do so, especially with respect to wom-
en's position within marriage, was one of her greatest strengths.
She chafed under the restrictions that the new role of organizer
imposed on her. Throughout her later career, she periodically
tried to bolt its obligations, only to be pulled back into them by
Anthony, who assumed them more comfortably.

On their midwestern tour, Stanton and Anthony got a mixed
response to the particular political position for which they sought
support. Their demand for the immediate constitutional enfran-

60. Noun, *Strong-Minded Women,* p. 116.
61. *HWS,* II, 389.
62. "What the People Say to Us," *Revolution,* April 8, 1869, p. 212.

chisement of women was well received. Midwestern women were ready to enlist in the drive for a sixteenth amendment. However, their audiences could not be convinced to oppose the Fifteenth. Although not abolitionists, these women were Unionists and Republicans, and as New England suffragists had predicted, were not very sympathetic to the explicit anti-Republicanism that Stanton and Anthony expressed. Elizabeth Boynton, later a suffrage leader in Illinois, considered Stanton's attack on the Fifteenth Amendment "able and eloquent," but "directly in opposition to the general sentiment of the convention, which was mainly Republican."[63] At each of the meetings on their tour, Stanton and Anthony submitted a series of resolutions against the Fifteenth Amendment, which charged the Republican party with "the establishment of an aristocracy of sex," and condemned the amendment as "retrogressive" legislation. Only Milwaukee suffragists endorsed the resolutions. At all the other meetings, they were voted down.[64] Mary Livermore reported that midwestern women found the *Revolution* suffragists' hostility to the Fifteenth Amendment "obnoxious," but accepted their leadership nonetheless.[65]

Therefore, when Stanton and Anthony returned from the midwest in the spring, they accelerated their efforts to secure a woman suffrage amendment, while deemphasizing their opposition to the Fifteenth Amendment.[66] Getting Congress to pass a sixteenth amendment seemed a program around which the badly divided suffrage movement might be reunified. As a vehicle for this effort, Stanton and Anthony turned to the Equal Rights Association. The association, nearly defunct as a result of the bitter conflicts that followed the Kansas campaign, had done little since late 1867 except hold its annual convention, at which hos-

63. *HWS,* III, 566.
64. *HWS,* II, 374. Stanton called these her "pet resolutions" (*HWS,* III, 641).
65. Livermore to Lucy Stone, August 9, 1869, NAWSA Collection, LC.
66. After the midwestern tour, Livermore recalled that she cautioned Anthony to avoid such attacks and Anthony agreed to "be silent on the 15th Amendment" (*ibid.*). Stanton, "The Sixteenth Amendment," *Revolution,* April 29, 1869, p. 266.

tilities between supporters of black and woman suffrage had nearly torn the organization apart. After a year and a half of political activity among women outside the Equal Rights Association, Stanton and Anthony now hoped to transcend old hostilities and rebuild the organization around the demand for a sixteenth amendment. After her return from the midwest, Anthony announced that the association would hold a convention in New York in May 1869. The call for the convention neither attacked nor praised the Fifteenth Amendment, but concentrated instead on the importance of immediate action on behalf of the sixteenth.[67]

Stanton and Anthony hoped to bring old and new suffragists together in a revitalized Equal Rights Association. They urged the women they had met on their tour to come east for the convention and were highly successful in convincing them of the importance of their participation. Delegations from Chicago, St. Louis, Milwaukee, and Dubuque, all composed of women new to national reform activities, attended the convention. New York women from the Working Women's Association were there as well.[68] Stanton and Anthony also sent invitations to "old friends," members of the New England association, from whom they had become estranged. "I hope we shall have the pleasure of seeing and hearing you in the Convention at New York," Stanton wrote to Elizabeth Buffum Chace of the Rhode Island Woman Suffrage Association. "New England must not withdraw her countenance from us . . . ; though we may differ a little as to ways and means, we are all together in the great principle that the safety of the nation demands that woman's voice be recognized in the government."[69] To Antoinette Brown Blackwell, Lucy Stone's sister-in-law, she wrote, "I hope you will be at the anniversary. . . . I wish so much all petty jealousies could be laid aside, for all that our cause needs now for a speedy success is union and magnanimity among the women."[70]

67. *Revolution,* March 18, 1869, p. 168.
68. *HWS,* II, 379.
69. Stanton to Chace, April 15, 1869, quoted in Wyman and Wyman, *Elizabeth Buffum Chace,* I, 315.
70. Stanton to Blackwell, May 20, 1869, Blackwell Family Papers, SL.

Stanton and Anthony overestimated the possibilities for a harmonious convention, however. The split in the Equal Rights Association was too deep, the conflict between its abolitionist and feminist priorities too strong to be remedied by a campaign for the sixteenth amendment. New England suffragists refused to yield the Equal Rights Association to Stanton and Anthony and instead tried to force them from the organization. Rather than beginning something new, the 1869 convention ended something old. It was the epilogue of the Equal Rights Association, the final moment in the transitional phase of suffragism between its prewar dependence on abolitionism and its emergence as an autonomous feminist movement.

Stanton opened the convention with a rousing call to organize around the sixteenth amendment.[71] Immediately after her keynote speech, Stephen Foster halted the proceedings by charging Stanton and Anthony with racism and demanding that they resign their offices in the Equal Rights Association. (Stanton was a vice-president and Anthony was on the executive committee.) He claimed that they had violated the principles of the association because they had "ridiculed the negro and pronounced the 15th Amendment infamous." Frederick Douglass substantiated Foster's indictment with specific charges: the *Revolution* suffragists had worked closely with a notorious racist, Train; they had slandered the intelligence and integrity of the freedman; and they had made degrading comparisons between "the daughters of Washington and Jefferson" and the daughters of bootblacks and gardeners.[72]

They also reiterated the position that not granting strategic priority to black suffrage was itself a major betrayal of the ex-slave. "With us the matter is a question of life and death," Douglass insisted. "When women, because they are women, are hunted down through the cities of New York and New Orleans; when

71. "Anniversary Address," *Revolution*, May 13, 1869, pp. 289–292.
72. Unless otherwise indicated, all quotations are taken from the *Revolution*'s stenographic report of the convention, May 20, 1869, pp. 305–308.

they are dragged from their houses and hung upon lamp-posts; when their children are torn from their arms and their brains dashed out upon the pavement; . . . then they will have an urgency to obtain the ballot equal to our own." Therefore, Stanton's and Anthony's enthusiasm for the sixteenth amendment was as intolerable to Douglass and Foster as their hostility to the Fifteenth. The only position satisfactory to supporters of black suffrage was the one that Julia Ward Howe had articulated at the New England Woman Suffrage Convention: "I am willing that the negro shall get [the ballot] before me."[73]

As she had done at the New England convention, Lucy Stone strongly challenged Douglass's contention that the black man's claim to the ballot was so much greater than the woman's. She and Blackwell defended Stanton and Anthony and tried to negotiate between their position and that of Douglass and Foster. With eloquence equal to that of Douglass, Stone cited details of women's oppression. "I want to remind the audience that . . . the Ku Kluxes here in the north in the shape of men, take away the children from the mother, and separate them as completely as if done on the block of the auctioneer. . . . The woman has an ocean of wrong too deep for any plummet, and the negro, too, has an ocean of wrongs that cannot be fathomed." She appealed to the convention to avoid comparisons between the sufferings of blacks and those of women. "We are lost if we turn away from the middle principle and argue for one class," she said.

Yet, if there was a "middle principle," there was no middle position. The only strategic alternatives were Stanton and Anthony's position, that the constitutional enfranchisement of women must be part of Reconstruction, and Foster and Douglass's, that it would have to wait until the Republican party had enfranchised the freedmen. Stone and Blackwell chose the Fifteenth Amendment and would not enlist in the drive for the sixteenth. "I thank God for the Fifteenth Amendment . . . ," Stone explained. "I will be thankful in my soul if *any* body can

73. "Woman Suffrage," *New York World,* November 21, 1868, p. 5.

get out of this terrible pit." When Ernestine Rose and Josephine Griffing proposed that the Equal Rights Association change its name to the Woman Suffrage Association and concentrate on the sixteenth amendment, Stone opposed the motion "until the black man had obtained suffrage."[74]

Stone's "middle principle" represented the predominant opinion at the equal rights convention,[75] and condemned it to inaction. The delegates passed a resolution, submitted by Blackwell, "That while we heartily approve of the Fifteenth Amendment . . . , we nevertheless feel profound regret that Congress has not submitted a parallel amendment for the enfranchisement of women."[76] They did not support Foster's demand that Stanton and Anthony resign from the association, but neither did they mobilize behind woman suffrage. After Stanton's keynote address, the sixteenth amendment was not reconsidered and the convention adjourned without any plans to organize support for it. For three days, all that the delegates could concentrate on was the unresolvable conflict between abolitionists and feminists. The convention's inability to resolve the question of suffrage priorities made it clear that the Equal Rights Association could not serve as a vehicle for the advancement of woman suffrage.

The obvious political bankruptcy of the Equal Rights Association led almost immediately to the formation of a new national reform organization, the National Woman Suffrage Association. It was founded two days after the equal rights convention had adjourned, at a reception for women delegates given at the Women's Bureau mansion by the editors of the *Revolution*.[77] The reception resolved itself into a business meeting and declared the formation of a national society "to discuss woman suffrage separate and apart from the question of equal rights and man-

74. "Equal Rights," *New York Times*, May 14, 1869, p. 5.

75. See Mary Livermore, "Editorial Correspondence," and A Midwesterner, "The New York Convention," both in the *Agitator*, May 22, 1869, pp. 4–5. (Livermore edited this paper from Chicago.) The point is also made in Kugler, "The Women's Rights Movement," p. 193.

76. "Equal Rights," *New York Times*, May 14, 1869, p. 5.

77. Harper, *Life and Work of Susan B. Anthony*, I, 326.

hood suffrage, so as to give greater strength and unanimity to call attention more directly to Congressman Julian's Sixteenth Amendment."[78] The principles of the National Woman Suffrage Association were simple—commitment to the sixteenth amendment and to a movement controlled and defined by women. Beyond that, its vitality, its breadth, and the kind of issues and tactics it would be willing to entertain remained to be determined. Nevertheless, its creation formalized and therefore advanced what Stanton and Anthony had been building for almost two years, an independent movement of women for their enfranchisement and emancipation. It can reasonably be called the first national feminist organization in the United States.

There are several contradictory accounts of how the National Woman Suffrage Association was formed, which reflect the political conflicts out of which it emerged. Blackwell charged that Stanton and Anthony planned ahead of time to organize a national woman suffrage society at the Women's Bureau reception, but did not tell New England suffragists about their intentions, to keep them from attending.[79] Both he and Stone had left New York by the time of the reception. Celia Burleigh remembered the *Revolution*'s role differently. She reported that during and after the equal rights convention, Stanton had refused proposals to form a national woman suffrage society, but had gone along with the nearly unanimous sentiment among women delegates at the Women's Bureau reception.[80]

No evidence exists to corroborate Blackwell's charges that the formation of the association was premeditated in order to exclude dissident suffragists. The gathering at the Women's Bureau was the first opportunity that women delegates to the equal rights

78. "Meeting of the National Woman Suffrage Association," *New York Times,* May 18, 1869, p. 5.
79. Blackwell to Martha Wright, December 10, 1869, Garrison Family Collection, Sophia Smith Collection (Women's History Archive), Smith College Library. This account was reported by Hannah Cutler, "Recollections of Woman Suffrage Affairs," unpublished manuscript, NAWSA Collection, LC.
80. Burleigh, letter dated November 21, 1869, reprinted in *Revolution,* May 26, 1870, p. 321.

convention had had to meet together and evaluate their common reactions. The decision to turn the reception into a political meeting might well have reflected a spontaneous upsurge of feminist rage, especially among the more recent suffrage converts whom Stanton and Anthony had brought to the equal rights convention. Margaret Longley of Dayton reported that the midwestern suffragists were dismayed at the convention because they had "supposed that they were going to a women's rights meeting . . . and that equal rights meant the equal rights of women with men." Many of the women were particularly disturbed at the dominant and disruptive role that men had played at the convention, and the disregard for woman suffrage and the sixteenth amendment demonstrated throughout its proceedings.[81]

On the other hand, Stanton and Anthony can hardly be considered passive in the formation of the National Woman Suffrage Association; undoubtedly they took the lead in giving their guests' discontent concrete political expression. Anthony chaired the Women's Bureau meeting. Stanton was elected president of the new association. She proposed that only women be permitted to join. This was the first time since the radical Salem, Ohio, women's rights convention of 1850 that any feminist had proposed the exclusion of men from women's rights activities. Stanton's motion produced heated debate. Henry Stanton spoke in its favor, because he "had been drilled for twenty years privately, and he was convinced women could do it better if left alone." However, other women replied that they wanted an organization into which they could bring their husbands, presumably for the same type of education. The meeting finally decided against Stanton's proposal.[82] Nonetheless, all were united in their com-

81. M. V. Longley, "Anniversary of the Equal Rights Association," *Woman's Advocate* (Dayton), May 29, 1869, pp. 4–5. See also Mary Livermore to Anthony, May 17, 1869, reprinted in Harper, *Life and Work of Susan B. Anthony*, I, 327.

82. Longley, *ibid.* There is no evidence to corroborate Henry Blackwell's claim (Blackwell to Martha Wright, December 10, 1869, Garrison Family Collection, Sophia Smith Collection [Women's History Archive], Smith College Library) that the National adopted a bylaw prohibiting men from holding office.

mitment to an organization "dedicated to the sole advocacy of the rights of 'lovely woman,' " and the National Woman Suffrage Association remained a women's organization, by virtue of the circumstances of its formation and the nature of its goals.[83] For forty years the great majority of its members and all its officers were women.

At the time of the organization's formation, much about it remained to be determined, especially the range of issues it would be willing to consider and the degree of radicalism it could tolerate. In forming the National Association, Stanton and Anthony joined with women whose feminism was not nearly as broad or as radical as their own. In particular, many of the new suffragists disagreed with their militant positions on marriage and domestic reform. When Anthony criticized the absolute control husbands had over their wives, Dayton women "took up the cudgel" in defense of marriage.[84] A New York City meeting of the association considered the liberalization of divorce law, but most of the women there found the topic "dangerous" and did not want to weaken the marriage bond.[85] Stanton and Anthony had before them the difficult and problematic task of educating these women out of their social conservatism to more radical ideas. The important thing about the formation of the National Woman Suffrage Association was that it represented the basic feminist consensus within which the work of political education could proceed.

Although much about it was still unclear, suffragists around the country were enthusiastic about the formation of the new association. It provided an organization to encourage and coordinate practical woman suffrage work on the national level. Frances Burr of Connecticut strongly supported the new organization's commitment to the sixteenth amendment and suggested that it organize "a body of five hundred women to storm the doors of the Capitol. . . . Anything to help it along," she urged.

83. A Midwesterner, "The Woman's Bureau Reception," *Agitator*, May 29, 1869, p. 3.
84. Harper, *Life and Work of Susan B. Anthony*, I, 331.
85. "The Bureau Suffrage Meeting," *Revolution*, December 16, 1869, p. 373.

" 'Push things.' " Mary Humphrey of Kansas "was indeed proud" to become a vice-president in the organization and approved of its decision "to concentrate all our efforts upon the one idea of Suffrage for women."[86] Even though she supported the Fifteenth Amendment, Mary Booth, a prominent New York author, joined the association because she believed "that the first practical thing to be done is to work in unison to get the ballot, irrespective of all other issues."[87]

The National Woman Suffrage Association developed on two levels. It held weekly meetings in New York City among local suffragists, and it continued the work Stanton and Anthony had begun on their midwestern tour, the organization of suffrage sentiment around the country. The New York City members were, for the most part, the same middle-class working women who had come to dominate the Working Women's Association. Sarah Norton, Clemence Lozier, Celia Burleigh, and others continued to meet regularly and discuss various reforms in women's sphere, but they now did so under the auspices of the National Woman Suffrage Association. This solved the programmatic dilemma that had plagued them in the Working Women's Association. The focus on woman suffrage and the drive for the sixteenth amendment provided them with the practical work for which they had been searching. They drew up and circulated petitions urging passage of the amendment to Congress, and considered other strategies for promoting woman suffrage, including a tax strike of women. The formation of the National Woman Suffrage Association permitted the New York City feminists to move from "thought and talk" about women's emancipation to "practical, positive action."[88]

Reorganized into suffrage work, the New York City feminists were also able to solve the dilemma of constituency, which had been unsolvable in the context of the Working Women's Associa-

86. "What the People Say to Us," *Revolution,* July 1, 1869, p. 406.
87. Booth to Antoinette Brown Blackwell, May 7, 1869, Blackwell Family Papers, SL.
88. "National Woman Suffrage Association," *Revolution,* June 24, 1869, pp. 393–394.

tion. The National Woman Suffrage Association led them to reach out, not as philanthropists to working women, but as organizers to women like themselves who were drawn to the suffrage demand. Soon after the formation of the National, they conducted a successful suffrage convention in the fashionable resort of Saratoga, at the height of the season, and formed the New York Woman Suffrage Association there.[89] The plan of organization that Matilda Joslyn Gage drew up for the New York association was ambitious. It called for vice-presidents from each of New York's sixty counties and an advisory council composed of one woman from each of the state's thirteen congressional districts. "Friends, this is work . . . ," Gage wrote of her plan. "Nothing effective can be accomplished by the guerrilla mode of action on which we have hitherto depended."[90] The implementation of Gage's organizational plan required a long-term effort. At first only thirty counties could provide active suffragists for the association's officers, and the majority of these were in the western part of the state where antislavery societies had flourished. It took several years for the woman suffrage movement in New York to extend into all the counties of the state. The original group of New York City suffragists stayed with the work and provided the leadership for the state suffrage association for almost half a century.[91]

The association simultaneously expanded outside New York. It provided a vehicle for organizing state and local woman suffrage societies around the country. "North, South, East, West, Pacific Coast, all! Have you heard the Call, and are you heeding it, to organize at once in behalf of the great cause of woman's enfranchisement?" the Revolution appealed.[92] Margaret Longley

89. *Revolution*, July 15, 1869, p. 25.
90. Gage, "Appeal to the Friends of Woman Suffrage in the State of New York," *Revolution*, July 29, 1869, p. 49.
91. See the New York Woman Suffrage Association Collection, Columbia University Library.
92. Parker Pillsbury, "Call to All Hands," *Revolution*, August 26, 1869, pp. 113–114.

returned home from the Women's Bureau reception to form the Ohio Woman Suffrage Association. Elizabeth Schenck was invited to become the California vice-president of the association. She accepted and proceeded to organize a Pacific coast branch.[93] In November 1869 Stanton left on another tour of the midwest to lecture and to organize local suffragists into the National Association. State and local affiliates were formed in the wake of her visit. In Minnesota the leading figures were two women who had worked for woman suffrage for some time, but whose effectiveness had been limited by their isolation. One was Mary Colburn, who had been speaking out on women's rights for a decade and had petitioned the state legislature to enfranchise women in 1867. The other was Sarah Burger Stearns, who had been a feminist since she was sixteen in 1853 and had been the first woman to petition for admission to the University of Michigan.[94]

The leaders of the New England association reacted to the creation of the National Woman Suffrage Association by forming their own national organization to continue their contest for the leadership of the movement. A few weeks after the Women's Bureau reception, the executive committee of the New England Woman Suffrage Association began to correspond with reformers around the country about organizing an American Woman Suffrage Association.[95] Stone, Blackwell, Higginson, and Julia Ward Howe were particularly active. In their letters they emphasized the importance of agitating for woman suffrage within a framework of support for the Fifteenth Amendment, and of proceeding in a more methodical and orderly fashion than had the National Association.[96] Their efforts culminated in the founding

93. *HWS*, III, 492 and 752.
94. *HWS*, III, 651.
95. "Editorial Correspondence," *Standard,* June 5, 1869, p. 2.
96. Just a few of the letters of invitation were: Stone to Gerrit Smith, October 26, 1869, Gerrit Smith Papers, George Arents Research Library for Special Collections, Syracuse University; Stone to Esther Pugh, undated, Blackwell Family Collection, LC; Stone to Lucy Larcom, August 20, 1869, Alma Lutz Collection, SL.

convention of the American Woman Suffrage Association, which was held in Cleveland in November 1869.

Like the New England association from which it grew, the American Woman Suffrage Association relied on strong support from Republican and abolitionist men. The call to the Cleveland convention was signed by prominent Republicans, and by many leading abolitionists, including Garrison, Samuel May, Jr., Aaron Powell, and Frederick Douglass.[97] Efforts were made to get the endorsements of Charles Sumner and Wendell Phillips as well, but these were unsuccessful.[98] Because they prized their connections with leading Republicans and abolitionists, the organizers of the American Association were particularly anxious to distinguish themselves from the hostility to male political influence that had been expressed in the National Association. They deliberately sought male supporters. "Our cause suffers today for the lack of organizing talent of *men* in its management," Stone wrote to James Freeman Clark to enlist his help.[99] The constitution submitted at the Cleveland convention specified an equal number of male and female officers, and it was agreed that the presidency of the association would alternate between a man and a woman.[100] Henry Ward Beecher, who was not present, was selected as the first president. From the floor, Olivia Hall, a Toledo suffragist, protested the appointment of a man to head a woman suffrage organization.[101]

97. "Woman Suffrage Call," August 5, 1869, Olympia Brown Willis Papers, SL. Lucy Stone to Franklin Sanborn, August 18, 1869, Alma Lutz Collection, SL.

98. Julia Ward Howe to Sumner, August 23, 1869, Sumner Collection, Houghton Library, Harvard University. Henry Blackwell to Lucy Stone, November 1, 1869, Blackwell Family Collection, LC. Phillips was deeply involved in labor reform politics in Massachusetts. He refused to sign the call "for reasons which are good to him" (Stone to Garrison, September 27, 1869, Boston Public Library).

99. Stone to Clarke, October 6, 1869, Blackwell Family Collection, LC. (Italics in the original.) Merk makes this point in "Massachusetts and the Woman-Suffrage Movement," pp. 374–375.

100. "Proceedings of the National [*sic*] Woman Suffrage Association," *Woman's Advocate* (Dayton), December 11, 1869, pp. 2–14.

101. The newspapers reported that the woman at the convention who

The American Association was designed to concentrate solely on the demand for woman suffrage and pledged itself to avoid any and all "side issues." Stone praised its commitment to the "simple straightforward advocacy of a principle on its own merits."[102] This explicit avoidance of all other aspects of women's oppression reflected the fact that the feminism that underlay its demand for woman suffrage was not initially as well developed as that of the National Association. The American criticized the National Association for being "too heterogeneous" and confounding woman suffrage with sexual and economic issues.[103] At the Cleveland convention, Higginson concentrated his opening remarks on how little social disruption the enfranchisement of women would bring.[104] Even more to the point, the American Association's single-issue approach to woman suffrage reflected the demands of abolitionist politics in this period. The major "side issue" that the American was pledged to avoid was the Fifteenth Amendment and black suffrage.[105] Rooted in the need to protect abolitionist and Republican priorities from feminist interference, the American Association began with a woman suffrage politics that was severely circumscribed and very defensive.

The Cleveland convention concentrated on forming an organization, rather than on planning strategy to advance woman suffrage. Its goal was to organize a nationwide suffrage society that was "more comprehensive and more widely representative" than

---

objected to the appointment of a man to head a woman suffrage organization was Mary Davis of New Jersey. Davis denied the charge and identified the protestant as Olivia Hall (*ibid.*).

102. Stone to Garrison, August 22, 1869, Boston Public Library.

103. Garrison to Elizabeth Pease Nichols, September 26, 1869, Boston Public Library. Stone to Amelia Bloomer, May 16, 1869, reprinted in Noun, *Strong-Minded Women,* p. 110. Clarina I. H. Nichols to Anthony, August 21, 1881, Susan B. Anthony Papers, SL. Paulina Wright Davis made this criticism in "Suffrage and Social Restrictions," *Revolution,* December 8, 1870, pp. 358–359.

104. "Woman Suffrage—The National Convention," clipping from an untitled Cleveland paper, November 26, 1869, NAWSA Collection, LC.

105. Thomas Wentworth Higginson to Elizabeth Buffum Chace, October 15, 1869, quoted in Wyman and Wyman, *Elizabeth Buffum Chace,* I, 323.

what it delicately referred to as "Associations already existing."[106]
The major order of business of Cleveland was adopting a constitution, bylaws, and a list of officers. Only Lucy Stone spoke
about particular strategic possibilities for woman suffrage. Contrary to the way that most reform conventions were conducted,
the planning committee submitted no resolutions and proposed
no petitions or memorials for circulation in the coming year.[107]
This reflected the fact that the organizers of the American Association, committed to the political priority of black enfranchisement, had an entirely different timetable for woman suffrage
agitation than that which led to the formation of the National
Association. The urgency behind the Cleveland convention came
not from the possibility of winning the sixteenth amendment and
the vote for women, but from the necessity of countering the
direction in which the National Association was leading the
woman suffrage movement.

A considerable number of the recent converts that Stanton and
Anthony had brought into the movement participated in the
Cleveland convention.[108] These women were much less partisan
about the split than leaders on either side of it, and did not see
their participation in the American Association as contradictory
to their involvement with the National. Not rooted in the tradition of abolitionism or involved in the conflicts that had driven
Stone and Stanton into rival camps, they were as impressed with
the similarities between the two factions as they were with their
differences and exerted considerable pressure for suffrage unity.
Members of the National convinced Anthony to come with them

106. Printed notice of intent to form an American Woman Suffrage Association, August 5, 1869, Olympia Brown Willis Papers, SL.
107. "Woman Suffrage—The National Convention," clipping, November
26, 1869, NAWSA Collection, LC.
108. Myra Bradwell of Chicago and her husband, Judge James Bradwell,
Celia Burleigh of New York, Olivia Hall of Toledo, and Mary Livermore
attended the Cleveland convention. For various efforts made there to unite
the two suffrage organizations, see "Proceedings of the National Woman
Suffrage Association," *Woman's Advocate* (Dayton), December 11, 1869,
pp. 2–14.

to Cleveland and offer her cooperation to the new organization.[109] She did so, although somewhat petulantly, offering her "blessing" on the American Association "though it nullify completely the National Association . . . for which I have struggled as never man or woman struggled before."[110]

For a few months after the Cleveland convention, there was some inclination, especially within the National, to try to unify into one organization. However, the political differences that had led to the split were becoming more, rather than less, intense, as the ratification of the Fifteenth Amendment seemed imminent, and pro-Republican suffragists were sure "the woman's hour" was just ahead. The American successfully resisted the efforts at unification, and by the end of 1869 two national suffrage organizations existed, competing for adherents and for the right to direct the way to victory.[111]

Events over the next three years aggravated the differences between the two associations, with the result that the split between them lasted twenty-one years. In particular, the process of political consolidation that marked the end of Reconstruction intensified the question at the heart of their strategic disagreement, the relationship of the Republican party to the future of reform. The American Association continued to expect the Republican party to take up woman suffrage, particularly after the Fifteenth Amendment was ratified in March 1870. In 1872 the American was able to secure a reference to women's enfranchisement in the national Republican platform, friendly, but vague and so noncommittal that some suffragists called it a "splinter" rather than a plank. This marked the high point of the Ameri-

109. Pillsbury to Martha Wright, November 24, 1869, Garrison Family Collection, Sophia Smith Collection (Women's History Archive), Smith College Library.

110. "Woman Suffrage—the National Convention," clipping, November 26, 1869, NAWSA Collection, LC.

111. Lucy Stone to Antoinette Brown Blackwell, October 31, 1869, Blackwell Family Collection, LC. Stone to Elizabeth Buffum Chace, November 6, 1869, quoted in Wyman and Wyman, *Elizabeth Buffum Chace*, I, 323.

can's Republican strategy, because the party never again even
considered woman suffrage, much less took it up as a partisan
issue. For its part, the National continued to believe in the necessity of independent political activity to advance the franchise for
women and reform in general. The high point of its efforts also
came in conjunction with the presidential election of 1872, when
it tried for a second time to form a woman suffrage/labor reform
alliance. The central figure in this effort was Victoria Woodhull,
around whom an eclectic group of labor reformers, free lovers,
and feminists had gathered. The National's effort to form an
independent radical party failed in the general political chaos of
1872, out of which surfaced a Republican party devoid of reform pretensions and intent on reestablishing stability in national
politics. The Republicans' victory in the 1872 presidential election signaled the beginning of a new period in American politics
and the end of all serious strategic opportunities for winning
women the vote, at least for the time being. After 1872 the strategic and ideological differences between the American and the
National Woman Suffrage Associations faded. However, the
early years of their rivalry had been so acrimonious that the two
societies were not able to unite until 1890.

Historians of the suffrage movement have tended to argue that
the split that began within the Equal Rights Association in 1867
and culminated in the rival formation of the National and American Woman Suffrage Associations in 1869 weakened suffrage
forces and prepared the way for the movement's decline in the
1870's.[112] This does not seem to have been the case. The failure
to achieve woman suffrage in the 1870's was far less a result of
hostilities within the movement than it was an aspect of the defeat of Reconstruction radicalism in general. Looked at from the
perspective of the growth of feminism, rather than the achievement of the vote, the political conflict of the late 1860's signifi-

112. See for example James M. McPherson, "Abolitionism, Woman
Suffrage and the Negro," *Mid-America,* 47 (1965), 47, and Flexner, *Century of Struggle,* p. 155.

cantly advanced the movement, liberated it from its subservience to abolitionism, and propelled it into political independence. The conflict between suffrage factions led both sides to create national organizations, to draw sympathizers into active participation, to search out new sources of support, and in general to begin the systematic work of organizing a mass movement of women for their own enfranchisement.

In many ways, American feminism was just beginning in 1869. The possibilities it held for American women all lay in the future; most of them still do. What did it mean that suffrage had become an independent feminist movement? Just this: that suffragists were no longer able to look to other reform movements to enact measures intended to benefit women; therefore, they had to look to women themselves not only to articulate the problem, but to provide the solution to women's oppression as well. This was suffragism's potential for affecting women's history—that increasing numbers of women would be transformed through the process of acting deliberately and collectively to achieve the equality and independence that enfranchisement seemed to promise. The historical agency of women had always been implicit in women's rights; but the prewar movement's relation to abolitionism had kept feminists from realizing their ultimate dependence on women themselves. Relying on the energies of another reform movement in turn placed an absolute limit on their power to affect women's lives. Reconstruction politics shattered feminists' dependence on abolitionism and opened the way for woman suffrage to develop into an organized movement of women, ultimately one of mass proportions. In retrospect we can see what suffragists only glimpsed in the 1860's, that it was women's involvement in the movement, far more than the eventual enfranchisement of women, that created the basis for new social relations between men and women. In other words, activity in the woman suffrage movement itself did precisely what Stanton and others had expected possession of the francise to do—it demonstrated that self-government and democratic participation in the life of the society was the key to women's emancipation. Therein lay its feminist power and its historical significance.

Stanton and Anthony were the leaders in establishing woman suffrage as an independent feminist movement. The basic premises of the political perspective that informed their leadership were the necessity of revolutionary change in women's position and the conviction that other women could come to understand and demand that change. These beliefs had led them to rebel against the Republican party's program for postwar reform and to cut themselves off from the abolitionist political community with which they had been affiliated for more than twenty years. Their feminist radicalism was also at the heart of their efforts to build a political alliance with labor reform and to organize a feminist movement among working women. Ultimately, their politics led them to establish the National Woman Suffrage Association, from which they could proceed to build an independent movement of women for their own enfranchisement.

It is sobering to reflect how long after the inauguration of this movement it took to win the ballot for women, and how much longer we shall still have to fight to win our emancipation. However, it would be a mistake to recognize the enormous scope of the struggle for women's liberation and not at the same time appreciate the extent of our resources for winning it. The process by which the woman suffrage movement emerged from the discontent of women, and the militant and radical feminism that its leaders brought to it is evidence of the ultimate capacity of women to liberate our sex. "It is wonderful . . . ," a Pennsylvania suffragist wrote in 1871. "Only twenty years ago even L. Mott doubted the wisdom of Elizabeth Cady Stanton claiming the ballot for women; now thousands joyfully follow her lead."[113]

113. Sarah Pugh to R. D. Webb, February 4, 1871, Boston Public Library.

Bibliography

Primary Sources

Manuscript Collections

American Antiquarian Society, Worcester, Massachusetts
  Stephen and Abby Kelley Foster Papers
George Arents Research Library for Special Collections, Syracuse University, Syracuse, New York
  Gerrit Smith Papers
Boston Public Library, Boston, Massachusetts
  William Lloyd Garrison Collection
  Higginson Autograph Collection
Buffalo and Erie County Public Library, Buffalo, New York
  Gluck Collection
Columbia University Library, New York, New York
  Josephine S. Griffing Papers
  New York Woman Suffrage Association Collection
Duke University, Durham, North Carolina
  Thomas Wentworth Higginson Papers
Library of Congress, Manuscript Division, Washington, D.C.
  Susan B. Anthony Papers
  Blackwell Family Collection
  Anna Dickinson Papers
  Frederick Douglass Papers
  Olivia Hall Papers
  National American Woman Suffrage Association Collection
  Elizabeth Cady Stanton Papers
Massachusetts Historical Society, Boston, Massachusetts
  Caroline Healey Dall Papers
Missouri Historical Society, St. Louis, Missouri
  Lillie Devereux Blake Papers
The Arthur and Elizabeth Schlesinger Library on the History of Women in America, Radcliffe College, Cambridge, Massachusetts
  Susan B. Anthony Papers
  Blackwell Family Papers

Mary Dillon Collection
Matilda Joslyn Gage Papers
Julia Ward Howe Papers
Alma Lutz Collection
May-Goddard Collection
Harriet Hanson Robinson Papers
Strickland Autograph Collection
Olympia Brown Willis Papers
Women's Rights Collection
Sophia Smith Collection (Women's History Archive), Smith College,
Northampton, Massachusetts
Garrison Family Collection
New England Women's Hospital Collection
Southern Illinois University, Carbondale, Illinois
Victoria Woodhull Martin Papers
Stowe-Day Library, Hartford, Connecticut
Isabella Beecher Hooker Papers
Joseph K. Hooker Papers
Vassar College Library, Poughkeepsie, New York
Autograph Collection
Paulina Wright Davis Papers
Elizabeth Cady Stanton Papers
Wisconsin State Historical Society, Madison, Wisconsin
Mathilde Anneke Papers

Newspapers and Magazines

Agitator, Chicago, 1869
Demorest's Monthly, New York, 1869–1870
Independent, New York, 1868–1870
Lily, Seneca Falls, 1853
National Anti-Slavery Standard, New York, 1865–1869
New York Times, 1865–1870
New York Tribune, 1867
New York World, 1867–1869
Packard's Monthly, New York, 1869
Revolution, New York, 1868–1871
Woman's Advocate, Dayton, 1869
Woman's Advocate, New York, 1869
Woodhull and Claflin's Weekly, New York, 1870–1872
Workingman's Advocate, Chicago, 1868–1869

Miscellaneous

American Equal Rights Association. *Proceedings of the First Anniversary.* New York: Robert J. Johnston, Printer, 1867.

Blackwell, Antoinette Brown. *The Sexes throughout Nature.* New York: Putnam's, 1875.

Blatch, Harriot Stanton, and Alma Lutz. *Challenging Years: The Memoirs of Harriot Stanton Blatch.* New York: Putnam, 1940.

Bloomer, Dexter C. *The Life and Writings of Amelia Bloomer.* Boston: Arena, 1895.

Clemmer, Mary. *Poetical Works of Alice and Phoebe Cary with a Memorial of Their Lives.* New York: Hurd and Houghton, 1877.

Commons, John R., et al. *Documentary History of American Industrial Society,* Vol. IX. Cleveland: Arthur H. Clarke, 1910–1911.

Croly, Jane Cunningham. *The History of the Woman's Club Movement.* New York: H. G. Allen, 1898.

Curtis, George William. *Equal Rights for All.* Rochester: New York State Constitutional Committee, 1867.

Dall, Caroline Healey. *Woman's Right to Labor.* Boston: Walker, Wise, 1860.

Davis, Paulina Wright. *A History of the National Women's Rights Movement for Twenty Years, from 1850 to 1870.* New York: Journeymen Printers' Cooperative Association, 1871.

Democratic Party. *Official Proceedings of the National Convention.* Boston: Rockwell and Rollins, Printers, 1868.

Douglass, Frederick. "Two Letters." Ed. Joseph Borome. *Journal of Negro History,* 33 (1948), 469–471.

Duniway, Abigail Scott. *Pathbreaking: An Autobiographical History of the Woman Suffrage Movement in the Pacific Coast States.* Portland: James, Herns and Abbot, 1914.

Emerson, Sarah Hopper, ed. *The Life of Abby Hopper Gibbons.* New York: Putnam's, 1896.

Greeley, Horace. *Divorce: Being a Correspondence between Horace Greeley and Robert Dale Owen, Originally Published in the New York Daily Tribune.* New York: R. N. DeWitt, 1860.

Grimké, Sarah. *Letters on the Equality of the Sexes and the Condition of Woman: Addressed to Mary S. Parker.* Boston: Isaac Knapp, 1837.

Hamilton, Gail. *Woman's Wrongs: A Counter Irritant.* Boston: Ticknor and Fields, 1868.

Howe, Julia Ward. *Julia Ward Howe and the Woman Suffrage Movement.* Ed. Florence Howe Hall. Boston: D. Estes, 1913.

——. *Reminiscences 1819–1899*. Boston: Houghton Mifflin, 1900.

Hunt, Harriot K. *Glances and Glimpses*. Boston: J. P. Jewett, 1856.

Livermore, Mary Ashton. *The Story of My Life*. Hartford: A. D. Worthington, 1897.

Memorial of Sarah Pugh—A Tribute of Respect from her Cousins. Philadelphia: Lippincott, 1888.

In Memoriam: Clemence S. Lozier. New York: Privately printed, 1889.

Mott, James, and Lucretia Mott. *Life and Letters*. Ed. Anna Davis Hallowell. Boston: Houghton Mifflin, 1884.

National Labor Union. *Proceedings of the Second Session*. Philadelphia, 1868.

National Typographical Union. *Proceedings of the Fifteenth Annual Session*. New York: Journeymen Printers' Cooperative Association, 1867.

——. *Proceedings of the Seventeenth Annual Session*. Cincinnati: Robert Clarke and Co., Printers, 1869.

Nichols, Clarina I. H. "The Papers of Clarina I. H. Nichols, 1854–1884." Ed. Joseph G. Gambone. *Kansas Historical Quarterly*, 39 and 40 (1973–1974).

Phillips, Wendell. *Speeches, Lectures and Letters*. Boston: Beacon, 1891.

Proceedings of the National Women's Rights Convention, held at the Cooper Institute, New York City, May 10 and 11, 1860. Boston: Yerrinton and Garrison, 1860.

Proceedings of the Women's Rights Conventions, held at Seneca Falls and Rochester, New York, July and August, 1848. New York: R. J. Johnston, Printer, 1870.

Report of the Women's Rights Meeting at Mercantile Hall, May 27, 1859. Boston: S. Urbino, 1859.

A Republican (not a Radical). *Universal Suffrage. Female Suffrage*. Philadelphia: Lippincott, 1867.

Shaw, Anna Howard. *The Story of a Pioneer*. New York: Harper, 1915.

Spencer, Sara Jane. *Problems on the Woman Question, Social, Political, and Scriptural*. Washington, D.C.: Langran, Ogilvie, 1871.

Stanton, Elizabeth Cady. *Eighty Years and More: Reminiscences, 1815–1897*. New York: T. Fischer Unwin, 1899.

——. *Elizabeth Cady Stanton as Revealed in Her Letters, Diary and Reminiscences*. Ed. Theodore Stanton and Harriot Stanton Blatch. New York: Harper, 1922.

——. Susan B. Anthony, Matilda Joslyn Gage, et al. *History of Woman Suffrage*. Rochester: Susan B. Anthony, 1881–1902. (Vols. I–IV). New York: National American Woman Suffrage Association, 1922 (Vols. V–VI).

Swisshelm, Jane Grey. *Half a Century*. Chicago: Jansen McClurg, 1880.

Train, George Francis. *The Great Epigram Campaign in Kansas: Championship of Women*. Leavenworth: Prescott and Hume, Daily Commercial Office, 1867.

———. *My Life in Many States and in Foreign Lands*. New York: Appleton, 1902.

Willard, Frances E. *Glimpses of Fifty Years: The Autobiography of an American Woman*. Chicago: Woman's Temperance Publication Association, 1889.

Willis, Olympia Brown. *Acquaintances Old and New among Reformers*. Milwaukee: S. E. Tate Printing Co., 1911.

———. "Olympia Brown, An Autobiography." Ed. Gwendolen B. Willis. *Annual Journal of Universalist Historical Society*, 4 (1963), 1–76.

Secondary Sources

Andrews, John and W. D. P. Bliss. *History of Women in Trade Unions*. Vol. X of *Report on the Condition of Women and Child Wage-Earners*. Washington, D.C.: Government Printing Office, 1911.

Anthony, Katharine. *Susan B. Anthony: Her Personal History and Her Era*. New York: Doubleday, 1954.

Baker, Elizabeth. *Technology and Women's Work*. New York: Columbia University Press, 1964.

Barnes, Gilbert H. *The Antislavery Impulse, 1830–1844*. New York: Harcourt, Brace & World, 1964, originally published in 1933.

Beldon, Gertrude May. "A History of the Woman Suffrage Movement in Illinois." M.A. thesis, University of Chicago, 1913.

Benedict, Michael Les. *A Compromise of Principle: Congressional Republicans and Reconstruction, 1863–1869*. New York: Norton, 1974.

Blackwell, Alice Stone. *Lucy Stone: Pioneer of Women's Rights*. Boston: Little, Brown, 1930.

Blair, Karen. "The Clubwoman as Feminist: The Woman's Culture Club Movement in the United States, 1868–1914." Ph.D. diss., State University of New York at Buffalo, 1976.

Blake, Katherine Devereux and Margaret Louise Wallace. *Champion of Women: The Life of Lillie Devereux Blake*. New York: Fleming H. Revell, 1943.

Bogin, Ruth. "Sarah Parker Remond: Black Abolitionist from Salem." *Essex Institute Historical Collections*, 110 (1973), 120–150.

Boston, Ray. *British Chartists in America, 1838–1900*. Manchester: Manchester University Press, 1971.

Bracey, John, August Meier, and Elliott Rudwick, eds. *Blacks in the Abolitionist Movement*. Belmont, Calif.: Wadsworth, 1971.

Brotz, Howard, ed. *Negro Social and Political Thought, 1850–1920*. New York: Basic, 1966.

Brown, Ira V. "The Woman's Rights Movement in Pennsylvania, 1848–1875." *Pennsylvania History*, 32 (1965), 153–165.

Buhle, Mari Jo. "Feminism and Socialism in the United States, 1820–1920." Ph.D. dissertation, University of Wisconsin, 1974.

Byrne, Elizabeth D. "The Struggle for Political Power: Tactics Used by the Massachusetts Woman Suffrage Association during the First Decade, 1870–1879." Unpublished manuscript, Schlesinger Library, 1970.

Catt, Carrie Chapman and Nettie Rogers Shuler. *Woman Suffrage and Politics*. New York: Scribner's, 1923.

Chester, Giraud. *Embattled Maiden: The Life of Anna Dickinson*. New York: Putnam, 1951.

Coleman, Charles. *The Election of 1868: The Democratic Effort to Regain Control*. New York: Columbia University Press, 1933.

Cott, Nancy F. *The Bonds of Womanhood: "Woman's Sphere" in New England, 1780–1835*. New Haven: Yale University Press, 1977.

Dorr, Rheta Childe. *Susan B. Anthony: The Woman Who Changed the Mind of a Nation*. New York: Frederick A. Stokes, 1928.

DuBois, Ellen, ed. "On Labor and Free Love: Two Unpublished Speeches by Elizabeth Cady Stanton." *Signs: Journal of Women in Culture and Society*, 1 (1975), 257–268.

——. "The Radicalism of the Woman Suffrage Movement: Notes toward the Reconstruction of Nineteenth Century Feminism." *Feminist Studies*, 3 (1975), 63–71.

——. "Struggling into Existence: The Feminism of Sarah and Angelina Grimké." *Women: A Journal of Liberation*, 1 (1970), 4–11.

DuBois, W. E. B. *Black Reconstruction in America, 1860–1880*. New York: Atheneum, 1969. Originally published, 1935.

Dye, Nancy Schrom. "Feminism or Unionism? The New York Women's Trade Union League and the Labor Movement." *Feminist Studies*, 3 (1975), 111–125.

Earhart, Mary. *Frances Willard: From Prayers to Politics*. Chicago: University of Chicago Press, 1944.

Elkins, Stanley. *Slavery*. Chicago: University of Chicago Press, 1959.

Farnham, Elsie Ann. "Isabella Beecher Hooker as a Reformer: The Vote for Women or a Quest for Personal Power?" M.A. thesis, University of Connecticut, 1970.

Filler, Louis. "Parker Pillsbury: An Antislavery Apostle." *New England Quarterly,* 19 (1946), 315–337.

Fisher, Marguerite. "Eighteenth Century Theorists of Women's Liberation." *"Remember the Ladies": New Perspectives on Women in American History,* ed. Carol V. R. George. Syracuse: Syracuse University Press, 1975. Pp. 39–48.

Flexner, Eleanor. *A Century of Struggle: The Woman's Rights Movement in the United States.* New York: Atheneum, 1968.

Foner, Eric. *Tom Paine and Revolutionary America.* New York: Oxford University Press, 1976.

Foner, Philip S., ed. *Frederick Douglass on Women's Rights.* Westport, Conn.: Greenwood Press, 1976.

——. *History of the Labor Movement in the United States,* Vol. 1. New York: International Publishers, 1947.

Galpin, W. Freeman. "Elizabeth Cady Stanton and Gerrit Smith." *New York History,* 16 (1935), 321–328.

Garrison, Wendell Phillips and Francis Jackson Garrison. *William Lloyd Garrison: The Story of His Life by His Children.* New York: Century, 1889.

Gettleman, Marvin. *The Dorr Rebellion: A Study in American Radicalism, 1833–1840.* New York: Random House, 1973.

Gordon, Linda. *Woman's Body, Woman's Right: A Social History of Birth Control in America.* New York: Grossman, 1976.

Grimes, Alan. *The Puritan Ethic and Woman Suffrage.* New York: Oxford University Press, 1967.

Grob, Gerald. "Reform Unionism in the National Labor Union." *Journal of Economic History,* 14 (1954) 126–142.

Grossman, Jonathan. *William Sylvis: Pioneer of American Labor.* Columbia University Studies in History, Economics and Public Law, No. 516. New York: Columbia University Press, 1945.

Grossman, Lawrence. *The Democratic Party and the Negro: Northern and National Politics, 1868–1872.* Urbana: University of Illinois Press, 1976.

Halm, Charles E., Jr. "The 1867 Woman Suffrage Referendum in Kansas: A Case Study in Voting Analysis." Unpublished manuscript, Johns Hopkins University, 1973.

Harper, Ida Husted. *The Life and Work of Susan B. Anthony.* Indianapolis: Bowen-Merrill, 1899. 2 vols.

Hartman, Heidi. "Capitalism, Patriarcy, and Job Segregation by Sex: The Historical Roots of Occupational Segregation." *Signs: Journal of Women in Culture and Society,* 1 (1975), 137–169.

Hays, Elinor R. *Morning Star: A Biography of Lucy Stone, 1818–1893.*
New York: Harcourt, Brace and World, 1961.

Henry, Alice. *The Trade Union Woman.* New York: Appleton, 1915.

Hugins, Walter. *Jacksonian Democracy and the Working Class: A Study
of the New York Workingmen's Movement, 1829–1837.* Palo Alto:
Stanford University Press, 1960.

Jacoby, Robin Miller. "The Women's Trade Union League and American
Feminism." *Feminist Studies,* 3 (1975), 126–140.

James, Edward T., Janet W. James, and Paul S. Boyer, eds. *Notable
American Women: A Biographical Dictionary.* Cambridge: Harvard
University Press, 1971. 3 vols.

James, Joseph B. *The Framing of the Fourteenth Amendment.* Urbana:
University of Illinois Press, 1965.

Johnston, Johanna. *Mrs. Satan: The Incredible Saga of Victoria Woodhull.*
New York: Putnam's, 1967.

Kerber, Linda. "The Republican Mother: Women and the Enlightenment,
an American Perspective," *American Quarterly,* 28 (1976), 181–205.

Kessler-Harris, Alice. "Where Are the Organized Women Workers?"
Feminist Studies, 3 (1975), 92–110.

Kraditor, Aileen. *Ideas of the Woman Suffrage Movement, 1890–1920.*
New York: Columbia University Press, 1965.

——. *Means and Ends in American Abolitionism: Garrison and His
Critics on Strategy and Tactics, 1834–1850.* New York: Pantheon, 1967.

——, ed. *Up from the Pedestal: Selected Writings in the History of
American Feminism.* Chicago: Quadrangle, 1968.

Kugler, Israel. "The Trade Union Career of Susan B. Anthony." *Labor
History,* 2 (1961), 90–100.

——. "The Women's Rights Movement and the National Labor Union
(1866–1872)." Ph.D. diss., New York University, 1954.

Lerner, Gerda. *The Grimké Sisters from South Carolina: Rebels against
Slavery.* Boston: Houghton Mifflin, 1967.

Lewis, Helen M. *The Woman Movement and the Negro Movement:
Parallel Struggles for Equal Rights.* Charlottesville: University of Vir-
ginia Press, 1949.

Litwack, Leon. *North of Slavery: The Negro in the Free States, 1790–
1860.* Chicago: University of Chicago Press, 1961.

Lutz, Alma. *Created Equal: A Biography of Elizabeth Cady Stanton,
1815–1902.* New York: John Day, 1940.

——. *Crusade for Freedom: Women of the Anti-Slavery Movement.*
Boston: Beacon, 1968.

——. "Susan B. Anthony for the Working Woman." *Boston Public Library Quarterly*, 11 (1959), 33–43.

——. *Susan B. Anthony: Rebel, Crusader, Humanitarian*. Boston: Beacon, 1959.

McKenna, Sister Jeanne. "With the Help of God and Lucy Stone." *Kansas Historical Quarterly*, 36 (1970), 13–26.

Macpherson, C. B. *The Political Theory of Possessive Individualism: Hobbes to Locke*. London: Oxford University Press, 1962.

McPherson, James M. "Abolitionism, Woman Suffrage and the Negro." *Mid-America*, 47 (1965), 40–47.

——. *The Struggle for Equality: Abolitionists and the Negro in the Civil War and Reconstruction*. Princeton: Princeton University Press, 1964.

McVicar, John. *Origins and Progress of the Typographical Union: Its Proceedings as a National and International Organization, 1850–1891*. Lansing, Mich.: Darius D. Thorp, Printer and Binder, 1891.

Matthews, John. *Legislative and Judicial History of the Fifteenth Amendment*. Baltimore: Johns Hopkins University Press, 1909.

Melder, Keith. "The Beginnings of the Woman's Rights Movement in the United States, 1800–1840." Ph.D. diss., Yale University, 1964.

——. "Ladies Bountiful: Organized Women's Benevolence in Early Nineteenth Century America." *New York History*, 48 (1967), 231–254.

Merk, Lois B. "Massachusetts and the Woman-Suffrage Movement." Ph.D. diss., Radcliffe College, 1956.

Montgomery, David. *Beyond Equality: Labor and the Radical Republicans, 1862–1872*. New York: Vintage, 1967.

Neu, Charles E. "Olympia Brown and the Woman's Suffrage Movement." Unpublished manuscript, Schlesinger Library, 1958.

Noun, Louise T. *Strong-Minded Women: The Emergence of the Woman Suffrage Movement in Iowa*. Ames: Iowa State University Press, 1970.

O'Neill, William. *Everyone Was Brave: The Rise and Fall of Feminism in America*. New York: Quadrangle, 1969.

Papashvily, Helen Waite. *All the Happy Endings*. New York: Harper, 1956.

Paulson, Ross Evans. *Women's Suffrage and Prohibition: A Comparative Study of Equality and Social Control*. Glenview, Ill.: Scott, Foresman, 1973.

Perry, Lewis. *Radical Abolitionism: Anarchy and the Government of God in Antislavery Thought*. Ithaca: Cornell University Press, 1973.

Quarles, Benjamin. "Frederick Douglass and the Women's Rights Movement." *Journal of Negro History*, 25 (1940), 35–44.

Rabkin, Margaret M. "The Silent Feminist Revolution: Women and the

Law in New York State from Blackstone to the Beginnings of American Women's Rights Movement." Ph.D. diss., State University of New York at Buffalo, 1975.

Riegel, Robert. "Split of the Feminist Movement in 1869." *Mississippi Valley Historical Review,* 49 (1962), 485–496.

———. "Woman's Rights and Other 'Reforms' in Seneca Falls: A Contemporary View." *New York History,* 46 (1965), 41–59.

Robinson, Harriet Hanson. *Massachusetts and the Woman Suffrage Movement: A General, Political, Legal and Legislative History from 1774–1881.* Boston: Roberts Brothers, 1881.

Rosenberg, Carroll Smith. "Beauty, the Beast and the Militant Woman: A Case Study in Sex Roles and Social Stress in Jacksonian America." *American Quarterly,* 23 (1971), 562–584.

———. "The Female World of Love and Ritual: Relations between Women in Nineteenth Century America." *Signs: Journal of Women in Culture and Society,* 1 (1975), 1–30.

———. "The New Woman and the New History." *Feminist Studies,* 3 (1975), 185–198.

———. *Religion and the Rise of the American City: The New York City Mission Movement, 1812–1870.* Ithaca: Cornell University Press, 1971.

Ross, Ishbel. *Crusades and Crinolines: The Life and Times of Ellen Curtis Demorest and William Jennings Demorest.* New York: Harper and Row, 1963.

Ryan, Mary P. *Womanhood in America from Colonial Times to the Present.* New York: New Viewpoints, 1975.

Scott, Anne F., and Andrew M. Scott. *One Half the People: The Fight for Woman Suffrage.* Philadelphia: Lippincott, 1975.

———. *The Southern Lady: From Pedestal to Politics, 1830–1930.* Chicago: University of Chicago Press, 1970.

Scott, Mary Semple. "History of the Woman Suffrage Movement in Missouri." *Missouri Historical Review,* 14 (1920), 281–384.

Sinclair, Andrew. *The Emancipation of the American Woman.* New York: Harper and Row, 1966.

Sklar, Kathryn Kish. *Catharine Beecher: A Study in American Domesticity.* New Haven: Yale University Press, 1973.

Sproat, John G. *"The Best Men": Liberal Reformers in the Gilded Age.* New York: Oxford University Press, 1968.

Stampp, Kenneth. *The Era of Reconstruction, 1865–1877.* New York: Vintage, 1967.

Stein, Leon, and Philip Taft, eds. *Labor Politics: Collected Pamphlets,* I. New York: Arno, 1971.

Stern, Madeline B. *We the Women: Career Firsts of the Nineteenth Century.* New York: Schulte, 1963.

Stevens, George. *New York Typographical Union No. 6: Study of a Modern Trade Union and its Predecessors.* New York: Department of Labor, 1913.

Stuckey, Sterling. *The Ideological Origins of Black Nationalism.* Boston: Beacon, 1972.

Suhl, Yuri. *Ernestine L. Rose and the Battle for Human Rights.* Clifton, N.J.: Reynal, 1959.

Swerdlow, Amy. "Abolition's Conservative Sisters: The Ladies' New York City Anti-Slavery Societies 1834–1840." Unpublished paper, presented at the Third Berkshire Conference on the History of Women, 1976.

Thornton, Willis. *The Nine Lives of Citizen Train.* New York: Greenberg, 1948.

Todes, Charlotte. *William H. Sylvis and the National Labor Union.* New York: International Publishers, 1942.

Tracey, George. *History of the Typographical Union.* Indianapolis: International Typographical Union, 1913.

Trout, Grace Wilbour. "Sidelights on Illinois Suffrage History." *Illinois State Historical Society Journal,* 13 (1920), 145–179.

Walters, Ronald G. *The Antislavery Appeal: American Abolitionism after 1830.* Baltimore: Johns Hopkins University Press, 1976.

Ware, Norman. *The Industrial Worker, 1840–1860.* Boston: Houghton Mifflin, 1924.

Welter, Barbara. "The Cult of True Womanhood, 1820–1860." *American Quarterly,* 18 (1966), 151–174.

Whitton, Mary Ormsbee. *These Were the Women, U.S.A. 1776–1860.* New York: Hastings House, 1954.

Willard, Frances E., and Mary A. Livermore, eds. *The American Woman: Fifteen Hundred Biographies.* New York: Mast, Crowell and Kirkpatrick, 1897.

Winant, Marguerite Dawson. *A Century of Sorosis, 1868–1968.* Uniondale, New York: Salisbury, 1968.

Wyatt-Brown, Bertram. *Lewis Tappan and the Evangelical War against Slavery.* Cleveland: The Press of Case-Western Reserve University, 1969.

Wyman, Lillie Buffum Chace, and Arthur Crawford Wyman. *Elizabeth Buffum Chace: Her Life and its Environments.* Boston: W. B. Clarke, 1914. 2 vols.

Zaretsky, Eli. *Capitalism, the Family, and Personal Life.* New York: Harper and Row, 1976.

Index

Library of Congress Cataloging in Publication Data
(For library cataloging purposes only)

DuBois, Ellen Carol, 1947–
 Feminism and suffrage.

 Bibliography: p.
 Includes index.
 1. Feminism—United States—History.
2. Women's rights—United States—History.   I.   Title.
HQ1423.D8   322.4′4′0973   77-90902
ISBN 0-8014-1043-6
ISBN 0-8014-9182-7 pbk.